Mother–Infant Attachment and Psychoanalysis

The issue of shame has become a central topic for many writers and therapists in recent years, but it is debatable how much real understanding of this powerful and pervasive emotion we have achieved.

Mother–Infant Attachment and Psychoanalysis argues that shame can develop during the first six months of life through an unreflecting look in the mother's eyes, and that this shame is internalized by the infant and reverberates through its later life. Mary Ayers further expands on this concept of the look through a powerful and extensive study of the concept of the Evil Eye, an enduring universal belief that eyes have the power to inflict injury. Ways of healing shame within a clinical setting are explored and a fascinating analysis of the role of eye contact in the therapeutic encounter is examined.

Mother–Infant Attachment and Psychoanalysis brings together a unique blend of theoretical interpretations of shame with clinical studies, and integrates major concepts from psychoanalysis, Jungian analysis, developmental psychology and anthropology. The result is a broad understanding of shame and a real comprehension of why it may underlie a wide range of clinical disorders.

Jungian analysts, psychoanalysts, and psychotherapists as well as all those interested in object relations and early emotional development will profit greatly from the theoretical and clinical analysis offered in this book.

Mary Ayers is a Graduate of the University of Maryland School of Social Work, and received her PhD in depth psychology from Pacifica Graduate Institute in Santa Barbara, California. She currently divides her time between being a mother to her four children, and a private practice in the suburbs of Washington DC where she specializes in analytic work with children and adults.

Mother–Infant Attachment and Psychoanalysis

The Eyes of Shame

Mary Ayers

 Routledge
Taylor & Francis Group

LONDON AND NEW YORK

First published 2003 by Routledge
27 Church Road, Hove, East Sussex BN3 2FA

Simultaneously published in the USA and Canada
by Routledge
270 Madison Avenue, New York, NY 10016

Reprinted 2004 and 2008

Routledge is an imprint of the Taylor and Francis Group, an Informa business

Typeset in Times by RefineCatch Ltd, Bungay, Suffolk
Printed and bound in Great Britain by
TJ International Ltd, Padstow, Cornwall
Cover design by Terry Foley, Anú Design

This publication has been produced with paper manufactured to
strict environmental standards and with pulp derived from
sustainable forests.

British Library Cataloguing in Publication Data
A catalogue record for this book is available from the British Library

Library of Congress Cataloging-in-Publication Data
Ayers, Mary, 1960–
    The eyes of shame/by Mary Ayers. – 1st ed.
        p. cm.
Includes bibliographical references and index.
    ISBN 1-58391-287-8 (alk. paper) – ISBN 1-58391-288-6 (pbk.: alk.
paper)
        1. Object relations (Psychoanalysis) 2. Attachment behavior. 3.
Gaze—Psychological aspects. 4. Shame. 5. Psychoanalysis. I. Title.
    BF175.5.O24A94 2003
    152.4—dc21
                                          2003004202

ISBN 978-1-58391-288-6 (pbk)

To my husband, Richard,
who helped me know my shame

And to our son, Sean,
who embodies its healing

Contents

Acknowledgements

Although a work such as this is authored by one person, its undertaking has been inspired and supported by others. Many people have contributed ideas and been generous with their time, and so this book is a result of them as well.

There are four individuals who directly influenced my writing. More thanks than can be expressed on paper go to my supervisor and mentor, the late Mara Sidoli, who with great skill opened my eyes to the world of infancy and the work of Michael Fordham. I truly miss her. Julie Bondanza gave unconditional and loving support to me in my own inner work, in addition to some wonderful book suggestions. My dissertation advisor, Cathy Rives, read all the chapters carefully, gave critical suggestions, and accepted my work without question. This not only made my dissertation process easier, but instilled in me the feeling that I had something worthwhile to say, which in turn gave me the confidence to pursue its publication. And last, Virginia Hendrickson, whose seminars on object relations and the work of Winnicott inspired many questions, and she generously read my work for a thorough clinical edit. To these four women I am truly indebted.

Thanks must also go to my husband, Richard, whose encouragement and support cradled me through my darkest times. My children, Kevin, Sean, Jennifer and Jeremy, tolerated my preoccupation and ill-temper, yet remained enthusiastic. I could entrust the care of my newborns to my niece, Sarah, who devoted herself to their care. And my fellow dream group members listened to me as I babbled loose thoughts and provided a container in which to explore my ideas.

Many other friends, colleagues and relatives gave encouragement and support. Sometimes it was the loan of a book, an article clipped from the newspaper, a dream, advice, or just the smallest word or two which illuminated my work. To each one of them I am deeply grateful. One last thank you must go to my anonymous reviewers who made valuable suggestions that enriched the content of the book.

Grateful acknowledgement is made for permission to reprint quotations from the following previously published material:

Excerpts from *The Words to Say It* by Marie Cardinal, © 1975/1996 Van Vactor and Goodheart, translated by P. Goodheart. Reprinted with permission of publisher, Van Vactor and Goodheart, Cambridge, Massachusetts.

Excerpts from *Myth and Symbol in Ancient Egypt*, by R. T. Clark, 1959. Copyright © 1959 Thames & Hudson, reprinted with permission of the publisher, Thames & Hudson, London.

"Snow White" by Bros. Grimm, translated by Lucy Crane in *Household Stories*, © 1963 Dover Publications, reprinted with permission of the publisher, Dover Publications, New York.

"Medusa" by Rachel Blau DuPlessis, © 1980 Rachel Blau DuPlessis, by permission of the author. Originally published in *Wells*, Montemora Foundation, New York.

"Medusa, Smiling" from *On Women Artists: Poems 1975–1980* by Alexandra Grilikhes, Cleis Press, Minneapolis 1981. Reprinted with permission of the author.

"Life in Death or Death in Life," p. 217; "Words," p. 219; "Mental Hospital," p. 218. In *Transference Neurosis and Transference Psychosis* by Margaret Little, © 1993, 1981 Jason Aronson Inc. Reprinted by permission of the publisher, Jason Aronson, New York.

"Black Mother Woman," Copyright © 1973 Audre Lorde, from *Collected Poems* by Audre Lorde. Used by permission of W.W. Norton, New York.

"The Myth of Narcissus" reprinted by permission of the publishers and the Trustees of the Loeb Classical Library from *Ovid: Volume II – Metamorphoses*, Loeb Classical Library Volume L 42, translated by Frank J. Miller, revised by G.P. Gold, Cambridge, MA.: Harvard University Press, 1916, 1977. The Loeb Classical Library ® is a registered trademark of the President and Fellows of Harvard College.

"The Moon and the Yew Tree" and "Mirror" in *Collected Poems* by Sylvia Plath, © 1981 Sylvia Plath. Reprinted with permission of Faber and Faber Ltd, London.

Five lines from "The Moon and the Yew Tree" from the collected poems of Sylvia Plath, edited by Ted Hughes. Copyright © 1963 by the Estate of Sylvia Plath. Reprinted by permission of HarperCollins Publishers Inc.

"The Salutation" by Thomas Traherne (1637–1674), pp. 123–4. From *The Penguin Book of English Verse*. In *Psychotic Anxieties and Their Containment* by Margaret Little, © 1990 Margaret Little. Reprinted by permission of Jason Aronson, New York.

"Tale of the Beautiful Wassilissa" from *The Feminine in Fairy Tales* by Marie Louise von Franz, Spring Publications, Dallas 1986, © 1972, 1986, 1993 Marie Louise von Franz. Reprinted by arrangement with Shambhala Publications, Boston (www.shambhala.com).

Kramer, S.N. Sumerian Mythology. *Memoirs of the American Philosophical Society*, Volume XXI, 1944 (pp. 86–93). Philadelphia: American Philosophical Society.

Excerpt from "Sultry," from *The Complete Poetical Works of Amy Lowell*. Copyright © 1955 by Houghton Mifflin Company, Copyright renewed 1983 by Houghton Mifflin Company, Brinton P. Roberts, and G. D'Andelot Belin, Esq. Reprinted by permission of Houghton Mifflin Company. All rights reserved.

Copyright © Stephanie Dalley 1989. Reprinted from *Myths from Mesopotamia: Creation, the Flood, Gilgamesh and Others* translated by Stephanie Dalley (1989) by permission of Oxford University Press.

"Self-Portrait in a Convex Mirror", copyright © 1974 by John Ashbery, from *Self-Portrait in a Convex Mirror* by John Ashbery. Used by permission of Viking Penguin, a division of Penguin Putnam Inc.

Illustration credits

1.1   Universe of Eyes. From Thomas Wright, *An Original Theory or New Hypothesis of the Universe* (1750). Photo from Edward Harrison, *Darkness at Night: A Riddle of the Universe* (1987) Cambridge: Harvard University Press.

2.1   Mother and four-minute-old infant in *A Child Is Born* by
       Lennart Nilsson. Photo Lennart Nilsson/Albert Bonniers
       Forlag AB, *A Child is Born*, Dell Publishing Group.
2.2   Frontispiece for Oscar Wilde's *Salome* by Aubrey Beardsley.
       © Victoria and Albert Museum, London/Art Resource, NY,
       Victoria and Albert Museum, London.
2.3   *Painted Object: Eye*, 1936 by René Magritte. © 2002 C. Her-
       scovici, Brussels/Artists Rights Society (ARS), New York.
       Copyright Phototheque R. Magritte-ADAGP/Art Resource,
       N.Y.
2.4   Patient's photograph of her mother's eye. Used with her
       permission.
2.5   Children's drawings of a face. From *Analyzing Children's Art*
       by Rhoda Kellog, © 1970. Reprinted with permission of The
       McGraw-Hill companies.
2.6   *The Difficult Crossing*, 1963, by René Magritte. © 2002 C.
       Herscovici, Brussels/Artists Rights Society (ARS), New York.
       Photo from Francis Huxley, *Eyes: The Seer and the Seen*,
       (1990) London: Thames and Hudson.
2.7   *La monde poétique*, 1926, by René Magritte. © 2002 C.
       Herscovici, Brussels/Artists Rights Society (ARS), New York.
       Copyright Phototheque R. Magritte-ADAGP/Art Resource,
       N.Y.
2.8   Venus of Willendorf from © Naturhistorisches Museum
       Wien, Photo: Alice Schumacher.
2.9   Paleolithic idol (Venus). Photo: Gerard Blot. © Réunion des
       Musées Nationaux/Art Resource, NY. Musée des Antiquités
       Nationales, St. Germaine-en-Laye, France.
2.10   Eye Idol, The Metropolitan Museum of Art, Gift of Institute
       of Archaeology, University of London, 1951.
2.11   Argus. Wall painting by Pinturicchio. Vatican Museums.
3.1   *Diego and I*, 1949, by Frida Kahlo. Used with the permission
       of the Instituto Nacional de Bellas Artes y Literatura,
       Mexico.
3.2   Mother and infant. Family photo.
3.3   Mother Earth figure. From Michael Maier. Atalanta fugiens.
       (Oppenheim: Extypographia H. Galleri, sumptibus Joh.
       Theodori de Bry, 1618.) Used with permission of Archives
       and Special Collections, Columbia University Health Sciences
       Division.
3.4   *The False Mirror*, by René Magritte. © 2002 C. Herscovici,

Brussels/Artists Rights Society (ARS), New York. Copyright
Phototheque R. Magritte-ADAGP/Art Resource, N.Y.
4.1   Eye spots on moths' wings. Reprinted from Paul M. Tuskes,
James P. Tuttle, and Michael Collins, eds, *The Wild Silk
Moths of North America: A Natural History of the Saturniidae
of the United States and Canada*. Copyright © 1996 Cornell
University. Used by permission of the publisher, Cornell
University Press.
4.2   Cyclocosmid Trapdoor Spider © Robert and Linda Mitchell.
Reprinted with permission of the photographers.
4.3   Venus of Lespugue, © Special Collections, American Museum
of Natural History. Used with permission of the museum.
5.1   Illustration from BABA YAGA by Ernest Small and Blair
Lent. Illustrations copyright © 1966 by Blair Lent, Jr.,
renewed 1994 by Blair Lent. Reprinted by permission of
Houghton Mifflin Company. All rights reserved.
7.1   The Soul and Her Tent. From *Scivias* (1141) by Hildegard
of Bingen. Rudesheim am Rhein, St. Hildegard. Used with
permission.

Introduction

> Everything became playacting and unreality under icy eyes watching her, while these in turn were watched by a pair [of eyes] behind them, which were watched by another pair, in an endless perspective.
>
> (Lagerlöf, 1978)

To the person who suffers shame, the world is full of eyes, crowded with things and people that can see. Bewitching eyes watch every movement and moment of self. The core of agony in shame is this element of exposure. One is visible and not ready to be seen, looking and not ready to see. There is a constant, excruciating feeling in shame of being looked at while hoping the ground beneath your feet will open and swallow you up.

Ancient and modern writers of all persuasions – psychologists, anthropologists, philosophers, and novelists – have long noted the visual and facial components in the phenomenon of shame. Recent authors title books *The Mask of Shame* (Wurmser, 1997), *The Many Faces of Shame* (Nathanson, 1987), or *Shame: The Exposed Self* (Lewis, 1995). Having a sense of shame saves one's face. We speak of being shamefaced, of hiding our face in shame, or a wish for shame might sound like "I hope he falls flat on his face." Someone who is ashamed might say, "I can't bear to look him in the eyes." Shame's presence in the Story of Creation, the Western world's depiction of the beginning of human history, is linked to the eye and was the reason Adam and Eve covered themselves with fig leaves. After eating the fruit of the Tree of Knowledge of Good and Evil, "the eyes of both were opened, and they knew they were naked; and they sewed fig leaves together and made loincloths for themselves"

(Genesis 3:7). On both a collective, archetypal level and an individual, developmental one, shame manifests itself most through the eye. It is mediated and conveyed by the idea of vision, and cannot arise without this perceptual element. In shame, we meet eyes and avoid eyes; the solitary, scrutinizing eye of our inner selves or the collective eyes of the world that will bear witness to our state of self-worthlessness, impotence, undesirability, ugliness, incompetence, filth, or damage.

Despite its prevalence as one of the deepest, most fundamental emotional experiences for all humankind, shame was rarely discussed, which made this subject a blind spot in psychological discourse. This may be because shame is a contagious affect, stinging the observer with the sheer visceral power of exposure. The feeling is hard to modulate, so one naturally seeks to avoid it. Jacoby (1990) says that the historically rare discussion on this subject could be because shame shows it most shameful side precisely when it is laid bare, so that whoever takes on the task of exposing it becomes vulnerable to its sting.

A growing awareness of shame is now evidenced in a large body of literature. In the last 25 years there has been a resurgence of interest and extensive psychoanalytic exploration into its phenomenology, definition, developmental considerations, and theoretical underpinnings in relation to various clinical disorders. Reasons for our present pursuit of a deeper understanding of shame are addressed in the Epilogue (after my theory is presented). For now, suffice it to say that shame's paramount significance and prominence in the world of affective experience has been firmly established. It is being hailed as the master emotion, the invisible regulator of our entire affective life (Nathanson, 1996). Its prevalence in the therapeutic encounter has been noted (although this area requires much more attention), with an increasing awareness that all aspects of the therapeutic process touch on the possibility of encountering shame. Not only is shame directly observed and expressed in psychotherapy, but even more pervasively lies hidden behind permeable veils. Shame is visible and invisible, occurs ubiquitously, intertwines with other feelings, and is laid bare in the shadows of the unconscious.

What remains neglected in this proliferation of material, however, is the amplification of shame's quintessential phenomenological image – the human eye. This study is a look into psychology's blind spot, the seemingly forbidden image of the eyes of shame. To my knowledge, no one has elaborated at any length upon the long-range significance of early eye interaction and its internalization in the developing object relations of shame. Examinations of shame have been split from its symbolic and developmental foundation, despite its natural connection in the psyche. This split masks the deepest and earliest developmental aspects of shame, by their very nature dark, elusive and instinctually wanting to stay hidden behind many faces and voices.

In order for the most primitive aspects of shame to be brought into full view for understanding, an investigation of the eye as its consummate developmental organ and archetype is required. By punctuating the eye as a natural symbol for shame, a portal of vision will be opened to the unconscious depths and intrapsychic dynamics of shame in the core of the self. Restoring this affect to its imaginal roots will also minimize reductionistic effects, and open up the earliest aspects of shame without the obscuring overlays of later childhood and adult experience, hence the more complex network of psychological organization.

Eye-to-eye contact is one of the most intimate relationships possible between human beings and a powerful vehicle of communication. Eyes have the power to repel, conceal, and destroy and, alternatively, attract, connect, and create. Physically speaking and in comparison with other areas of the body surface, the eye has a wide array of fascinating properties. These properties are instinctually based. From the moment of birth the human infant responds in a compelling fashion to mother's eyes, and she responds in kind to capture her baby in eye-to-eye contact. These qualities and the feelings conveyed through the medium of eye contact make it a major vehicle for, and point of intimacy in, intrapsychic and interpersonal development. These properties may also be the reason why the eye, in the course of tens of thousands of years of evolution, has come to have a wide range of archetypal meanings of profound proportion.

Shame also carries dual meanings. It has the power both to annihilate and disintegrate the self, and safeguards psychic life by making self-awareness possible. Shame is always sparked by consciousness. In looking at shame through the image of the eye, an indissoluble bond is forged between the fear of being exposed and destroyed, and a searching curiosity invested in looking, seeing, and knowing. The image of the eye provides a means of metabolizing shame's presymbolic, concrete object representation into a conscious, archetypal symbol of the totality of the self.

In the pages to come, I will be exploring the role that the eye plays in the early generation of shame and, consequently, the distorting images that dominate the self as a result of its introjection. In attempting to single out and animate a topic that has hitherto been overlooked, I am guilty of two related things: devoting my attention to one part of an entire body of literature on shame, which in turn unfortunately creates what may feel like hostile scrutiny of the mother or mother blaming. My theory is maternally biased, and informed by the work of Winnicott, Fordham, and Jung whose theories are also maternally biased. It focusses on the infant's development in the first six months of life, and the role that eyes play in the construction of mother's presence and as a psychological center of their relationship. This short time frame and focus on eye-to-eye contact necessitates a close look at the mother to the exclusion of other factors. Good enough mothering and accurate reflection of the infant's needs result in strong ego development and concept of self; false mirroring results in shame. Good or poor mothering depends on the mother's level of emotional maturity; in some cases a mother's disturbance with a particular child outweighs her capacities for love.

I must also emphasize at this point that I am writing about the inner world of shame and the self, so that "bad mother" must also be understood as the negative pole of the mother archetype called the Terrible Mother. This is an emotionally charged, internalized form of mother in a complex psychic situation that takes on the collective unconscious force of terribleness when the infant has a negative experience of her real mother, who in actuality unites both good and bad. To put it another way, the infant is controlled by the absolute dimension of the archetype so that the lack of reflection that may appear in mother's eyes, emotionally separate from the infant and the mother's love for her baby (which every mother experiences), becomes for the infant petrifying, terrible, and attacking. Thus, the mother's eyes that generate shame are hollow eyes that become an empty mirror, her face a skull with burning, annihilating eyes, or simply a camera that sees only the surface. The inner experience of the infant in the face of such eyes, a subjective life that no one can know with any certainty, is imagined.

The single-minded perspective in this book is broadened by ample literary, mythical and philosophical quotations. These are not only added in support of my theory, but to incite the reader to pause and wonder about the prevalence of absolute shame, and the contemporary realities being reflected by these works. A feast for the eyes is offered through illustrations. Oftentimes, more information can be obtained at a single glance, occupying only an instant of time, than in pages of description addressed to the mind through reading. This work is also about what eyes see and the imagination creates, which necessarily entails seeing images. Pictures also give nonverbal expression to content that is preverbal or unable to be verbalized.

Lastly, this work represents a felt need to journey through shame freed from the eyes of scientific scrutiny – those same objectifying eyes that can generate shame in the first place. It is hoped that this look into shame will reveal its earliest development, primitive state of being, and raw primordial forms, provide an image to mitigate its toxicity, and unveil shame's transformative powers to ultimately humanize its most petrifying elements.

Chapter I

The eyes of shame

We should keep our eyes on eyes themselves
Eyes to see how they see.

(Gracian, 1642)

To those who can see them, there are eyes,
Leopard eyes of marigolds crouching above red earth,
Bulging eyes of fruits and rubies in the heavily-hanging trees,
Broken eyes of queasy cupids staring from the gloom of myrtles.
I came here for solitude
And I am plucked at by a host of eyes.

(Amy Lowell, 1874–1925)

Shame defined

Shame is a concept that has only fully entered the vocabulary of psychological inquiry within the last 25 years. People are ashamed of even experiencing shame, so that the emotion which produces hiding due to a fear of exposure has until relatively recently hidden itself from psychologists. Shame is not a word in the general index to Jung's 20 volumes of *Collected Works*, nor in the index to Klein's *Envy and Gratitude* (1975), *Love Guilt and Reparation* (1975), or a glossary of her working terms. The index to *The Standard Edition* of Freud's work contains 36 references to shame, compared with the 140 references to guilt (Wharton, 1990: 284). In *Interpretations of Dreams*, shame is connected with embarrassment, as in dreams of being naked (Hultberg, 1986: 159).

Prior to the recent surge of interest, theorists subsumed shame under other emotions, mainly guilt, whereas shame as an independent affect was overlooked and underestimated. A few theorists who included shame as a concept only touched on its myriad facets lightly, never able to fully explicate its phenomenology. Wurmser (1997) has commented on the tendency to treat shame in a splintered way "as if viewed through a prism" (p. 51). He states that the broad spectrum of shame feelings had previously been divided into fragments to be considered separately: social anxiety, sense of inferiority, narcissistic injury, embarrassment, or dread. Though not always synonomous with shame experience, all of these affects at least touched on it or formed some segment of the spectrum. Nathanson (1996) has criticized many writers for the nonsense they have made of shame. He states that "everybody has a different definition of shame, embarrassment, humiliation, mortification, the experience of another's contempt, or the experience of being put down; every single writer made it clear that their personal experience of shame incorporated universal truths" (p. 4).

As the study of shame has evolved, the word has come to have multidimensional and far-reaching connotations. It is difficult to know at this point what one is talking about when the shame word is used. Numerous writers have looked at it as a defense or as the affect behind the defense. Wurmser (1997) suggests that we consider as cognates the many words by which shame experience is described. This leads to the concept of a "shame family of emotions," inclusive of embarrassment, humiliation, shyness, or modesty, as well as the put-down feelings of disgrace, degradation, and dishonor. As he puts it:

> Shame in its typical features is complex and variable, a range of closely related affects rather than a simple, clearly delimited one. It shades into moods on one side, into attitudes on the other. Moreover, it is clear that anxiety is a cardinal part of it. Yet evidently shame is more than anxiety, and anxiety is more than shame.
>
> (Wurmser, 1997: 17)

Extensive articles have been written to differentiate shame from guilt (Piers and Singer, 1953), shame from anxiety, contempt from shame, aggression from shame, actual shame experience or being ashamed from a sense of shame. It has been pointed out that shame functions at a number of different levels or acts differently within the context of various pathologies. It is believed that hidden dimensions of shame underlie clinical phenomena as widespread as narcissism, social phobia, envy, domestic violence, addictions, identity diffusion, post traumatic stress disorder (PTSD), dissociation, masochism, and depression (Lansky and Morrison, 1997). Shame is also implicated in complex affective states such as rage, envy, despair, and hopelessness (Morrison, 1989; Wurmser, 1997), pride, conceit, and ambition (Broucek, 1982; Nathanson, 1992). Nathanson (1996) states that "the study of shame teaches much about everything that is beautiful and everything that is ugly within the human soul; this study is central to the development of competence as a contemporary psychotherapist" (p. 13). Broucek (1991) writes, "in my clinical work I have come to the conclusion that if one knows shame one knows psychopathology (and also something about health)" (p. 5). I concur with this, and will add that knowing shame also leads to a deeper understanding of what it means to be a human, vulnerable self.

Several authors in the clinical literature make a distinction between types of shame, although these types differ according to the writer. Lewis (1971) delineated three types of shame experience: overt, consciously experienced shame; unidentified or unacknowledged shame, where it is obvious shame has been experienced but the individual remains unconscious; and bypassed shame, where shame has obviously been experienced but where it is circumvented into obsessiveness about the self in the moment of shame. Kaufman (1992), on the other hand, distinguishes between primary and secondary shame. For example, the shame that 12-step programs deal with is called secondary shame – that is, the shame of being an addict. Beyond this, he states, are the core feelings of shame that may have caused an individual to become an addict in the first place. Levin (1967) also discusses primary and secondary shame. Primary shame is intrapsychic and internal, whereas secondary shame is described as "feeling ashamed of reacting strongly with shame" (p. 357). The cycle goes something like this. A sexual inclination leads to primary shame; this kind of shame results in inhibition of the impulse, or in regression (or both), and this results in secondary shame, which may lead to a denial of the inhibition and an acting out; this enactment (depending on its nature) can lead to further shame.

Wurmser (1997) distinguishes between the affect of shame and shame anxiety. He postulates that the affect of shame always involves the superego, and therefore is developmentally possible only after the formation of the superego system, which is to say after the resolution of the Oedipus complex. The more archaic, primitive form of shame

– its anxieties – come long before the oedipal stage. Shame anxiety is the fear of a total object loss and self loss. He further differentiates shame by dissecting its layers: "an important phenomenological aspect of shame is that it may affect the *functions* of self exposure or looking or merely a particular *content* that is exposed" (p. 56).

Societal and personal issues intersect in the affect of shame. Shame is both an intimate feeling of self-conception as well as a social conception of facing others. Most languages have at least two words for our English word *shame*: one to denote the feeling, one to denote the healthy attitudes that define a wholesome character. For example, French *pudeur* refers to the admirable qualities of modesty, chastity, shyness, a sense of shame, and in biblical uses the genitals. The emphasis in this form is on the inner, personal experience. The words *schande* in German and *honte* in French refer to disgrace, scandal, criminality, and the shame of crisis. The emphasis in this meaning is on social customs and standards.

A functional distinction is made by Hultberg (1986) between one form of shame that is directed at the environment (the object) and serves social adaptation, and a second form referring more to the subject which protects one's integrity or self. One guarantees – by conformity – the individual's belonging to the society; the other takes care that the collective does not intrude too deeply into the personality. Shame is closely linked to both the persona and the shadow, that is to say to both the social personality and the personal experiencing of the integrity of the self. To illustrate his point, he offers an example from Heller's work on a New Guinea tribesman who knows that shame is either "skin shame" or "deep shame." A person who is observed when urinating or having sexual intercourse feels "shame on the skin," but the one who hurts the spirit of his or her forebears suffers from deep shame.

Despite the broad range of meanings and numerous attempts at definition, experience reveals that every instance of shame is a time of painful incapacity, an endless moment when one is overcome with the existential feelings of defect and unlovability. There is the momentary, fleeting kind of shame in the normal range of human experience that will affect everyone to some degree throughout the life cycle as an inevitable part of growing up. This kind of shame is easily overcome. With some individuals, however, these feelings may conceal some deeper aspect of shame, a fundamental notion involving the whole self that one is in some way defective and unlovable down to the core of one's being. An individual burdened with this type of shame goes far beyond the normal, everyday kind of shame with which anyone can readily relate; one stops being a human being and is petrified by the movements of life. Early infancy is the place where this type of shame, which I will call absolute shame (a term first used by Wurmser, 1997), develops, and, if solidified into a sense of self, will only complicate secondarily the shame experienced at progressive developmental stages and moments in life. Shame at this level is more than just a momentary reaction; it is a way of being that is plagued by the polarized feelings of nonexistence and the fear of having one's existence destroyed by a glance. Although shame is an innate, normal feeling, an excessive amount of it considered maladaptive and a developmental pathology, while missing it altogether also points to an even deeper disturbance (Lowenfeld, 1976). One lives in a crippling space of alienation, craving to be seen in the eyes of the world beyond the false protection of shame.

Although the scope of shame is broad, the focus of my exploration into shame will be very narrow and precise. Like looking at a tree in the forest, my selective attention will be limited to the internalized form of shame where the whole self experiences on a chronic basis the kind of paralysis that others experience only in isolated moments of exposure. For these individuals, normal experiences of shame prompted externally end up massively amplified by inner shame, with the result that at a very deep level what gets obstructed is the ability to show oneself. This results in a feeling of nonexistence and the inability to see that because of this one is actually rejecting the world, imposing a punitive self-exile. Absolute shame requires no audience, but occurs through the observations made by a staring, critical internal eye that objectifies and poisons the other parts of self being scrutinized. The shaming other exists within, although it does get projected and populates the world with staring eyes that magnify and distort one's self-image, and from which one frantically seeks escape. One pictures oneself in the eyes of the other through a scrupulous study of facial expression, and is turned to stone by her gaze. These intrusive, internal eyes make it hard to realize oneself mirrored through another's eyes. The only reflection one gets back is one's own vision of oneself staring back. This individual perishes through her own persecuting eyes, annihilating a lively and feeling self through the power of the Gorgon's stare. Morrison (1996) emphasizes this internal self aspect of shame when he states that "shame is fundamentally a feeling of loathing against ourselves, a hateful vision of ourselves through our own eyes – although his vision may be determined by how we expect or believe other people are experiencing us" (p. 13). Shame becomes most pathological, yet can take on its symbolic qualities, when it becomes intrapsychic. Internalized shame is far more menacing, primal, and compelling than shame instigated by an external situation. This idea is a pivotal one that will be amplified throughout this work.

A phenomenological description of shame

Shame has been described in many ways and with many faces. This phenomenological consideration of shame will reveal when, where, why, and how we feel when we are ashamed. The experience of shame is explored as an individual experience that contributes to a sense of self as well as a collective one, a fact of social existence which serves adaptive functions.

It may appear contradictory that while the focus of this inquiry is on the primitive, internal states of being in shame, the phenomeno-logical descriptions focus primarily on its more common, external aspects within the normal range of human experience. The develop-ment of shame has been analyzed in the earliest months of life the-oretically, and through infant research and observations, but shame experienced at this infantile level has not yet been phenomenologic-ally described at any length in the literature (with the exception of Wurmser's 1997 book entitled *The Mask of Shame*, where he pro-vides vivid clinical material on what he calls archaic shame). This type of shame is unimaginable and nameless, beyond speech. The most infantile aspects of shame are masked and dissociated, hence reside almost completely within the domain of the unconscious. In a therapeutic process, it is at first difficult to communicate, residing at a preverbal level. Being preverbal, it is difficult to put into words and inevitably becomes disconnected. It only reveals itself through an exploration of the deepest levels of inner life (or poetry and other evocative forms). Its articulation requires the language of the inner-most self, a regressed, infantile part of the patient speaking and acting through an adult ego, as well as the therapist's holding response, eye contact, and interpretations of the vivid impressions left by the patient's raw and "unmentalized" material (Mitrani, 1996). Mitrani offers this definition of an unmentalized experience:

> Elemental sense data, internal and external, that have failed to
> be transformed into symbols (mental representations, organized

and integrated) or signal affects (anxiety that serves as a signal of impending danger, requiring thoughtful action), but are instead perceived as concrete objects in the psyche or as bodily states that are reacted to in corporeal fashion . . . Such experiences are merely "accretions of stimuli" that can neither be used as food for thought nor stored in the form of memories. These experiences, which have not been kept in mind, cannot be repressed. Instead, they are isolated as if in quarantine, where they remain highly immutable. These unmentalized experiences therefore represent one of the most challenging aspects of our work.

(Mitrani, 1996: 207)

Shame at this level is hard to understand other than through experience and working with it in order to help the patient find words to fit what is unthinkably horrible. At this point I only hope to bring the reader into the flavor of the kind of experiences with which we are dealing and make it clear that, regardless of what dimension of shame is examined phenomenologically, the eye is consistently central to its experience. It is hoped that this material is sufficiently graphic to involve the reader at an experiential level.

The individual's experience

Prominent in the experience of shame is the sense of profound, inhibiting alienation from the world and ourselves – shame makes us want to hide from others. These moments of painful incapacity break communicative bridges of open exchange with others (Broucek, 1982; Kaufman, 1992). Shame and its inexpressible, dissociative elements interrupt, paralyze, take over, inconvenience, trip up, and make incompetent anything that had previously been felt as pleasurable (Nathanson, 1992). Whatever communication has only shortly before been produced by interaffectivity is severed, and speech becomes impossible. One moment you can feel like a worthwhile human being, and the next second banished to oblivion, your total identity disintegrated. It can be an all-encompassing experience, obliterating all other thoughts and feelings. Continuity and coherence are forfeit, and you are suddenly unpleasantly self-aware. Shakespeare's Richard III articulates these feelings of alienation in his opening soliloquy. Once the glory of the wars are over, Richard III, an isolated figure starkly exposed against a bleak background and overwhelmed by this exposure, plots his villainous deeds, seemingly in defense of his agony:

> But I, that am not shaped for sportive tricks,
> Nor made to court an amorous looking-glass;
> I that am rudely stamp'd, and want love's majesty
> To strut before a wanton ambling nymph;
> I, that am curtailed of this fair proportion,
> Cheated of feature by dissembling nature,
> Deformed, unfinished, sent before my time
> Into this breathing world, scarce half made up,
> And that so lamely and unfashionable,
> That dogs bark at me as I halt by them;
> Why, I, in this weak piping time of peace,
> Have no delight to pass away the time,
> Unless to spy my shadow in the sun,
> And descant on mine own deformity:
> And therefore, since I cannot prove a lover,
> To entertain these fair well-spoken days,
> I am determined to prove a villain,
> And not the idle pleasures of these days.
>
> (Shakespeare, quoted by Lansky, 1995: 1079)

Although in shame we plunged into self-absorption, destroy interpersonal contact, and desperately want to hide, shame is nonetheless visible, highly reactive and difficult to control. Part of its self-exposure aspects include the very obvious autonomic responses of shame, which reveal that facial and visual contact is disconnected. Many writers, ancient and modern, have noticed the rapid eye motions of shame. Ezra (9: 6) cries "O, my God, I am too ashamed and blush to lift my face to thee, my God, for our iniquities have risen higher than our heads, and our guilt has mounted up to the heavens." Tomkins (1962) notes that eyes turn away from the other to the self. Darwin, the first to develop a compendium of emotions, describes shame as:

> The habit, as with every one who feels ashamed, of turning away, or lowering his eyes, or restlessly moving them side to side ... directed towards those present, bringing home the conviction that he is intently regarded; and he endeavors, by not

looking at those present, and especially not at their eyes, momentarily to escape from this painful conviction.

(Darwin, 1965: 329)

Sylvan Tomkins (1962), who followed in Darwin's steps and was the first to develop a theory of affects by closely observing faces, describes the importance of the face in expressing shame. He states that the common countenance is a shrinking from the world, hoping the ground beneath your feet will open and swallow you up. To be ashamed of feeling is to hide the eyes, lest the eyes meet and reveal the feeling.

As a physiological mechanism, shame is an averted gaze with tonus in neck and shoulder muscles reduced, eyebrows furrowed, and the head slumping with eyelids drooping; the vasculature of the facial skin dilates to produce the blush (Nathanson, 1996). Sustained eye contact with another becomes impossible. Extreme shame may further entail turning pale, fainting, dizziness, and rigidity of all the muscles (Wurmser, 1997: 83). Tomkins and Izard (1965) believe that the averted gaze may serve both to hide shame and reduce its excruciating feelings by attenuating involvement. Feldman (1962) suggests that blushing is the "flowing over" of the flaming look of the other that puts one into shame. Hultberg (1986) comments on the link between shame and the vegetative nervous system and suggests that this in itself indicates that shame is connected with the deepest layers of the psyche. The blush, a visible expression of shame, offers a clue to shame being distinctively human. As Nietzsche (quoted in Wurmser, 1997: 98) declares, "Man is the creature who blushes."

The agony and overpowering aspect of shame is its element of unexpected self-exposure, which leads to the need to hide. For Schneider (1977) and Lynd (1958), the key to understanding the shame experience is its element of exposure and overwhelming sense of visibility. One is visible and not ready to be visible. The feeling of exposure is connected to the fact that shame always entails the feeling of being observed, which can be based in internal or external reality (Yorke et al., 1990). Because of this awareness, it is doubtful whether shame is ever completely internalized. The perception of exposure can derive from a possible observer, a former one, or a fantasized one. Shameful experiences are not easily forgotten, and when recollected the affect surfaces strongly.

It can be seen from these descriptions that the element of visibility in shame and its phenomenological connection to the eye appear to entail a malevolent, destructive force. Shaming eyes humiliate. We hide our faces, want to run away, and long to vanish from the powerful eyes of contempt and disgust, which stare and induce these intolerable feelings. The world of shame is a world of staring eyes, not unlike an 18th century drawing of a galaxy of innumerable seeing eye stars (Figure 1.1).

In this world of vision, one feels unloved, indeed unlovable. Wallace (1963) links the exposure aspect of shame with the threat of being despised. Wurmser (1997) quotes a patient who put it this way: "I'd be better off dead. I can tell what people think of me because I can see it in their eyes" (p. 110). Champion Jack Dupree, a renowned blues singer, depicts the significance of these feelings in his song entitled "Have Mercy on Me".

Donne, in a poem entitled "Witchcraft in a Picture," captures the eye's destructible element:

> I fix mine eye on thine, and there
> Pity my picture burning in thine eye:
> My picture drowned in a transparent tear,
> When I look lower I espy;
> Hadst thou the wicked skill
> By pictures made and marr'd, to kill,
> How many ways mightst thou perform thy will?
> (Donne, quoted in Huxley, 1990: 26)

Wurmser (1997) reports a client's dream which dramatically depicts the deadening (as well as petrifying) aspect of shame and its connection to the eye. The patient, a girl who has suffered an acute catatonic breakdown and watched her parent's shock at seeing her look so dead, dreams the following: "I was eating the eyes of the world. I was eating the eyes of Christ, blinding him by my eating and drinking. My eating created the darkness" (p. 120). Erikson (1950) theorizes that the self-exposure aspect of shame is actually rage turned against the self, which is avoided through invisibility: "He who is ashamed would like to force the world not to look at him, not to notice his exposure. He would like to destroy the eyes of the world. Instead he must wish for his own invisibility" (p. 28). In *Hippolytus*, Euripides writes: "We seek to turn shame into nobility . . . What is hidden is revealed. You are destroyed." Adam and Eve's shame was

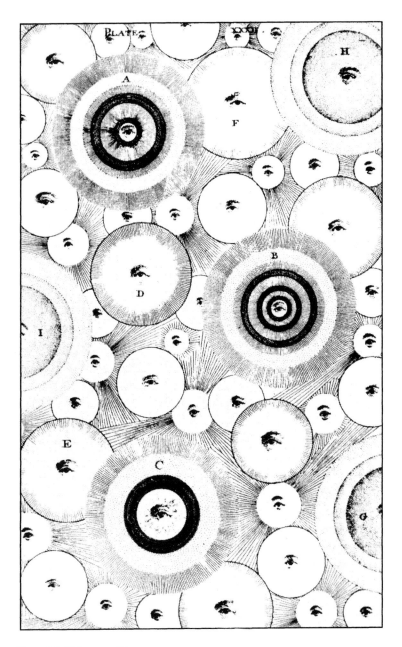

Figure 1.1 Universe of Eyes

the eye-opening discovery that they were naked, after which they were expelled from the Garden of Eden:

> Then the eyes of both of them were opened, and they knew they were naked; and they sewed fig leaves together and made loincloths for themselves. They heard the sound of the Lord God walking in the garden . . . and the man and his wife hid themselves from the presence of the Lord God among the trees of the garden. But the Lord God called to the man, and said to him, "Where are you?" He said, "I heard the sound of you in the garden, and I was afraid because I was naked."
>
> (Genesis 3: 7–11)

A central theme around shame, then, is about seeing and being seen when one wishes to hide, or of not being seen in the way one wants to be seen, or in a way that is congruent with what one is trying to show. Looking and self-exposure are dangerous activities for which one can be punished.

There are the poignant elements of estrangement and the need to hide as the self becomes a spectacle. This aspect of shame brings us to the etymology of the word. The origins of this word are obscure, but scholars believe it is derived from a Germanic root *sham/skem* (Old High German *scama*), meaning sense of shame, being shamed, disgrace (*schande*), which can in turn be traced back to the Indo-European root for our English word shame *kam/kem*, meaning to cover, veil, or hide. The prefix (*skam*) gives the reflexive meaning "to cover oneself." The word *schmen* in modern German means shadow or ghost and may refer us to shame's elusive, dark qualities. Pines (1995) notes that we also derive words for structures that protect us, for chambers and cameras, from the Indo-European root *kam/kem*. For example, camera is a word for room, also given to photographic apparatus, "for the exposure of sensitive film to light must be done within a dark protective chamber" (p. 346) – a nice therapeutic metaphor for revealing shame. An interesting note here is that, opthamologically speaking, the human eye is a camera type, defined as one with an iris diaphragm and variable focussing or accommodation which forms excellent images. It appears, then, that etymologically through the root *kam/kem* shame is connected to the eye.

The experiences that can generate shame cluster around several issues. Shame is apt to occur when telling a bad story or overstaying one's welcome, or in walking down the street only to realize that one's skirt is tucked in one's underwear. Here shame is contagious and can sting the observer as well. One can also be ashamed of likes, dislikes, assets, or deficits, even success or genius. The catalyst for shame seems to be what is revealed about one's character or the way one's characteristics seem to divide oneself from others. Tomkins writes on the interpersonal sources of shame:

> If I wish to touch you but you do not wish to be touched, I may feel ashamed. If I wish to look at you but you do not wish me to, I may feel ashamed. If I wish you to look at me but you do not, I may feel ashamed. If I wish to look at you and at the same time wish that you look at me, I can be shamed. If I wish to be close to you but you move away, I am ashamed.
>
> (Tomkins, 1963: 192)

What we are ashamed about immutably links shame to character formation, the essence of self-definition. Shame has been described as the affect of inferiority; when ashamed the individual says "I am weak, I am a failure, I can't compete, I have shortcomings." The content of self is looked at with disdain and disgust and accompanied by such thoughts as "I am dirty, I am foul and messy, I am defective, I have lost control." It is an emotion that comes upon the individual suddenly and is out of proportion to its cause. A small thing can evoke intense shame, and, vice versa, a large thing may not cause shame at all. Because shame is so inextricably tied to one's self-identity, the feeling reaction of shame may not be commensurate with its precipitator. To have magnitude the catalyst need only reveal some subjectively experienced darker aspect of self. Lynd concurs on the inconsequential catalysts for shame:

> It is the very triviality of the cause – an awkward gesture, a gaucherie in dress or table manner, "an untimely joke" always "a source of bitter regret," a gift or a witticism that falls flat, an expressed naivete in taste, a mispronounced word, ignorance of some unimportant detail that everyone else knows – that helps give shame its unbearable character.
>
> (Lynd, 1958: 40)

Sartre captures this dimension of shame in *Being and Nothingness*:

I am ashamed of what I am. Shame therefore realizes an intimate relation of myself to myself. Through shame I have discovered an aspect of my being . . . I have just made an awkward or vulgar gesture. This gesture clings to me; I neither judge it nor blame it. I simply live it. I realize it in the mode of for-itself. But now suddenly I raise my head. Somebody was there and has seen me. Suddenly I realize the vulgarity of my gesture, and I am ashamed.

(Sartre, 1956: 301–2)

Shame is experienced as a blow to one's self-image, which leads to secrecy and concealment of one's being. In shame we want to lose our "painful self-consciousness, the painful awareness of a hateful identity" (Pines, 1995: 346).

Shame and society

Culture plays a decisive part in the construction of an emotion and views of shame from a societal perspective focus primarily upon it as a means of adaptation. Shame both connects and disconnects us from significant others, regulating human distance and direction. Tomkins (1963) and Lewis (1971) suggest that shame is the master emotion in all societies. We cannot live outside society; we are born from it, depend on it, and are sustained by it. To be shamed and thrust outside society is to become psychically annihilated. Psychoanalytically speaking, shame is an important part of an internal structure of forces that control the instinctual drives to facilitate the process of socialization (Piers and Singer, 1953).

Agnes Heller (1985), in her book entitled *The Power of Shame*, delineates a general theory of shame that scrutinizes the ethical regulation of human action and judgment whose authority is social custom represented by the eyes of others and the Ideal Eye, or Eye of God. Practical reason can become manifest as an internal voice. It is her opinion that, like all other affects, the shame affect is integrated into cognition during socialization. Intersubjectively, shame seems to play a great part in the development of moral norms, actively promoting adaptation to society's ethical and social factors. It has even been postulated that it is the affect of shame that supports society, for without it we would be asocial animals (Heller, 1985; Hultberg, 1986). The main thesis of Heller's book appears to be:

Shame affect is the very feeling which regulates a person's
actions and general behavior in conformity with the norms and
rituals of his or her community. Given that we are social beings,
yet born into a world in which the norms and values are external
to us, coming to conform to these norms is identical with becoming human. In this respect shame is an inescapable part of our
humanity.

(Heller, 1985: 7)

Turner (1995) has pointed out that the foundation myths of any
culture depict some terribly shameful act at the point of origin of the
human world. Of course the story of Adam and Eve has been mentioned, but there is also the Shinto story of the shaming of the sun
goddess Amaterasu by her violent brother Susa-no-wo, who threw a
flayed horse through the roof of her weaving hall. She fled ashamed
to the safety of a cave which deprived the world of sunlight – as did
the shame rage of Ceres in the myth of Persephone. These myths are
expressive of the truth that lies at the core of our human predica-
ment. Human life is by its very nature shameful, and the repression
of this fact becomes the hidden cause of much cultural damage.
Turner states:

The coexistence of a reflective mind with a smelly, sexed, and
partly autonomous body; the horror of death; the ambiguous
relationship of human beings and the rest of nature; the
incestuous paradoxes of kinship and parenthood; the crimes of
our ancestors against the peoples or species they displaced; the
capacity to lie given us by our language . . . Our aboriginal
human philosophy tended . . . to divide the cultural from the
natural.

(Turner, 1995: 1061)

That shame is a fundamental factor of human existence and serves
the functions of upholding the structure of society is illustrated by
the Greek myth about its genesis (Stone, 1988). Protagoras said that
when man was first created he lived a solitary existence, unable to
protect himself and his family from what was stronger than he was.
Consequently, men banded together for security, creating cities that
were torn with strife because their inhabitants "did wrong to each
other." This caused the men to scatter once again. Zeus then feared
that the human race was bent on destruction, and to ensure their

survival sent his messenger Hermes down to earth with two gifts that would enable men to live together amicably and in safety. These gifts were Aidos and Dike. Aidos, the Greek Goddess of Shame, denotes both sexual shame and that of the genitals. As the source of decency and the restraining force of public opinion, she was also linked with integrity, respect, and piety. Her companion was Dike, Natural Law and Justice, or Nemesis, Due Enactment. Zeus further instructed his messenger, "Make thereto a law of my ordaining, that he that cannot partake in respect (Aidos) and right (Dike) shall die the death of the public pest." Hesiod prophesied that Aidos and Dike/Nemesis would abandon mankind due to their evil, wicked nature. This loss would mean a fatal hardening of character where good repute would be forfeit. The inevitable fate in such a situation is nemesis, the retribution that falls on the justly disapproved.

Shame has also been well known in the work of anthropologists; in fact this discipline has historically emphasized the importance of shame. Throughout Western history, this emotion has been responsible for major changes in culture and society. Ruth Benedict (1977) made a distinction between two types of cultures: shame cultures and guilt cultures. Shame cultures, according to her theory, are those in which the highest goal is not a clear conscience but a good reputation among people, honor, renown, and respect. About these kinds of culture Graves (1962: 91) has said "in a shame-culture the voice of one's peers has indeed the power of a god". Guilt cultures, on the other hand, rely upon an inner conviction of sin. According to Jacoby (1990), shame is a driving force behind cultural development. Shame guards boundaries, and anyone who crosses them runs a personal risk and invites social sanctions.

Religion is a powerful cultural force, and the primary message from a religious perspective is that shame is a fear of disgrace and that a lack of it destroys. The Talmud says: "Jerusalem was destroyed because its people had no shame" (quoted in Jacoby, 1990: 5). Church tradition identifies so-called original sin with the violation of God's prohibition. Yet this God is unique. He can see us, but we cannot see Him. No one can hide from God. He can put us to shame and this has no reciprocity. What is shameful before God is sin, and if we sin we hide our face in vain. There is no place to hide from the Eye of God that can see what is visible and invisible, sees everything and exists everywhere, and can penetrate to the depths of one's soul. From a more humanitarian perspective, Scheler (quoted in Emad, 1972) speaks of shame as a passageway to resolve the conflict between the human's spiritual and bodily domains. He concludes that shame is natural for a human being, and that neither God nor beast is capable of experiencing shame. Culturally, the experience of shame has undergone many shifts. Hultberg (1986) hypothesizes that due to the decline of conventional Christianity in the Western world, the values of good and evil have become emptied of meaning, which leads to a dominance of shame at the expense of guilt. Heller, commenting on the demise of the community and the overestimation of human conscience, takes this view:

> Loss of the Ideal Eye tended to come about simultaneously with the loss of the real eye of the community, and that (over-estimation) failed to face the further fact that we need the crutch of an external authority not in spite of our being human but because of it.
>
> (Heller, 1985: 7)

Conclusion

In summary, shame is primarily object relational, so closely connected with human nature and collective life that even biologists have considered it to be our main characteristic. In social interchange, the presence of shame is pervasive and necessary for functioning, though it is all too often unrecognized or dealt with directly. Heller (1985) states that shame is the only inborn moral feeling in us, and that it is due to the emergence of practical reason as an independent authority of human conduct and conscience that shame has become increasingly ambiguous (p. 6). Darwin adopted the point of view that humans have moral instinct, an essential human characteristic that separates us from other species, because they have shame. Even in the Old Testament Story of Creation, it appears that it was the capacity of Adam and Eve to feel shame that let Yahweh know they were conscious. Shame will never be overcome because "it is the price we pay for becoming increasingly conscious human beings" (Frantz, 1986: 177).

An analysis of the developmental origins of shame

So far in this review of the phenomenology of shame, its distinctions as an affect with which anyone can readily relate, as well as its cultural and religious influence, have been discussed. This part of the review has provided a working definition that aims at recognizing aspects of shame as a group of felt experiences in relation to the human eye. The remainder of this chapter will focus on the varied explanations in the literature of its origins and role in development. Is shame a manifestation of pathological narcissism, the failure to maintain good object relations, and the absence of good enough mothering? Or is shame part of the structure of the personality, the result of failure to attain an ego ideal or the consequence of a hyperactive superego? Or is it a sadomasochistic enactment, the powerful imprinting of early traumatic events such as incest and sexual trauma, or brutal parenting? The following review surveys some of the many theories that have been added to the literature in recent years and reveals the considerable controversy surrounding the development of shame as a key aspect to human behavior.

Early on in the history of psychology there were isolated contributions on shame made by Erikson (1950), Fenichel (1945), Edith Jacobson (1965), Wallace (1963), and Piers and Singer (1953), and an analysis of shame in relation to blushing by S. S. Feldman (1962). Helen Block Lewis (1971) is the individual who rediscovered shame through a careful analysis of therapeutic failures, the people who had gone through a so-called successful analysis only to return later with more intense symptoms as if psychoanalysis had done little for them (take special note of these regressive tendencies). These were the patients with the greatest shame pathology. Her study of this phenomenon eventually led to her groundbreaking book *Shame and Guilt in Neurosis*, inspiring new interest in this pivotal emotion which continues to reverberate in psychoanalytic circles to this day.

More recently, significant works on the etiology of shame delve deeper into earlier developmental patterns and have come from an exploration of superego and drive theory (Wurmser, 1997), of narcissism (Morrison, 1989), affect theory (Nathanson, 1992; Tomkins, 1962, 1963), identity (Erikson, 1950; Lynd, 1958), separation and autonomy (Erikson, 1950; Sidoli, 1988) and as a core affect in disorders of the self (Broucek, 1991). These theories will be explicated briefly in the following pages. I will again ask the reader to take particular note of the role that the eye plays in its formation, regardless of what theory is presented.

The basic affect theorists, exemplified by Tomkins and followed by Nathanson, believe that shame is a core affect that is innate, evidences itself on the face of an infant, and remains unaltered throughout life. Tomkins (1963, 1987) believed that we are all born with an innate group of nine normal emotional mechanisms, or facial responses, which he named innate affects. Each affect has its own subcortical address or hardwired brain location that contains its triggering program. These affects operate to bring things into consciousness, and the ways we learn to handle these affects are central to the formation of personality. Tomkins's shame theory is based on the idea that shame is an auxiliary affect and specific inhibitor of the basic positive two-part affect mechanisms of interest–excitement or enjoyment–joy. Shame comes forth and operates as an inhibitor only after interest or joy has been activated. The shame barrier may arise because, for example, "one is suddenly looked at by another who is strange; or because one wishes to look at, or commune with, another person but suddenly cannot because s/he is strange" (Tomkins, 1987: 143). Basically, emotional involvement with another is diminished due to a reduction in satisfaction. The differences in the experience of shame are explained as variations of intensity of the experience given different settings. Magnification of shame happens, for example, by combining multiple affects aroused by the same occurrence as well as multiple sources for shame in relation to the same event. Shame, if magnified in frequency, duration, and intensity, can become malignant in the extreme. This is due to the fact, Tomkins emphasizes, of the consequence of the magnification of the affect and not the nature of the amplifier. Because shame is viewed as an inhibitor to excitement or joy, even in a chronic state of shame the hope to resume a full state of enjoyment or excitement is maintained. Tomkins's idea that shame counters the movement towards engagement "is getting at something important, something that represents one of the warp threads that bind a number of shame theories" (Miller, 1996: 24). Regardless of what functions shame plays in the process of development, or at what developmental crisis it emerges, the idea that shame acts as an inhibitor is central. This inhibiting (or petrifying) dimension of shame is one that we will return to in a later chapter.

Nathanson (1992) built upon the work of Sylvan Tomkins by combining Tomkins's theory of affects and ideas on shame with the contributions of neurophysiology, psychopharmacology, classic psychoanalytic thinking, and infant observation. Linking Tomkins's concept of affect interest to attachment theory and affective communications, Nathanson develops what he calls a timetable for shame. He begins his construct of shame by building on Tomkins's concept that the innate affect of shame is a mechanism that inhibits enjoyment or excitement, and explains the enormous variations of mature manifestations of shame and its tie to the self as the result of its combination with drives, cognitions, and personal experience over time. Nathanson insists that shame is not essentially social but is connected to self and sparked by any impediment to the more pleasurable affects of engagement. Shame is simply the response to anything that interferes with positive affect and occurs at all levels of child development along with a multitude of concerns.

The majority of the theorists who address the origins and function of shame in the developmental process do so from a psychoanalytic perspective, yet the diversity within psychoanalytic theories of development create extensive variation in its explanation. One idea, however, where there appears to be agreement is the connection between shame and the eyes. This is, for example, in the insistence that shame is a motive for defense against scoptophilia (the desire to look at). Otto Fenichel, a spokesman for orthodox psychoanalysis, states:

> I feel ashamed means "I do not want to be seen." Therefore, persons who feel ashamed hide themselves or at least avert their faces. However, they also close their eyes and refuse to look. This is a kind of magical belief that anyone who does not look, cannot be looked at.
>
> (Fenichel, 1945: 56)

Most of the theorists agree that developmentally shame precedes guilt, but differ with regard to the point at which shame first appears. This discrepancy is due to several factors: the debate over whether shame is innate (Wallace, 1963) or learned (Grinker, 1955); the function of shame as a defense (Freud, 1905) or an experience which may elicit defensive strategies (Fenichel, 1945); and finally, emphasis on shame as a part of drive theory versus structural theory, or drive regulation versus several object relations positions. Those theorists who focus on the structural dimensions of shame differ on which structure is most important. For example, Piers and Singer (1953) view shame as the tension between the ego and the ego ideal; the theorists who focus on the interpersonal dimensions of shame relate it to a concept of self and debate the timing of its emergence. Issues around identity are pronounced in shame due to the awareness of self in the experience. Several theorists emphasize identity as the primary consideration in shame, although some regard shame as necessary to identity formation, and others regard shame as the result of poor identity formation. For the sake of brevity and in the hopes of not being too pedantic, I will focus only on those theories that form a time line, so to speak, that depicts the progression (or regression) of theoretical thinking on shame's development back to the earliest days of life.

Spero (1984) places the development of shame in the second year of life, in the context of "anal organization," on the border between self-awareness and object awareness, and follows the beginning of internalization of external, shaming parental attitudes. Several theorists point out that some parents force their children to be ashamed, and show how shame is provoked and maintained by parents in particular, along with teachers, peers, and siblings. This is done through comments like "what will the neighbors say," "you will be the death of me yet," "one day you are going to kill me," and "shame on you." These kinds of comments, according to some theorists, are a major social derivative which contributes in due time to a shaming superego. Feldman graphically describes the internal scenario a child can experience in relation to such comments:

> The eyes of the angry parent mobilize the primordial trauma of the fiery eyes. The child feels that the parent will destroy him, devour him. Like a dog, he is threatened with having his face rubbed in urine and feces. He is afraid that he will be thrown into the toilet and that he will lose his freedom. He who is forced to be ashamed . . . is not allowed to cling and is without support. He has no will. He is paralyzed and close to fainting. He is subdued like a slave and forced to serve. He loses ground, casts down his eyes, and wants to hide. The strong have dominance over him.
>
> (Feldman, 1962: 381)

Erikson (1950) relates the development of a sense of shame with the long period of dependency in infancy. It is specifically developed during the stage of autonomy vs. shame and doubt as the psychosocial dilemma of the toddler at the anal stage. During this time the child must perform functions that are visible to others, and the tension between what the child can do and what is expected of him are most intense and create doubts. The child is particularly vulnerable to shame around the toddler stage, when he learns to stand upright and to walk. At this moment of great achievement, of standing on his own two feet, he is also paradoxically confronted with an increased awareness of his own relative smallness, helplessness, and potential for failure. Toilet training is also occurring during this time.

In her article entitled "Shame and the Shadow," Mara Sidoli (1988) explores the development of shame during the growing child's process of separation. According to her, shame seems to occur from the young child's recurrent experiences of shortcomings, inadequacy, and dependency in youthful attempts to discover an increasingly larger world. Sidoli states that the child must have developed sufficient ego to be able to experience being separate from parents and other people in his or her environment in order to have an experience of shame (p. 128). This separate ego is established towards the end of the first year of life and reaches its peak during the anal and oedipal stages of development, during which time jealousy of and rivalry with the parent of the same sex is at its highest. This period is accompanied by feelings of shame over one's inadequacy. Shame is linked with a feeling of smallness and inadequacy because of being small, and since children are in fact small, they suffer severe blows to their narcissism and may compensate these shameful feelings through an over-identification with adults. Shame may also develop out of weaning and the realization of being separate, inasmuch as the child attributes the loss of the breast to personal inadequacy and badness. The baby might feel that there "must be something wrong with me if mother pushes me away."

Developmentally, shame engenders the awareness of self and its vulnerabilities. Most theories appear to center on the issue of an emerging identity (described above), which in turn is linked to the concept of self. New theories that locate shame in the earliest days of infancy have been added to the literature in recent years. These origins link the phenomena of shame with the self and narcissism,

identity and ideals (Broucek, 1991, 1997; Kaufman, 1992; Morrison, 1989; Wurmser, 1997).
Kaufman (1992) discusses both identity and the self in relation to shame. In contrast to many of the theorists who have discussed shame as preceding and hindering the formation of the self (Broucek, 1982; Lewis, 1971; Spero, 1984; Wurmser, 1997), Kaufman proposed that "it is precisely following the internalization of shame as a major source of one's identity that the self becomes able to both activate and experience shame without an inducing interpersonal event" (p. 37). In other words, shame and identity do not become linked prior to the mature capacity to articulate a shame experience. Only then can we create meaning about ourselves. The critical event in shame is a significant person rupturing the interpersonal bridge that severs the vital processes of mutual enjoyment, understanding, growth, and change of relationship. Kaufman describes shame as an ambivalent affect in which the other is both desired and hated. This view of shame necessarily entails rage as a correlate of shame, which increases alienation and prevents reestablishment of the relationship. This loss of the interpersonal bridge is the original source of pain. I will return later to a deeper exploration of the dynamics involved in disconnecting from the vital processes of relationship, and how this can result in terror and rage.

Seeking to explain the internal development of shame, Kaufman delineates both the vehicle of identification and its outgrowth, internalization of attitudes and behaviors, which combined gradually lead to identity formation. The process of identification is rooted in the visual process and, he states, visual imagery plays a significant role in mediating the movement from outer to inner. If shame is internalized to a large degree, in order to adapt to outer reality the self may resort to characterological defensive processes as protection from shame. Moreover, the defective self is dealt with by disowning the self. Various needs, feelings, and drives are denied, creating a distorted sense of identity which often leads to splitting, which inevitably hinders integration. The core of Kaufman's thinking is that this splitting leads to the internal perpetuation of shame by part of oneself attacking the negative aspects of self.

Kohut, writing about narcissistic patients, describes how shame originates in a failure of the mirroring and approving response which is expected and needed by the infant to contribute significantly to a sense of self. For Kohut, shame is a reflection of the self over-whelmed by its infantile and split off grandiosity. Morrison (1987, 1989) builds on Kohut's work and the framework provided by self psychology for an understanding of shame, which to his mind lies at the very center of narcissistic pathology. He contends that a defin-ition of shame must involve more than a self overwhelmed by gran-diosity; it must account for disappointment, failure, and deficit (1987: 276). He begins by amplifying the function served by the construct Kohut called the selfobject, and the relation between the ego and the ego ideal. The mother serves essentially a selfobject function and "when the infant looks at mother s/he does not see the mother as we would see her, but as a reflection of the infant, the self mirrored on the face of the mother" (Morrison, 1987: 271). The age-appropriate mirroring of infantile grandiosity, as well as its self-affirming presence, is necessary to self-cohesion. Morrison contends that not only is shame caused by the breakthrough of unmirrored grandiosity, but it also occurs "when the self fails to attain its ideals through the unresponsiveness of the idealized parental imago to pro-jective identification of the ego ideal . . . the ideal self" (Morrison, 1987: 278). Shame is the result, then, of an insufficiency of idealized selfobject's responsiveness to the need for mirroring, affirmation, merger and idealization. This experience leads to a primary internal shaming eye focussed on the depleted, fragmented self with its fail-ures and inadequacies.

Broucek (1991) explores shame in an intersubjective context. Drawing many examples from infant research, which he contends provide evidence of primitive shame experience, he describes the rhythmic interactions of attention and non-attention between mother and infant. From his observations, he suggests that shame is evoked in the infant as a result of the mother's failure to recognize and respond to her child. Shame experiences are particularly painful in terms of the infant's sense of inefficacy, incompetence, and lack of control. Failure may induce a sense of profound helplessness and unlovability, and lead to the withdrawal evident in shame. The infant is striving to fascinate the mother through her own self-exposure, struggling to recognize that she is lovable, hoping that she will recog-nize her when the child begins to experience mother as a stranger. Shame at this level leads the individual to believe that something has been wrong with them since the beginning.

Broucek (1991) then focusses on what he calls objective self-awareness and the objectifying dimensions of shame. He describes this as when the self is viewed as a collection of functions that are executed without regard for the inner life as something to be valued. The image of objectification is a camera which "looks always at and never into what it sees" (Barfield, quoted in Broucek, 1991: 40). "Shame frequently has to do with experiencing oneself being treated as an object when one is attempting to relate to the other in an intersubjective mode" (p. 39). External shaming experiences only exacerbate an already shame-weakened self. For children who arrive at the stage of objective self-awareness with an already shame-ridden sense of self, realizations of being small and weak vis-à-vis adults will overwhelm their already taxed shame tolerance, necessitating defensive maneuvers (p. 57). Strong shame propensities result in the dominance of objective self-awareness over a subjective sense of self and a thwarting of the separation–individuation process.

Wurmser's (1997) work also addresses shame in the infant, but his approach differs from Broucek's in significant ways. He outlines the archaic and partial drives of theatophilia and delophilia, which he defines respectively as the desire to watch and observe, and as the desire to express oneself and fascinate others by one's self exposure – to see and be seen. These partial drives take place in a zone Wurmser has called the "perceptual and expressive interaction with the environment" (p. 163), and he goes on to say that the infant does much more than feed in his waking state. He begins to establish a relationship with the mother with his eyes, both to express himself and to elicit a response from her, usually in a very powerful way. Wurmser postulates that the core of one's self-concept and object world is formed by theatophilia and delophilia, drives which are evidenced at birth. If there is interference in the interchange between mother and infant, either due to environmental factors or the intensity of the inherited drives, the infant is predisposed to early forms of shame. He delineates a developmental line of premature separation due to the distortion of these partial drives: the line starts with re-actions, as early as the first few days of life, of displeasure and withdrawal, finds more highly developed expression in stranger anxiety at age eight months and results in outward shame 18 months later. The outcome of this development culminates in the core feelings of shame.

Both Broucek (1991) and Wurmser (1997) are looking at the infant's thwarted intentions as the earliest forms of shame phenomenology. Whereas Broucek refers only to the child's intention of engaging and seeking facial responses, Wurmser emphasizes the infant's active use of eye contact to engage mother and the world, and the network of complexes that can develop around the infant's core drive activities of looking and showing if their attempts at engagement are frustrated. Wurmser calls the catalyst for the catastrophic feelings of shame the face of contempt, whereas Broucek talks about the still faced adult. Either way, these faces result in a profound alteration in the early sense of self (the birth of narcissism) which will haunt the individual through every subsequent developmental stage. For Broucek, the result of such a maternal face is a shriveling, curdled infant; Wurmser describes a wordless, frozen infant with searching eyes (p. 83).

Conclusion

My exploration into the world of shame began somewhat pedantically in order to give the theoretical underpinnings for understanding and precisely distinguishing the kind of shame that is the subject of this work. A review of the literature examined the phenomenology of shame on both individual and collective levels in order to establish a clear relationship between the eye and shame. A theoretical analysis of the developmental origins of shame led to the work of Wurmser and Broucek who both identified the cold, rejecting face of the mother and wondered at its potential impact on the vulnerable infant. These works comprise the cutting edge of psychoanalytic work on shame, and bring us face-to-face with mother's eyes.

The remainder of this work is an effort to explore the reverberations within the self of the experiences of early shame generated through these faces, the felt experiences behind the petrifying function of shame symbolized by the "eye of the self gazing inward" (Morrison, 1987: 273). We internalize objects in the form of images, and the psychic world of infancy is reflected in images and what are called symbols of the self (Fordham, 1965). It is my contention that the infantile experiences of shame are captured in the image of the eye. This eye, originating in the face of the mother, is internalized and personified by the archetypal world that dominates the inner world of the infant.

The myth of Medusa provides a metaphor for looking into these eyes. With this in mind comes a means of approaching its earliest, most infantile aspects. Like Perseus's bright bronze mirror-like shield that protected him from looking directly into Medusa's face (which would turn him to stone), and facilitated his ability to behead her, the facts in the literature will reflect the eyes of shame, leading to important insights for disempowering shame's petrifying effects and, ultimately, to its remedy.

Chapter 2

Mother's eyes

Eyes which see are the same thing as a heart which understands.
(Deuteronomy 29:4)
Look at them looking, their eyes meeting the world.
(William Carlos Williams, 1883–1963)

Eyes are readily detectable. From the moment of birth the sight of an infant's searching eyes will magnetically attract mother's gaze. The infant's eyes, in fact, seem to have been designed by evolution to seek out mother's eyes – finding her eyes gazing back is the infant's primordial desire. Not only are eyes the most richly fascinating and appealing feature of mother's face (and baby's eyes to the mother), shining, colorful, and rotating balls with contrasting sizes of big and small; it is by looking into each other's eyes that the bonds of love between infant and mother can be formed. This rapturous moment of falling in love, if ever witnessed, becomes an unforgettable sight. Mother and child gaze deeply into each other's eyes, mutually mesmerizing each other to dispel any strangeness between them. This connection is beautifully expressed in a custom practiced by the Tamils of India, a tribe who are so endeared to their babies that they call them "Eye."

Mutual gazing has been called a world within a world (Stern, 1990), and it is to this aspect of the inner world of mother and infant that we turn now in our exploration into the deepest aspects of shame in infancy. This world is an eye world, a place where the infant, in her highly vulnerable and dependent state, has a direct, albeit unconscious, line to what mother is thinking and feeling through their intimate eye contact. At this level of development, mother's inner emotional life will be experienced by the infant with a drama and intensity unique to a psychic life dominated and personified by archetypal energies. The infant instinctively struggles not to be taken over by it. In *Diary of a Baby*, Daniel Stern imagines a four and a half-month-old baby's internal, rapidly changing experience in the face of mother's eyes:

> I enter the world of her face. Her face and its features are the sky, the clouds, and the water. Her vitality and spirit are the air and the light. It is usually a riot of light and air at play. But this time when I enter, the world is still and dull . . . Where is she? Where has she gone? I am scared. I feel that dullness creeping into me. I search around for a point of life to escape to.
>
> I find it. All her life is concentrated into the softest and hardest points in the world–her eyes. They draw me in, deep and deeper into a distant world. Adrift in this world, I am rocked side to side by the passing turbulence that ripples the surface of her eyes. I stare into their depth. And there I feel running strong the invisible currents of her vitality . . . I call after them to surface, to see her face again, alive.
>
> Gradually life flows back into her face. The sea and sky are transformed . . . Her face becomes a light breeze that reaches across to touch me. It caresses me . . . Suddenly her wind shifts. The world of her face tilts up, new spaces open, and she approaches me with a fresh, strong breeze . . . I slip forward quickly in effortless delight . . . It is upon me. It strikes. I try to meet its force, to run with it, but it jolts me through and through. I quake . . . I turn my back to her wind. And I coast into quiet water, all alone. This quiet place quells the turmoil inside of me. It dies down and comes to a rest.
>
> (Stern, 1990: 58–60)

This passage graphically depicts a contained experience of mother's lively eyes. Poetic, metaphorical, and certainly not an infant's words or thoughts, these are the feelings Stern imagines that Joey is experiencing from his facial expressions. I imagine that a repeated experience of shame at Joey's age would sound more like the desolate inner experience of having to mirror mother rather than be reflected as a self by her, becoming for mother whatever she feels. This disturbing experience is described beautifully by Sylvia Plath in her poem entitled "Mirror":

I am silver and exact, I have no preconceptions.
Whatever I see I swallow immediately.
Just as it is, unmisted by love or dislike.
I am not cruel, only truthful –
The eye of a little god, four-cornered.
Most of the time I meditate on the opposite wall.
It is pink, with speckles. I have looked at it so long
I think it is a part of my heart. But it flickers.
Faces and darkness separate us over and over.

Now I am a lake. A woman bends over me,
Searching my reaches for what she really is.
Then she turns to those liars, the candles or the moon.
I see her back, and reflect it faithfully.
She rewards me with tears and an agitation of hands.
I am important to her. She comes and goes.
Each morning it is her face that replaces the darkness.
In me she has drowned a young girl, and in me an old woman
Rises toward her day after day, like a terrible fish.

(Plath, 1981: 173)

What happens to the infant internally when there is foreboding, pensiveness, hatred, or vacancy in mother's eyes? What happens when the mother is misattuned, withdrawn, rejecting, depressed, envious, or empty, and sees nothing of the excited, craving infant who is left cringing and unable to engage the mother's depriving eyes, or see her own self reflected in them? What happens to a nascent sense of self when the infant meets that still or contemptuous maternal face? The answer to all three questions is shame about one's very being, and an attempt to demonstrate how this is true will be made in the pages to come.

Just as shame has been neglected historically, the role of the eye in psychological development and the formation of attachment between mother and infant has been glaringly minimized or overlooked. There is an extensive developmental line that takes place through vision that psychologists have barely noticed, let alone incorporated into clinical theory and practice. Given the obvious prominence of eyes, this is hard to understand. Vision is of prime importance in humanity's struggle for survival. The time schedule of physical development in the human species follows a pattern laid down in prehistory, and eyes are one of the first organs to develop in utero at five weeks. The embryo's growth takes place from the head down, and at this time the head is grotesquely large compared to the rest of the body. Only much later does the body catch up. We can appreciate the intellectual significance of eyes when we realize that optical stimulation, more than other senses, produces changes in electroencephalographic rhythms. Embryologically, it is derived from the brain, becoming the only part of the nervous system exposed to the outer world. First the forebrain issues a hollow stalk on both sides, and the end of this stalk thickens and forms a small sphere. This stalk thrusts forward, and when it meets the inside of the skin, turns inward on itself like a cup. The base of this cup becomes the back of the eyeball, and the skin surface covering it the retina. Inside the cup, skin cells form for the lens and cornea, and finally the surrounding skin folds over to form eyelids. We don't know if infants can see in utero, but we know that eyes are sensitive to light and the fetus will shield its eyes with its hands when light intrudes. By week 13, the eye is well developed (Nilsson and Hamberger, 1990: 112).

The event of birth brings the child who is being born into direct eye contact with the mother. Figure 2.1 is a picture of a four-minute-old newborn and mother enjoying their first moment of eye-to-eye contact after their birth struggle together. It was at one time thought that an infant's visual capacities were limited. It is now firmly established that the perceptual capacities at birth are well developed, and by two and a half to three months are functioning at adult capacity.

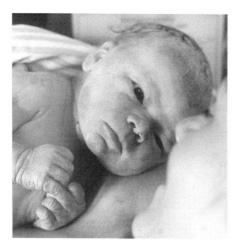

Figure 2.1 Mother and four-minute-old infant's first moment of eye contact

Eye-to-eye contact is reciprocal from the moment of birth and, unlike the other tasks of raising a baby and senses involved, is a part of every phase of interaction. When the mother is touching, holding, or breastfeeding, for example, she is gazing upon her baby, and the infant will hopefully be returning the gaze. Infant research, as will be demonstrated later, clearly reveals that the mother's face configuration, specifically her eyes, comes to have a unique stimulus value for her infant and plays a significant role in the developing early object relationship, becoming the first primary object.

Eyes and vision are also rich in meaning. Eyes are one of mankind's most precious organs, because through them reality is more comprehensively perceived. Eyes are considered organs for actual sight, and have long been considered the mirror to the soul and vehicles for emotional expression, especially between mother and infant. One glance from an eye can tell us more than hours of auditory or tactile description. Hand–eye coordination gives us mastery over the world, and when we say we understand a thing, we mean that we grasp and see it.

Strangely enough, the eye has been overlooked as the point of contact between a mother and an infant in favor of the breast. Perceptual experiences of infancy and childhood have been obscured by the Kleinian ideas of good and bad breast. The infant not only relates to the breast as a part-object from the time of birth, but to mother's eyes as well. Robson (1967) has argued that "despite the fact that psychoanalytic theory has emphasized the mouth as an early focus point of body image, in terms of their salience the eyes should have priority" (p. 17). It is during breastfeeding that mother's eyes become most prominent due to their proximity (eight inches away) and come to be fused with the breast. It may actually be the eyes to which the infant emotionally cathects. The connection between mother's eyes and her breasts is illustrated by a Slovak injunction never to give a child the breast after it has been weaned, for fear that her desires will become implacable and that she will develop an evil eye towards the things that are forbidden to enjoy (Huxley, 1990: 73). The identification of the breast with the eye is also a collective truth revealed in the etymological roots of our language. Almansi (1960) points out that the Latin word *papilla* (for pupil of the eye) is the diminutive of *pupa* or *puppa* which means girl. *Puppa* was also used in vulgar Latin to indicate the nipple, hence the Latin *poppina* which indicates the bud, the eye of plants. The modern Italian *puppa* or *poppa*, a vulgar word for the female breasts, is derived from the same Latin word, as is the common verb *poppare* or *puppare*, which means to suckle. Similarly, the Italian word *capez-zolo*, meaning the nipple, derives from the Latin *capetium*, which in turn comes from the word *caput* meaning head. In one of the Malay dialects, the nipple is called *mata susu*, literally the "eye of the breast." Another connection between eye and breast may be in the notion that eyes can eat, as in the phrase "to look at" and "devour with the eyes" (p. 61). Figure 2.2 shows clearly the fusion of the eye with the breast – a demoniacal figure of a woman whose nipples and navel are depicted as eyes.

Shame dwells in the eye. Eye-to-eye contact is evocative of shame so that its exploration in infancy necessarily leads to restoring the prominence of the eyes of both infant and mother. In the previous

Figure 2.2 Frontispiece for Oscar Wilde's *Salome* by Aubrey Beardsley

chapter a review of the clinical literature led to the determination that the deepest, most primitive aspects of shame are connected to the caregiver's face. The darkness or hollowness in the mother's eyes can be intolerable to the infant who will avert her gaze and hide her face (pathogenic for shame), and this very early experience continues into adulthood. In ordinary life, the face plays a significant role in interpersonal communication. Emotional messages are led by the face that becomes the center of a person, a primary expression of character and individuality. For the person who suffers from the earliest dimensions of shame, the evocative power of eyes and faces is massively amplified. On a conscious or unconscious level, this individual concentrates more intensively on faces, scrupulously studying the subtleties of emotional expressions to see past the mask of social manners and graces which can conceal the true face of feelings. The cringing impact of shame can be activated at any moment by a look in the eyes, a shadow that crosses a face, knitted eyebrows or simply eye contact. Picturing oneself in the eyes of the other will instill such a horrible feeling that this individual will hope to wipe her existence off the face of the earth.

In this chapter, we will be looking at the specific patterns of experience in the mother–infant relationship that contribute to the generation of shame in the first six months of life, from an infant research point of view. These first months of an infant's existence are the most vulnerable, dependent times that are critical in laying the foundation for further development. Infant researchers such as Rheingold (1961) have pointed out that during this time the infant's primary activity is the visual exploration of the environment. The infant's looking and gazing at the caregiver increases after birth due to maturation of physiological and neurological systems up until about four months, when this behavioral system is mastered. The general developmental course of infant's gazing at mother's face is similar across cultures with only minor variations (Super and Harkness, 1982). When sensorimotor abilities are vastly more developed, and reaching, grasping, and manipulation have enormously extended the infant's range of controllable activities, the mother's face, voice, and actions are no longer the main source of interest. Gaze behavior begins to serve other functions, and orientation to objects outside the dyad becomes possible (Trevarthen, 1979, 1982). By this time, the infant has also developed schemas of the human face, and most importantly knows the specific face of mother and is very familiar with the various changes it undergoes to form different emotional expressions. Stern (1977) states that this initial time period is one in which the infant is first being shaped into a social being, learning the skills of interactive processes by inviting mother for engagement and play, maintaining and regulating the exchange, and achieving the ability for ending the engagement. These interactive events take place mainly through face-to-face interaction and are the most crucial experiences in the first phase of "learning about things human." What is clearly revealed through infant research and observation is that the face subsumes a whole range of early experiences with the mother, both satisfying and unsatisfying. Mother's facial expressions give information to the infant about her growing self, just as in adulthood we tend to see ourselves through the eyes of others. By the end of this first six months the groundwork has been laid for reading basic human expressive displays (an art that the shamed individual develops with acuity and precision).

Whatever the physical side of development that infant research can track, there is also the emotional side, which is far less clear. The early days of life must be theorized from what patients present of their unconscious emotional life in a process of psychotherapy. Infants do not think or understand things as we do; nevertheless they are all the time having experiences which add up in a memory system. Even Carl Jung (1951/1959), who was not very interested in infancy, wrote that "the child had a psychic life long before consciousness" (p. 178). The infant state of consciousness is pure sensation with no capability for thought, reflection, or judgment. Shame occurs long before verbalization has come to have any meaning. The psychic world of infancy and experiences of shame can, however, be reflected directly in the preverbal manifestations acted in the transference or provocative countertransference reactions (both of these are explored in relation to shame in Chapter 6). This world is also made visible in facial expressions and responses to facial expressions. Darwin (1765) was the first to note that the pure affect states observable on the face of a newborn infant were the same expressions showing on the face of the more sophisticated, controlled adult. What he missed, however, was the inner emotional experience to which psychologists now attend. We cannot know directly what an infant feels simply because it is unable to communicate with us in words, yet the adult who can articulate feelings with words is wearing the same facial expressions.

Several clinicians have pondered and played with understanding these powerful, regressive elements in the adult's experience. From a clinical point of view, the first six months of life have been described as a time when the mother's bad feelings can be directed against the infant, while in the second half of the first year, the infant's reciprocal feelings of ambivalence, love, and hatred towards the mother make their first appearance (Herman, 1989). Spitz and Wolf (1946) have shown how the first smile specific to the approach of the mother's face from the front constitutes a first organizing element in the construction of preobject mental life. During the first six months, the relationship between mother and child is reciprocally organized on the basis of situations which set positive and negative affects. At around six months, the phobia of a stranger's face sets in and testifies to the differentiation of a permanent object. To a certain extent, it is an actual phobia, since the mother's absence is equivalent in that moment to danger, new experiences and strangers, which awaken all the negative affects. Winnicott (1992c) argues that the vitally important early period of infant emotional development, called the "symbiotic phase" or "stage of absolute dependence," is one before which "the infant knows himself (and therefore others) as a whole person that he is (and they are)" (p. 149). However, during this time, important emotional processes are developing. If they go awry, the result will be the solidification of psychosis and psychotic anxieties within the developing personality structure. At five or six months, a new phase he calls "the stage of relative dependence" develops and is marked by significant changes occurring in the infant that make it easier to refer to emotional development in terms that apply to human beings in general. Lacan (1977) theorizes that in the first six months there is no differentiation between infant and mother, and self-recognition does not exist. Only gradually does this emerge, beginning at age six months during a time he calls the "mirror stage of development" which is complete by 24 months. If these theories from research and clinical work were put together, one could say that the first six months of the infant's existence, during the time core shame can develop, are not experienced as separate from mother and are a time before self-awareness is acquired.

The eye as face

Of course many things are going on in the world of the infant and mother at the same time. According to Stern (1977), the infant's first exposure to the world of humanity consists of what the mother does with her face, eyes, voice, body, and hands (p. 9). Among many other things, mother is smiling, gazing, gently singing, cuddling, cooing, and soothing her baby as she goes about the tasks of breastfeeding, bathing, changing diapers, dressing, and rocking her baby to sleep. The baby is coming to know her mother through the touch of her skin, the warmth of her caressing hands, the sight of her face, the smell of her body, the taste of her breast and milk, and the sound of her voice. Each of these separate senses makes up the coherence of the mother's presence to her child, and thus the infant's experience of mother.

For the purpose of this work, however, the role that the eye plays in the construction of mother's presence will be singled out for closer understanding. A science teacher once taught me that we perceive objects more distinctly if we look through a hole in a card or other apparatus which acts like the pupil of an eye, narrowing the aperture for greater precision of focus. Like the artist who wishes to examine a singular point in a picture and looks through a tube to exclude all the other objects painted on the canvas, I will be separating out the eyes and vision to examine them with singular focus, delving deeply into the eye world of mother and infant, despite the many other factors that go into the development of their fascinating, intricate and complex relationship. Figure 2.3 is a painting by René Magritte entitled *Painted Object: Eye*. Not only does this painting depict exactly what I am attempting to do through words, but also conveys viscerally what happens when the eye is punctuated and other features of a face are excluded.

Artistic license is taken with the word eye, expanding its meaning to include the concept of face. Face and eye will be used interchangeably to convey the idea that a face becomes an eye, or an eye becomes a face, when all the senses and emotions are compelled into looking (Huxley, 1990). The concept that a face and eyes work in unison is supported by modern physiological/psychological research. Paul Ekman (2003), a researcher who has identified 18 kinds of smiles, states that the only kind of smile that activates the brain centers for enjoyment is the same grin that spontaneously crinkles the eyes into crow's-feet during a chuckle (pp. 206–7). This fact conveys the idea that eyes themselves are the center of facial expression. One can see the genuineness of the smile through the smiling eyes, which is to say that true facial expression involves engagement with the eyes.

The idea that an eye can also mean a face is further supported by the ancient wisdom in the etymological roots of our language. The pupil of the eye is so called because of the doll-like reflection of the

Figure 2.3 A painting by René Magritte entitled *Painted Object: Eye*

one who looks into the pupil of another's eye. The word pupil gets its name from the Latin *pupilla*, meaning a little girl, a doll, a puppet. This etymology is widespread; in Spanish the pupil is called *el nina del ojo*, the young girl of the eye; in German it is called *des Mannlein*, the little man; in Greek *kore*, the maiden (Huxley, 1990: 26); in Hebrew *ishon*, little man; in Sanskrit *kanna* meaning young girl (Almansi, 1960: 60). Essentially, the ancients conceived of a little child in the eye, a "pupil" who receives and learns about the outer world, visually mediating experience.

Gazing into another's eye, one sees in its darkness the infant-like image that is a miniature mirroring of oneself. This capturing of oneself in the pupil of the eye could be telling one that an eye is shorthand for a face (Huxley, 1990). Figure 2.4 is a picture taken by a patient who collected eye photos, and this one is of her mother's eye

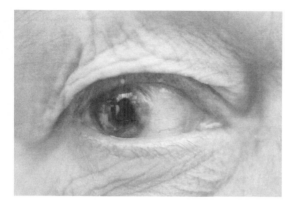

Figure 2.4 Patient's photograph of her mother's cold, lidless eye

(she will be discussed in more detail in Chapter 6). By looking closely at the pupil, one is able to spot her "tiny doll" reflection (as well as that of the world behind her) in her mother's pupil while capturing her eye with the eye of the camera.

The importance of eyes to a face is captured in the visual logic of very young children, who when asked to draw a face will represent the eyes alone (see Figure 2.5). It is thought that children draw this way because they include only the features they see (Kellogg, 1969). Magritte has done practically the same in his painting entitled *The Difficult Crossing* (see Figure 2.6), which depicts a man standing with a head which is an eye, its color and pupil creating what would be the face. Looking at this painting leaves me wondering what his

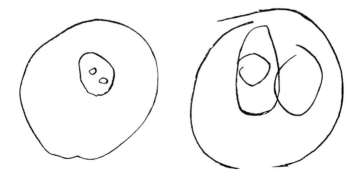

Figure 2.5 A 3-year-old's drawing of a human face

Figure 2.6 A painting by René Magritte entitled *The Difficult Crossing*

"difficult crossing" is. The "eye face" seems to peer directly at the gaping jaws of the ocean where a ship is being rocked side to side not far away. In surrealist fashion, it feels like the eye is staring at an image of the devouring mother. When we face a thing we look at it, and this fact is captured in such words as the German word *das Gesicht* and the English word visage, which comes from the Latin *didere* meaning to see, as well as the Greek *ops* and the Mende *ngame*, both of which mean at once eye and face (Huxley, 1990).

Eye or face – both bring life to whatever they are a part of. The eye and the face are equally the most expressive, communicative organs. The fascinating power of the eyes is hardly confined to the pupil's reflective qualities and capacity to vary in diameter, for an eye without a face does not express much of anything (see Figure 2.7). Despite the remarkable brilliancy of its structure, which is astonishing, alone an eye is nothing more than a slimy, mobile, shiny globe of fluid with a touch of color. Only its removal from the position it occupies in a living face reveals its round dimensions, yet an eye

Figure 2.7 A painting by René Magritte entitled *La monde poétique*

needs a face (and a mind) to come to life. Greenacre (1926) points out that the eye is the least expressive facial feature, and that the neurological foundation of the observation that eyes are expressive is really a function of facial muscles and nerves. She speculates that it is not the eyeball itself but intricate movements of facial muscles, most especially the eyelids, which enhance the eye and give it its reputation for being so emotionally expressive. For example, coldness of glance is really immobilized facial muscles. On the other hand, a face without eyes is lifeless and mask-like. Take for example the Paleolithic images of the Great Mother Goddess whose faces were rarely given expression through the eyes (Figure 2.8 and 2.9), with the goddesses of Neolithic times, whose eyes start to open with compelling effect (Figure 2.10).

Figure 2.8 Venus of Willendorf, limestone, Austria

Figure 2.9 Paleolithic idol (Venus), soapstone, Austria

Figure 2.10 Eye idol from Tel Brak, Syria, about 3000 BC

A note about blind infants

There is yet another preliminary remark to prepare the way into the eyes of shame. In this exploration I am referring only to persons who have sight. Individuals with congenital blindness are beyond the scope of this work. I suppose that no one can really understand the mental processes of the person born blind unless she has been blind herself, so that my insight into a blind person's mind is that of a psychologist interested in eyes. A sketchy thought from my point of view, however, is that blind infants will need to accentuate the development of another sense to arrive at the equivalency of sight. Although inborn, the capacity for vision is not ready-made from the start; it is developed gradually (albeit rapidly) through repetitious experiences of eye contact with people. From the moment of birth, looking and touching, eye contact and skin contact, are the two major ways infants can explore the world directly, as well as being the two means mother has of getting to know her baby. When the eyes can't see, the activity of the tactile sense must compensate for the absence of vision. So much information is obtained through touch, and in later life the blind person, in order to be mobile, touches her way through the world with a stick. Perhaps for the blind, sight manifests through what is felt in the skin, and can account for the visceral qualities experienced in shame. Tactile contact may even arouse a visual image or schema for the object touched. It may be as though a blind infant, like the Argus (see Figure 2.11), has many eyes on its skin. A mother is also bound to interact differently with a blind infant, which could in itself create a greater propensity for the development of shame. A blind person is already to some degree an outcast and alienated from the normal world. But early forms of shame could get generated through mother's sterile, rejecting, or unempathic touch and would have to be therapeutically analyzed through interactive bodily experiences and sensations.

Infant research

The first part of this exploration into eyes is a look at the research specifically focussing on the infant's development of vision, and the crucial role that it plays in forming an attachment to the mother and the world of human stimuli. These scientific facts about vision are presented to show how important the eye and face are to an infant's visual development, and to provide a basis of support for the exploration of the eye as a psychological center of the mother–infant relationship, hence a major factor in intrapsychic and interpersonal development. As you read, note how infant research reveals the importance in particular of mother's face to visual training and how her eyes become the infant's first selfobject.

Current research reveals the newborn infant to be a "tiny replica

Figure 2.11 Argus, Hera's many-eyed watchman. Wall painting by Pinturicchio

of self," a social being born with a complex internal state actively seeking engagement with the world. Neonates are now considered biologically predisposed to search for stimulation, and neonatal research details the readiness of both mother and infant for immediate postnatal interaction. The baby offers coos and gurgles, cries, head movements, smiles, and eyes as big as saucers to reinforce and provide feedback for mother's modes of interaction (Lichtenberg, 1991). Eye contact is one among the many signals the infant has available for indicating need and endearing herself to mother. This is a dramatically different view of the infant from the tabula rasa or undifferentiated state depicted by Freud's drive theory of preprogrammed instincts. Research supports an object relations perspective which sees the internal development of the infant shaped by a human social context. This position is best stated by Winnicott's (1960) often quoted remark "There is no such thing as an infant," by which he meant that whenever one finds an infant one finds maternal care, and without this care there is no infant.

Finding that infantile psychological and visual development is much more than what psychoanalytic drive theory supposes opens up the possibility of a deeper exploration of shame and an awareness that this affect has a much earlier onset than at first believed by psychoanalytic theorists. In the previous chapter, we saw how views of shame have moved from an analysis of instinctual events which occur within the child to a developmental, object relations perspective which shifted attention to an earlier time and what goes on in the space between mother and infant. Shame could then be linked to early mother–infant attachment and the infant's experience of mother's face. That research demonstrates that the infant begins extrauterine life supplied with demonstrable functional capacities to engage mother lends weight to Broucek's theory that shame is the result of the infant's inefficacy in her attempts to engage mother; hence being looked at as an Other or becoming an object in mother's eyes. However, his conclusion that shame is at core a narcissistic defeat does not capture the depth of the disturbance in this affect. Later in this chapter, a theory is developed that identifies shame as an affect in psychotic anxieties, in that shame is disintegrating to and annihilating of the self.

Eye-to-eye contact

Infant researchers have extensively explored the evolution of perceptual and attentive capacities in the infant. At birth, the visual motor system (looking at and seeing) comes immediately into operation. The newborn can not only see, but also arrives with reflexes that allow her to fixate her gaze upon an object and visually pursue it. Infants also begin life with preferences for visual stimuli (Fantz, 1961), and Stern (1990) has pointed out that these innate preferences for certain features add up to a face. The infant's early perceptual skills and preferences for curves over straight lines (shape of the eyes and eyebrows), strong light/dark contrasts (the black pupil against the whites of the eye), acute angles (the corners of the eyes) and love of motion add up to a preference for looking at eyes. Experimental situations reveal that neonates can visually discriminate brightness, form and pattern, and contrast levels of complexity and movement (Kessen, Haith, and Salapatek, 1970). Infants react selectively to human and non-human objects, indicating that they have "inborn pre-coordinations" for each of these interactions (Lichtenberg, 1991). The baby has an inbuilt bias to respond to features that have human significance, and mother's face is the first face ever to be recognized. This finding indicates that the neonate is screening perceptual input in combination with information stored from everyday experiences. When presented with mother, the neonate will "open his mouth, circle and purse his lips, and sustain this for several seconds. This is often accompanied by tongue thrusts as well as body quivers and small thrusts of the head forward . . . These responses, especially when accompanied by the widening of the eyes, are as compelling as the social smile at six weeks" (Bennett, 1971: 87). Brazelton and Als (1979) put it this way: "the contrast of the infant's behavior and attention span when he was interacting with his mother, rather than an inanimate object, was striking as early as four weeks of age . . . You could indeed tell from looking at a toe or a finger whether the infant was in interaction with an object or a parent – and by four weeks of age, even which parent it was" (pp. 357–9). Stern (1977) has offered an interesting interpretation of this different behavior, postulating that interactions with humans lead to internalized affectively charged units of experience, while reactions to objects contribute to the formation of what Piaget called sensorimotor schemata.

Greenman (1963) has determined that of all the neonatal reflexes, visual fixation and following, two of the first acts of the infant, are the only ones that do not disappear over time and show increasing facility. These visual abilities are precocious compared to the infant's other abilities and will maintain their form throughout life. The infant's early control of gaze gives her a large measure of control over her perceptual input. In a social interaction this means control and regulation of the amount and timing of visually focussed social interaction (Robson, 1967). This early visual motor control has been described as an important early ego mechanism to accomplish coping and defensive operations in an interpersonal situation (Spitz, 1955; Stern, 1974). As for mother's reaction to visual fixation, she experiences for the first time the very certain reality that her infant is really looking at her, and even more into her eyes. With the feeling that her baby can see her, a new level of dramatic connection can be experienced, and she seems to spend much more time with her baby.

By the age of one month, infants demonstrate an appreciation for the non-featural aspects of the human face such as animation, complexity, and configuration (Sherrod, 1981). They scan faces fluidly, and when scanning behave differently than when scanning inanimate objects. They squirm, vigorously move their arms and legs, open and close their hands and feet in smooth movements (Donne, 1973) and emit more sounds (Brazelton et al., 1974).

Up to two months of age, infants predominantly scan the periphery of objects, and thereafter they shift their gaze to look more intently at internal features (Salapatek, 1975). There are two important differences, however, when the object is a living face. Infants even younger than two months shift their gaze from the peripheral to the internal features of the face when there is movement in facial features (Donne, 1973). This same phenomenon is observed when a voice is added (Haith et al., 1977), and neonates are able to discriminate their own mother's voices (DeCasper and Fifer, 1980).

In addition to the infant's visual capacities, the role of mutual gazing or eye-to-eye contact between mother and infant has come under the scrutiny of many researchers (Jaffe, Stern and Perry, 1973; Robson, 1967; Stern, 1974). They have found that, in their awake states, infants spend much of the time in quiet attentiveness to the mother's face in the midst of squirming, gurgling, and other gestures to engage the mother. Infants will interrupt their feeding, whether it is by breast or bottle, to focus their eyes on mother's face, particularly her eyes about eight inches away (Stern, 1977). During feeding, mothers spend about 70 percent of the time facing and looking at their infants. At such times the infant will perform no expressive or social behaviors except eye-to-eye contact, which is an extremely important and powerful event for the mother (Stern, 1974, 1977; Wolff, 1963).

The first and most important object seen then is mother's eyes, rather than the breast, which many earlier psychoanalytic theorists assumed. Infant research has clearly shown mother's face to be the initial focus of concern in the infant's early construction of the visual world and human relatedness. It has also been thought from these observations that the mother's visually perceived face comes to be fused with the breast, which only contributes to its sense of power (Spitz, 1955). The nipple is thought to behave like an eye, and the infant looks at it as though it is looking into mother's eyes (a good example of how these two objects come to be paired is shown in infant observation material later in this chapter). From the very beginning mother's face is central to the process of attachment. Infants will actively seek their preferences for mother in order to stimulate responses. Ideally, mother will provide the correct reciprocal feedback to capture the baby in its need for eye-to-eye contact. According to Lichtenberg (1991), by seven to ten days of age, the mother can rely on consistent eye-to-eye contact. By four weeks the infant is giving clear cues to the mother to lengthen this engagement, and by three months these periods of eye-to-eye contact have become conversational games. All these developments make the face the heart of interaction and human development.

At two and a half to three months, a dramatic difference in perceptual organization and eye-to-eye contact emerges (Lichtenberg, 1991). The eight-inch gaze focus observed during breastfeeding nears adult capacity and vastly expands the infant's visual communicative capacity (White, Castle and Held, 1964). When a favored stimulus is offered, like the mother's face, the baby will prolong the alert period rather than falling asleep. At nine weeks, the infant's way of looking at mother changes from simply searching to an active scanning that looks for her eyes on which to visually fixate with eyes widening and brightening (Wolff, 1963). The infant searches the face, peering at the mouth, hairline, and then the whole facial gestalt. As soon as eye-to-eye contact is made, she smiles. After this change, the infant's interest in and responsiveness to the environment can be considerably heightened (Emde, Gaensbauer and Harmon, 1976).

Infants are born with an innate preference for the human face (or at least eyes). Experiments with masks confirm that the eyes are the most important facet of the visual gestalt (Wolff, 1963). For example, at two months a pair of black dots on a face-sized card will elicit the child's searching response. Gradually, however, the complexity of the gestalt must be increased, until at eight months nothing short of an actual human face will do. Infants of about three months showed more interest in a moving human face, seen frontally, compared to a profile or one where the eyes cannot be seen. Kagan et al. (1966) found that four-month old infants smiled far more often to the presentation of a realistic face stimulus than to those where the features were either scrambled or lacking eye representations. In a study by Goldstein and Mackenberg (1966) children of four and a half to ten and a half years of age were given the task of identifying peers from photographs showing isolated facial features, and were far more successful when part or all of the two eyes was displayed.

According to Robson (1967), if the bond through eye contact is not established, or if it is characterized by disruption or distress, the infant's ability to form human relationships will be damaged. He supports this idea with a quote from Ahrens: "the absolute stimulus which must stand at the root of social behavior is the eye part (of the mask or an observer's face)" (pp. 17–18). Robson goes on to quote Schaffer and Emerson, who have observed with increasing frequency during the first year of life that situations in which "visually maintained contact" is interrupted are the most provocative of separation protest (p. 18). They further find that a mother who provides perfectly adequate bathing, changing, feeding, and soothing but does not provide significant eye contact during these interactions is depriving her infant of the optimal conditions for developing a "face tie," hence a good attachment. Maternal responsiveness must accurately meet the baby's needs; obviously a significant need of the infant is for mother's eyes. The mother's face has an emotional climate, and depriving maternal behaviors must become a part of the infant's gestalt of the mother's gaze. Behaviorally, this may be defined as the degree of animation and modulation of facial expression, particularly around the upper half of her face.

By the third to fourth month of life, the infant has become remarkably social with an established repertoire of facial expressions (Ambrose, 1961; Emde and Harmon, 1972; Spitz and Wolf, 1946). Stern (1990) points out that from the age of two months to six months, the baby's social world is limited to a face-to-face one, and "as a way of interacting with others and reading their behavior, it will last all his life" (p. 47). Several major lines of social behavioral development converge (gaze, smiling, vocalization). It is also around this time that the infant is fully able to distinguish mother's face from the face of a stranger. This appears to promote the full development of shame out of its prior partial manifestation of gaze aversion:

> Many people have had the experience of seeing someone in a crowd and eagerly trying to greet and communicate with the individual only to find suddenly that the person whose attention has been claimed is a total stranger. The shame experienced in such a situation may be mild, or intense, depending upon the circumstances. Since an unanticipated friend–stranger differential can elicit shame, Tomkins hypothesizes that as soon as the

infant learns to differentiate the face of the mother from the face of a stranger . . . the infant is vulnerable to shame.

(Izard, quoted in Broucek, 1991: 31)

Gaze aversion

When visual behavior does not exist in the relationship between human beings, something deviant or pathological is present. One of the earliest forms of relating and consolidating a relationship is via eye contact, and, therefore, interaction disturbances are frequently characterized by infant gaze aversion. Most researchers interpret gaze aversion in terms of the infant's reaction to over- or under-stimulation (Brazelton, Koslowski and Main, 1974; Field, 1977; Stern, 1974), intrusive controlling (Stern 1977), or unresponsive and insensitive (Keller and Gauda, 1987) caregivers. Gaze aversion develops as a failure to achieve an optimal range of attention and arousal, a keystone in the establishment of attachment between mother and infant. Until motor abilities are developed, the only control the infant has is to shut her eyes or avert her gaze. As Lichtenberg (1991) puts it, "just as infants respond in a compelling fashion, with eye fixation, to a face, they will, from the second week, react defensively to a looming head. They will move their heads back and away, widen their eyes, and show a 'negative' facial expression" (p. 53). In the range of negative responses, they may withdraw attention (Aleksandrowicz and Aleksandrowicz, 1976; Bridger, 1961), shut their eyes or turn away to avert their gaze (Beebe and Stern, 1977), or become fretful and cry. These experimentally induced displeasure responses are suggestive of pathological interaction sequences that may occur with mothers who are depressed, withdrawn, or hyperanxious. Violations in this kind of interaction can affect both mother and infant, and engender a powerful repetitious pattern.

In order for the mother to elicit behaviors of engagement in addition to eye-to-eye contact, she must keep the infant in a range of attention and arousal in which these behaviors may occur. Each relationship has different means to achieve this goal. The infant's primary means are control of visual motor skills that allow visual attention. The mother's means of achieving engagement involve the ways she can modulate the stimulation through a continually changing array of sounds, motions, facial expressions, and tactile events.

The infant does not orient and remain attentive to any and all stimulation. Instead, it appears that infants are innately disposed to orient, remain attentive to, and find pleasurable only certain stimulus quantities and qualities that fall within a given range (Kessen et al., 1970). In a project by Stern (1974) with four-month-old infants, the major clinical issue was how much and what kind of stimulation the mother provides for the infant, and in turn, the infant provides the mother. All of the interactive events were performed with the high potency valued face. The extent to which these behavioral acts are absent and she is exposed to normal adult behavior, the infant will experience stimulus deprivations, lack of social play and responsiveness, and withdrawal.

In general, if the level of stimulation is too low, an infant will either not attend or "lose interest" quickly, and, if it is available, she will seek more stimulation elsewhere. If the level of stimulation is too high, she will avoid it (Stern, 1974: 404). Infants do not like to be encroached upon frontally and react in an aversive manner to objects which loom towards their face and eyes (Bower, 1965). If an infant is shown a stimulus that is of low intensity or low complexity, or almost identical to one she has seen enough before to have formed a schema, it will elicit relatively little visual attention and arousal. Positive affect will follow as the intensity of the stimulus increases, in turn raising attention and arousal. However, when a pronounced range is reached, the infant will attempt to shut out stimulation coming at her primarily through the organ of the eye with signs of gaze aversion. This movement supports Tomkins's definition of shame as reducing excitement enjoyment, and now we can add arousal system and attachment.

An experiment called the still faced study done by Tronick and his colleagues (1975) shows clearly the result of restricted facial displays on the infant, and is of particular importance in demonstrating the early onset of shame in relation to mother's face. Researchers asked mothers to alternate between normal, active, and lively facial displays and a flat, deadpan expression. In the experiment, a mother fixes her gaze above the infant's eyes, keeping her face expressionless and immobile. The infant would first attempt to recapture the mother's expected response by trying to meet her eyes, moving her hands and eyes, and groping with her arms, legs, and indeed her entire squirming body. When this was unsuccessful, the baby averted her gaze and collapsed into an attitude of total withdrawal. The cycle of attempts to engage followed by collapse was repeated, each time with mounting distress. Initially the infant's main reaction to the inhibited facial looks was to do remarkable things to get the mother's attention. When this was not forthcoming, the infant dis-integrated and collapsed into shame, evidenced by gaze aversion and a limp body which "cringes in *apology* for her very existence" (Morrison, 1996: 7).

Having the mother interact with her infant while looking at another adult instead of her infant also tends to increase both maternal activity and infant gaze aversion (Trevarthen, 1974). In studies which have manipulated face-to-face interactions (Field, 1977), an interesting finding emerges. When the mother engages in attention getting behaviors, the infant is gaze averting, overloaded by the stimulation. Conversely, during imitation, the mother replicates more closely the infant's behavior, making it less discrepant and more readily assimilated by the infant, who has less need to take pause in the interaction.

Early maternal behavior has a clear impact on visual and arousal systems (Moss and Robson, 1968; White et al., 1964). This evidence suggests that the caregiver who is affectively "alive" (talking, chan-ging facial expressions, moving, etc.) provides stimulation that cor-responds more closely to the range of stimulus events to which the infant is constitutionally preset to respond than most other stimulus events in an average expectable environment (Ainsworth, 1969). The average mother during a social interaction will seek to maintain the infant in a state of attention and arousal by performing social behaviors such as smiles and coos, which in turn produce in her infant those behaviors that maintain her attention and arousal. Drastic variation in a mother's behavior may be experienced as too discrepant, and this will predictably influence the flow of the mother–infant interaction. The eventual result of these interruptions of regulation is a lack of attunement and attachment, which can in turn lead to shame.

Conclusion

This chapter has provided an analysis of infant research specifically related to the development of vision and the role that eye contact plays in facilitating attachment between mother and infant, and socialization. Findings that emerge from infant research clearly demonstrate that the mother's face and eyes are of primary import-ance in the infant and mother's interaction. To summarize the most salient features of the infant research just delineated, studies show that the moment-to-moment interaction between mother and infant is far from random; the actions of the two participants show a marked degree of behavioral rapport. At a preverbal stage, the overall interaction is indirect and face-to-face contact regulates the interactive process. The neonate has a unique personality from the start and is an active participant in interaction with the mother. The infant's visual behavior and facial movements suggest affect and approach responses. This construct is obvious by the second week of life (Bennett, 1971). Infant research clearly reveals that the mother's face configuration, specifically her eyes, comes to have a unique stimulus value for her infant and plays a significant role in the developing early object relationship, becoming the first primary object. The mother's expressions have uncontested primacy as far as the infant's interest and attention are concerned, and she is led to attract as much interest as possible to her already stimulating face. Reciprocally, the infant's gaze is a social signal indicating readiness to engage in interaction, and gaze aversion signals a need for alteration or termination of the engagement. The mother's still face has a particularly strong impact on the infant's withdrawal responses. It is noteworthy that shame is evidenced as early as the first six months of life, during the development of visual competence.

Chapter 3

Mother's eyes as false mirrors

Have you seen your face before your parents were born?

(Zen koan)

Never have I been in control of myself or even belonged to myself from the hour she let me gaze into her eyes: – that mirror which pleases me so greatly. Mirror, since I saw myself reflected in you, deep sighs have been killing me. I have destroyed myself just as the beautiful Narcissus destroyed himself in the fountain.

(Bernard de Ventadour, 1145–80, quoted in Nichols et al., 1962: 168)

Visual contact is one of the most intense and binding interactions in the world of the mother and infant. One could say that for a young infant, the face, most particularly the eye area, is the mother. The mother's eyes create a potent emotional presence for the infant and form the raw material from which the infant begins to experience her relationship to the world and others. Winnicott puts it this way: "The paradox has to be accepted that what the baby creates was already there, and that in fact the thing that the baby creates is part of the mother which was found" (Winnicott, 1987: 65). Eyes are an emotional center of the mother–infant relationship and a pivotal factor in intrapsychic development. The mother's face is the infant's first reflection of her inner self, and it is through her mother's mirroring and responsiveness that the child begins to develop a sense of being and integrate intense emotions and instincts. Wright (1991) points out that "within this social interchange it is the visual channel that appears to have particular importance – it is through smiling, eye-to-eye contact and playful face-to-face interaction between mother and baby that attachment proceeds" (p. 9). Mother–infant interaction grows through a positive dialogue of visually perceived gestures. These early face-to-face moments are almost purely social in nature and are crucial in the formation of experiences. Eye contact is the beginning of object relating, which is in turn forming a template for how the individual will ultimately relate to the world. For the mother and infant, "gazing back and forth, rather than talking back and forth, is the action" (Stern, 1990: 49).

Imagine the impressions, then, that mother's eyes can make upon an infant's unformed, fragmented mind. Infant research has clearly shown that the baby is a human being from conception, immature and highly dependent yet a storehouse of experiences. Mother's facial expressions, the sparkle or darkness in her eyes must, then, dominate and define the infant's immediate world and sense of being. Everyone finds meaning in the expressions of another's eyes, and we tend to see ourselves in the eyes of others. What traces of the experience of mother's eyes are left behind? How does her baby internalize the inner emotional life reflected in her eyes? How does this experience live within the infant in the first six months of life and reveal itself later in adulthood?

In this first section, we will be looking at the growth-sustaining functions that the mother contributes, both as a mother and through her eyes, to the infant's core sense of self in the earliest phase of psychological development according to two similar theories: Winnicott's theory, which focuses on the interaction between mother and child; and Jungian developmental theory developed through the work of Michael Fordham which addresses the internal mental structure of the infant mind in interaction with the mother. Fordham's material is less specifically related to the mother's eyes, although it brings important collective unconscious dimensions in the form of archetypes into play. My presentation of Winnicott's work relates most directly to the mother's presence, hence specifically her eyes and face, and the infant reflected in them, while my explication of Fordham's work is directed more towards the infant's intrapsychic mechanisms and, therefore, how mother's eyes and face are bound to be internalized. In either theory, however, the primary factor that contributes to strong and healthy psychological development is the responsiveness and empathy of the mother. Later, in the section entitled "The Eye as False Mirror", the mother's empathic failures that damage the infant's growing mental structure according to these two theories are explicated. As before, eye-to-eye contact, the role of the mother's face, the infant's response to it, and the nonverbal expressions that transpire through these organs will be emphasized while being fully aware that eye contact is just one component in the vast matrix of mother–infant interactions.

The eye as mirror

Winnicott (1971) has said "in individual emotional development the precursor of the mirror is the mother's face" (p. 111). A pediatrician who became a psychoanalyst, Winnicott focuses on the central role of the mother (or maternal figure) and her contributions to the infant's psychological development. For him, the nature of maternal care determines the quality of the baby's development. He states: "It is not possible to talk about an infant without at the same time talking about infant-care and the mother" (1965b: 233).

According to Winnicott (1971), the mother and her face play a vital mirroring role from the moment of birth. The infant is, paradoxically, both dependent and independent. There are all the potentials that are inherited, including maturational processes which have a reality of their own and cannot be altered. At the same time, these independently existing inherited potentials depend upon environmental provision for their evolution. The mother facilitates or makes possible the infant's realization of inherited potentials through her empathic reflections of her infant.

During the initial stage of emotional development, the environment is "not yet separated off from the infant by the infant" (Winnicott, 1971: 111). This phase is marked by the infant's absolute dependence upon the mother that exists in a psychological as well as physical sense. He calls this first stage the "holding phase," described as a period when the infant lacks knowledge of the existence of anything other than the self. The infant is absolutely dependent but not able to know about dependence. The infant is in a "facilitating environment," relating to mother in a merged state. In this state, "the environment is holding the individual, and at the same time the individual knows no environment and is at one with it" (Winnicott, 1992b: 283).

In earliest infancy, indistinctness between self and object prevails. At this stage, there is also no internal differentiation between consciousness and unconsciousness; these two states of mind do not yet exist in the infant, although experiences do. At the beginning, the baby has not separated off what is not me from what is me, so that what is a part of the environment (i.e., the mother) is the baby. What is called a baby at this point is the cumulative experience of the baby with the mother. The mother is a subjective object to the infant, or in Kohutian terms an archaic selfobject. This means that the object providing care is experienced as an extension of the self of the infant. The subjective object is "the first object, the object not yet repudiated as a not-me phenomena" (Winnicott, 1971). This form of object relating, which he compares with primary identification, is an essential precondition for the development of a sense of self and promotes an initial sense of existence for the infant. The baby feels as if the object of primary identification is a subjective one, created by the baby and within her control. Mother and baby, eye to eye, work together to create the illusion of continuity and sameness.

For her part, the mother plays in holding, handling, and presenting herself as an object to her infant for her use, all the while holding the infant's "inherited potentials" (Winnicott, 1971). These potentials are what comprise the infant's true self and contain the "continuity of being" or "going on being" elements that create a sense of a continuous, and eventually, differentiated self. These potentials cannot become manifest unless linked to good maternal care.

Therefore, the mother's role is to give back to the infant its own self. The baby should look at the mother's face and catch a glimpse of her self reflected in it. In Winnicott's words:

> What does the baby see when he or she looks at the mother's face? I am suggesting that, ordinarily, what the baby sees is himself or herself. In other words the mother is looking at the baby and what she looks like is related to what she sees there. All this is too easily taken for granted . . . that which is naturally done well by mothers who are caring for their babies shall not be taken for granted.
>
> (Winnicott, 1971: 112)

Bion (1962), in particular, increased our understanding of the early and crucial interplay of the maternal mind with the mind of her infant. Through a process of what he calls "maternal reverie," the mother uses her mind to contain her infant's primitive terrors, a process that lies at the heart of all good infant care. Just as the mother will bathe away the infant's bodily mess, she will also clean up the infant's mental messes as a prerequisite to growth. Through a process of projection, these anxieties enter her mind, where they are decontaminated and returned to her infant in a new, less lethal form. This is performed through what Bion called the "alpha function." In this way the gap that these primitive anxieties can produce between mother and her infant is slowly metabolized so that the dyad is only gradually acclimated to the dimly apprehended fact of separateness. Maternal reverie enables the mother to contain her infant through the turbulence arising from their actual physical and mental separateness. Slowly the infant will internalize these experiences of reverie and develop her own "alpha function" to contain extreme feelings, with the result that this child will reflect positive feelings about herself. Hendrickson (1999) has said that in Bion's thought, the alpha function also leads to the formation of a contact barrier which creates differentiation between the conscious and the unconscious, a semipermeable membrane that regulates the flow, and maintains a connection, between the two.

Figure 3.1 is a painting entitled *Diego and I* by Frida Kahlo. It is a splendid depiction of what the holding of another in the mind's eye can look like in an intimate relationship; hence what an infant held in mother's mind must look like too. The mother, through holding the infant in her mind and her capacities of relatedness, awareness, and empathy, shows the infant her love and comes to an exact, almost magical understanding of the infant's needs. The infant lives in the mother's intuitive third eye. The good enough mother looks at, admires, and reflects her infant in her mind as shown in her eyes, and this in turn facilitates the creation of the infant's mind and concept of self. Winnicott puts the infant's thinking this way:

> When I look I am seen, so I exist
> I can now afford to look and see
> I now look creatively and what I apperceive I also perceive.
> In fact I take care not to see what is not there to be seen (unless I am tired).
>
> (Winnicott, 1971: 114)

To be perceived by the other and to perceive that one is looked at by the other evokes a sense of self. The infant looks into mother's face and gets back evidence that she is recognized as a being. It is this kind of synchrony in the initial interactions and eye-to-eye contact between mother and infant that provides the infrastructure for the deepest level of empathic contact (Stern, 1977). The craving, openness and responsiveness of the baby to her mother is depicted in

Figure 3.1 Painting by Frida Kahlo entitled *Diego and I*

Figure 3.2, which shows a mother in synchronous interaction with her eleven-day-old infant.

The eyes of mother serve to hold the infant emotionally together just as her skin holds the infant somatically together. Our most

Figure 3.2 Mother and child in a synchronous union

intense moments of inseparableness and wholeness occur when we look into the accepting and responding face and eyes of the other, an experience which begins in infancy. When the infant is held in mother's eye, she is contained in mother's mind. By holding her baby in mind, by reflecting her during a state of reverie, the mother relates directly to the mental life of the infant and helps to transform the anxieties plaguing her baby. Eye contact ensures direct communication, play, and reciprocal empathy between the two. This shared space becomes a unique medium that resonates with the sensations, thoughts, emotions, and mental images of the two.

When containing, eyes are a vital presence creating a unity for identity of being and existence. The eye's shininess and reflective qualities can also literally be viewed as a mirror. The infant becomes the little child residing in the chamber of mother's pupil, contained in the mind of the mother so that the infant can take in the outer world as itself through mother's eyes (remember Figure 2.4.). That this child becomes a self through mother's eyes is a concept emphasized in the words of Socrates while pondering the meaning of the Delphic inscription "Know Thyself." It is, he says, as though someone were to say to the eye:

> "See thyself," which it should do in a mirror, especially in the mirror of another eye. If the eye is to see itself, therefore, it must look at the eye, at that part of the eye – the pupil – where sight which is the virtue of the eye resides.
>
> (Socrates, quoted in Huxley, 1990: 32)

Seeing oneself reflected in another's eye is to know one's self, and to exist.

Although the infant has been shown to be biologically primed for immediate interaction, she is in a state of total dependence and unable to gain control over what mother does well or poorly, only to be taken care of or suffer disturbance. The maternal ego implements the infant's ego, so to speak, making it powerful and stable. The ego support provided by the mother enables the infant to live and develop, despite her inability to control what is good and bad in the environment, and provides simple, stable, "going-on-being" (Winnicott, 1971) elements that derive from the infant's own true self.

During this period of absolute dependence, the mother is serving as a container for an enormous amount of primitive, deeply rooted anxiety related to survival. The baby is an immature being on the brink of unthinkable anxiety all the time; every infant begins life under these circumstances. These anxieties are kept away by the vitally important containing functions that the mother serves. The infant escapes mental death only through the constant satisfaction of her needs, which are satisfied through her dependency on the mother's care, from which she does not distinguish herself. The maternal role of holding includes reliable aid in helping the infant to become able to experience and survive this kind of disintegrative, psychotic anxiety.

Under favorable circumstances, the infant establishes a continuity of existence despite these anxieties, and then begins to develop the sophistications that make it possible for impingements to be gathered into an area of omnipotence which develops eventually through the separation of the "me from the not-me" (Winnicott, 1971). The mother–infant unit begins to disentangle itself, the pace varying according to the dynamics between infant and mother. This differentiation of the infant into a separate personal self opens up the capacity for object relationships, and the mother–infant relationship changes "from a relationship of a subjectively conceived object to a relationship of an object objectively perceived" (Winnicott, 1960: 45). As maturation proceeds, the mother becomes an objectively perceived environmental feature, outside the omnipotent control of the baby. For the infant, it is essentially a period of ego development and integration.

Michael Fordham is a Jungian analyst who based a theory of infant development on Carl Jung's structure of the psyche and Melanie Klein's ideas on the infant's unconscious fantasy life of good and bad objects. He begins his theory by postulating that the infant mental structure is the same as an adult's, although in infancy it exists only in a germinal state. An explication of Fordham's theory of infant development must begin, then, with a brief detour into Jung's description of the structure of the psyche.

Jung theorized that the psyche is divided into conscious and unconscious aspects. The ego is considered the center of consciousness and the starting point for all empirical psychology. It is the seat of individual identity, and all conscious contents are connected with it. The unconscious includes all psychic elements which are outside conscious awareness, or, in other words, not connected to the ego. The self is, paradoxically, both the center of unconsciousness and the totality of the psyche. The unconscious consists of two layers, the personal unconscious and the collective unconscious. The personal unconscious contains unknown personal contents which can be integrated by the ego, whereas the collective unconscious contains transpersonal, universal elements called archetypes, which cannot be assimilated by the ego and of which we can only have indirect knowledge. Archetypes are a priori conditioning factors or predispositions, the substructure for all forms of mental functioning. An archetypal energy can never be known in its totality, only its images that appear symbolically in dreams, myths, religions, literature, art and other collective, cultural forms. The ego's developmental task throughout life is to adapt to both the outer and inner world, and this growth takes place through what is called the process of individuation.

Of particular importance to Fordham's theory are the archetypal shapes and patterns present in the infant's mind at birth that will form the infant's psychic life and regulate behavior. These proto-images are contained within the initially integrated and whole primal self (in Jung's theory called the self). In this primal state of wholeness, scarcely separate from the wholeness at all, the infant experiences and is controlled by the absolute dimension of the archetypes that are getting stimulated through affect driven instinctual discharges which promote development (Sidoli, 1989). The activity of the archetypes at this stage is tremendously intense, largely due to the weakness of the ego, giving rise to anxiety states linked to fears for survival and threats of disintegration. Fordham (1965) writes that archetypal activity at this stage is "natural, ruthless, absolute, in the ebb and flow of their need to discharge themselves . . . expressed anthropomorphically, the archetypes attack, persecute, seduce the ego" (pp. 98–101). The "primal self," the original state of wholeness, preserves the infant's continuity of being and individuality during a time when these big forces are at work in the little world of the baby.

Being a whole, intrapsychic, and closed system, the primal self must come into relation to the environment, and this occurs through the functions Fordham calls deintegration–reintegration. The infant is in a state of total dependency upon the mother, who is containing these catastrophic fears and anxieties. The infant deintegrates and opens to the environment so that mother can metabolize and humanize the instinctual, archetypally empowered collective elements internally bombarding the infant. In this essential capacity, the mother is the one person who can introduce the real world to the baby in a way that makes sense (integration). Similar to Winnicott's thinking, Fordham assumes that deintegration leads to a state of fusion between mother and the baby:

> Mother and infant become a unit thus reflecting the primary unity of the self from which the baby has begun to emerge. For his part the infant has not yet learned how to distinguish himself from the object world, and so all objects are treated as part of the self, but the state of fusion is participated in by the infant's real mother also.
>
> (Fordham, 1965: 107)

Fordham believes that the mother's love and care of her baby facilitate the infant's dependence to allow a fluid rhythm of integration, deintegration, and integration. This will help contain the infant's primal self while the ego unfolds and is shaped by these individuating processes to form a psychic structure which evolves into conscious and unconscious, inside and outside, good and bad. Infant observation, Fordham surmised, supported his theory:

> The integrative–deintegrative sequences stared me in the face. It was only necessary to observe a good feeding to see the baby unpacking, as it were, itself, approaching the breast and feeding until satisfied, and after which returning to an integrative sleep.
> (Fordham, 1985a: 4)

Infant research also supports Fordham's theory that there is an inbuilt capacity for organizing experience which, from the moment of birth, is creating psychic organization through its findings that the neonate is innately equipped to regulate stimuli and tension within optimal threshold limits. For example, Emde (1981) points to what he calls a biological predisposition "such that there are built-in self-righting tendencies after a defection due to adverse environmental circumstances" (p. 213).

Fordham gives the following example of a deintegration–integration sequence in a two-week-old baby. This particular example was chosen due to the prominence of eye contact:

> Baby N was lying in his bassinet on his right side . . . His eyes were open and he was moving his whole body slightly as if a little restless. F (mother) said he was probably hungry as it was near feeding time. N then suddenly quieted and for several minutes he lay absolutely still with his black eyes staring at the bassinet . . . F picked up N and gave him to me (the observer). N lay in my arms looking intently in my face and often opening his mouth and making noises. I talked to him and he responded by fixedly looking at my face. Several times he looked as though he was trying to smile . . . Then he looked away as if exploring the room and when I spoke he turned his head back to me looking in the vicinity of my face but not able to immediately focus directly . . . Then N took the baby and put him to her right breast to feed . . . N sucked vigorously occasionally stopping for a rest. At first his eyes were wide open but after a couple of minutes they shut while he continued to suck . . . F put him to her left breast and he sucked vigorously with lots of little grunts looking intently upwards. I thought he was trying to see her face but F said he was looking at her red jumper. He then fell asleep and stopped sucking.
> (Fordham, 1985b: 51–2)

One can see from this observation that vision can in itself be an image for the process of deintegration–integration. The infant's looking is an active exploration and opening up of the primal self to the environment. Closing the eyes, looking at an inanimate object, or averting the gaze can be seen as an integrative, digestive process. Robson (1967) states that "vision is the only modality which, by closure of the eyelids, gaze aversion, and pupillary constriction and dilation is constructed as an on–off system that can easily modulate or eliminate external sensory input, sometimes at will, within the first months of life" (pp. 13–14).

Differentiation and the gradual emergence of consciousness are acquired through good interaction with the mother. States of identity with self alternate with states of awareness of separateness. Archetypal images, enriched and humanized through interaction with the real world, will in time develop into proper images of objects and people (Sidoli, 1989). Deintegrates provide the groundwork for the development of ego. Thinking in a similar vein as Winnicott, Fordham states that mother provides containment for these deintegrative processes and must not violate the wholeness of the infant's primal self. Progress and maturation depend on the infant's capacity to elicit a response from the mother and relate to her, as well as the mother's capacity to empathize and relate to her infant. Eventually a movement from an undifferentiated stage to the stage of permanent and differentiated object is achieved, and the division of conscious and unconscious takes place.

In order to survive the intensity of these archetypal forces, the infant needs to receive the repeated and progressively refined attention of a mothering environment, to be able to signal the mother to better adapt to its needs and receive an attentive response. The infant quickly develops techniques to bring the surrounding environment into existence. Prolonged staring into the mother's eyes is one way the baby attempts to engage her.

The eye as false mirror

At the beginning, babies are absolutely dependent creatures necessarily and profoundly affected by everything that occurs, large or small. All that happens in the small world of the infant is extreme. Contentment is blissful, frustration is cataclysmic, sounds are cacophonous or harmonious, and mother's eyes can be petrifying or loving. With no precedents to qualify impressions, the baby is more vulnerable, and all experiences are bewildering and new. With time so undefined, states of want and need must seem to go on interminably. The infant must feel at times that she lives in a world without end.

Winnicott (1965b) proposes that Mother Nature makes natural provision for the high degree of unconditional adaptation that the infant needs to contain and define her otherwise limitless world. Like Alice, at first large but then growing small in the White Rabbit's house in Wonderland, the baby cannot expand to fit into the world of adult sophistication; a better fit is achieved when the mother can shrink herself into infancy. During the course of pregnancy and for a few months following birth, the mother enters what he calls a state of "primary maternal preoccupation," a time when she is given over to the care of her baby in such a way that the infant feels like a part of her own being. Feeling herself at the same time separate, a part of her regresses to her own experiences as a baby and as a mother she draws on these experiences. The infant literally becomes a part of her mind, and through this identification she is able to know directly what the baby is feeling and needs. When the mother is doing this well, when there is a harmonious synchrony between the mother's infant self and her own baby, the infant has no means of awareness of maternal provision and her ego support is taken for granted. The infant will simply experience a magical, undifferentiated "me–not me" state of being. In the best of situations, a mother protects her infant's own unique inherited potentials so well that the true self can evolve and mature. The good mother is able gradually to let go of her identification with her infant as the infant's need to become separate requires less and less adaptation.

Nature is also wise in making mother–infant eye-to-eye contact so prominent at the early stages of development, especially with its effect in evoking a smile. Eye contact has survival value for the relationship, and good eye-to-eye contact is critical to the development of positive, harmonious maternal feelings. Mothers take the greatest pleasure when their infants begin to see and recognize them, and when the infant gazes lovingly at her mother it enhances the mother's care. Mothers get little satisfaction from an infant who is helpless, crying, and defecating, and who may appear physically repugnant at times. The very helplessness of the newborn baby has survival value, awakening deep emotions in the mother that can facilitate the creation of an enduring attachment.

A certain proportion of babies, however, have experienced their mother's failures of adaptation while dependence is absolute, and then damage is done – damage which is at best difficult to repair. Problems arise when a pattern develops in the infant's life of mother projecting her own mental content upon her infant, rather than using it to relate to and reflect her baby. When a mother fails in this crucial holding phase, she creates a traumatic and premature sense of separateness that seriously interferes with the natural tendencies that exist in the infant, who instead becomes a "collection of reactions to impingements." The mother is no longer the infant's creation, but a separate person not under her control, someone whom the infant is in no way prepared to contain. The necessity of reacting to a mother's psychic content breaks up the infant's going-on-being. The automatic, reflexive reaction creates a trauma. Object relations become a threat. The infant withdraws from relating to objects.

The fate of the baby whose being becomes merely a "collection of reactions to impingements" produced by premature separateness during a symbiotic union with mother is states of disconnection characterized by "unthinkable anxieties." These anxieties, clinically known as "psychotic anxieties," have been defined as "relating to survival, identity, or loss of something which is not perceived as separate from the self or differentiated out from the rest of the self" (Little, 1993: 154). When psychotic anxieties predominate, everything relates to survival, and these ideas are fixed with an intensity which must be recognized as delusional (survival is the key when dealing with the regressive core of shame). When an infant is reacting, she is not being, and reacting at this very early stage of development means a temporary loss of identity, an extreme sense of insecurity and a loss of continuity of self. Without continuity of being the infant cannot come into her own existence. Even though a mother may be providing physical care, if she is not mentally adapting to her baby, she cannot metabolize the primitive, deeply rooted anxieties related to survival. An infant cannot psychically survive without her mother, so she suffers mental death. Psychotic anxieties, according to Winnicott (1965a), have only a few varieties, which he enumerated as "going to pieces, falling for ever, having no relationship to the body, and having no orientation" (p. 58). I would like to add to this list "not existing," a form of psychotic anxiety most relevant to the type of failure in holding and impingement that can result specifically from a mother's unreflecting eyes; in other words, shame at its core. Shame is the annihilating affect that lies at the heart of a psychotic schizoid element related to survival hidden in an otherwise sane personality.

Our relationship to the actual world is founded on the way things begin and the pattern that gradually develops in the relationship between a baby and its mother. During the initial symbiotic state it is assumed that the infant's experience of self is defined by parts of both the mother and the baby. The infant believes that the mother is her creation, and the good-enough mother plays at creating and supporting this illusion. Even though the infant is not a part of the mother's psyche, she is providing conditions for the confused perception between subject and object to occur. For this reason, mother's psychic content is bound to get mixed up with the infant's developing self during eye-to-eye contact. This is because eyes are consummate organs of emotional expression, "windows of the soul" and portals of vision into another's innermost thoughts and feelings. Eyes convey every emotion the human soul is capable of, and have the capacity to impart information to the mind that the other senses cannot grasp. "When a man speaks," said Mencius (quoted in Huxley, 1990: 4) "watch the pupils of his eyes, for there what can be concealed." Shakespeare's Berowne cries, "Behold the window of my heart, my eye" (quoted in Huxley, 1990: 26). "The eyes," Culpeper says, "are next in nature unto the soul, for in the eyes is seen and known the disturbances and griefs, gladness and joys of the soul" (quoted in Huxley, p. 56). In everyday language, there are hundreds of common expressions referencing the eye, like "flashing eyes," "glad eyes," and "glancing daggers." The Bible speaks of "the eye of pride," the "eye of pity," the "eye of wrath," the "eye of anger" and the "eye of mockery."

Eyes not only allow one to see into another's mind, but enable one to affect what one sees, to bend or persuade another to one's will. This is the importance of the eye in magic and symbolism. Literature is replete with a profusion of eyes that are bright, melting, glittering, twinkling, hard, commanding, envious, or cold. One glance from an eye can tell us more than a thousand words, and it is for this reason that eyes are one of the most powerful forms of nonverbal communication. A single look can have the force of violent hatred, and the power in the mere act of looking can be so intense that it can turn a human being into a naked, shriveling spectacle.

That eyes take on this symbolic significance corresponds to the psychological truth that the unconscious has a certain autonomy; that there is a largely unconscious element connected to eyes. It is through eye contact that one can experience the mental life of the other beyond the individual's conscious will. This is true for adults at any time, and even more for the infant during the initial merged conditions.

When a mother's mind is preoccupied with her own infantile insecurities or emotional content, she will invade the infant's psychic space with her own emotional state. Herman (1988) put it this way: "The infant mind will sense acutely, and be set awash by terror, when a mother's mind is reeling, or is wildly out of kilter, the more so since it will be hijacked to serve as a container for maternal distress" (p. 153). When the maternal intrapsychic conflicts that influence the mother–infant relationship become impingements that in turn become a pattern, the details of the way in which the impingement is sensed by the infant are significant, as well as the infant's reaction to them. Winnicott says that "object relating matches with object-presenting" (1965a: 60). If mother's face is unreflecting, the infant becomes walled off from her own emotional self and inherited potentials by a similarly rigid and impervious internal facade. A mother becomes a faceless moon described so eloquently by Sylvia Plath in her poem entitled "The Moon and the Yew Tree."

> The yew tree points up. It has a Gothic shape.
> The eyes lift after it and find the moon.
> The moon is my mother. She is not sweet like Mary.
> Her blue garments unloose small bats and owls.
> How I would like to believe in tenderness –
> (Plath, 1981: 172)

What happens next depends on the personality and temperament of the infant. The range of affective responses is vast, and includes rage and aggression (as will be seen in Baby N shortly), depression, autism, and numerous others. Culture and gender may play a part here. Universal aspects of social interaction, such as eye-to-eye contact, are given form and structure within a given culture, whose ultimate goals for behavior should be considered specifically. No social class is immune, and no matter what the culture, the behavioral expectations for men and women are different. Women are more prone to suffer core shame for at least two reasons (although this is not to say a man can't develop it). Historically, Western culture has favored masculine characteristics over feminine traits, and this naturally has certain repercussions for emotional development. Eurich-Rascoe and Kemp put it this way:

> In their extreme forms, the feminine has been associated (and confused with) the vulnerability of the vanquished and the masculine with the invincibility of the conqueror. Because of these experienced extremes, feelings of shame have come to be associated with "femininity."

> (Eurich-Rascoe and Kemp, 1997: 52)

Second, core shame develops in relation to the mother, and the relationship a mother provides the daughter is different than that provided to a son. Surrey (1991) states that a woman will have more of a tendency to lack separation from others, and that the daughter may learn how to mirror for her mother, while a son's developmental processes emphasize separation and disidentification. Given the way absolute shame can develop, this distinction would certainly make a female more prone to develop it. This distinction may also make it less accessible in a male, who may be more likely to project it onto a woman. It might look more like narcissism and shamelessness, or manifest as either aggression, castration anxiety, or misogyny. Behavioral differences, however, are only secondary to shame, and sons as well as daughters can fall victim to shame. A man must come to terms with his own weak, small self or, as Wurmser puts it, heroically transcend shame, while a woman must come to terms with a bad, ugly self. Gender differences are exemplified by the figures of Narcissus and Echo, which we will come to presently. In either instance, an unloved self needs to separate self out from a complete symbiotic tie to a Terrible Mother.

Back to the case where shame develops in the core of the self. Two related processes occur. On the one hand, the infant introjects the mother's eyes, the most powerful and disturbing aspects of mother, as part-objects. She does not separate, but clings to those unreflecting eyes for something to hold onto in the face of catastrophic anxieties that threaten extinction and in defense against the mother's absence. Holding onto the eyes becomes a substitute for the mother's holding the infant in her mind. However, the infant is holding onto the very eyes that annihilate, so she ceases to exist and be seen, petrified by shame (it is interesting to note that it was once thought that the eye had a power of emitting some peculiar principle from itself upon external objects that would render them invisible). Shame protects the tie to the internal bad object, leaving the mother unsoiled and perfect. Holding undergoes a distortion, and now becomes holding onto the object of impingement. The true self retreats further, building an impenetrable wall that keeps anything from entering or escaping. Shame, in other words, is the impenetrable wall of separation that protects a fragile, true part of the self against mother's intrusive looks that exert such horrendous power, holding the infant self captive. The infant instinctively guards against any imprudent reaching out and self-uncovering, yet at the same time is vulnerably, prematurely exposed in a negative light, without the mother's holding and protection. These are the dual aspects of shame: annihilating the self while protecting the self.

This lack of holding creates "the unmentalized experience" of shame (Mitrani, 1996). There occurs what Winnicott called a "freezing of the failure situation," and it is this phenomenon that lies at the core of the shamed infant self. This means being petrified by mother's unseeing eyes that look and turn the infant into a mere thing, a no thing, a despicable, unlovable object without humanity – turned to stone by the Gorgon's stare. The self becomes a separated object, and this change "feels indelible, eternal, engraved in granite on our memories" (Pines, 1995: 346). Psychotic anxieties manifesting as a lack of existence begin to dominate the inner world of the infant. The mother is a part object – her eyes – which makes integration of the experience all the more difficult. Good mother disappears and bad mother comes into rulership. A gesture, a cry, a protest – all these things are missing because the mother's annihilating eyes stare hideously.

Shame originates interpersonally but gets internalized so that the infant self can activate shame without an externally inducing event. The eyes turn inward, gazing upon the self, this time not facing outward towards the object, but inside. What does this frozen failure situation look like in the life of an adult individual experiencing shame? This individual ends up petrified by eyes because the mother could not meet the very specific needs for love and reflection that her eyes can convey. Eyes quickly become objects of terror, symbolizing the invasion of others into the perimeters of one's personal space. Perhaps the petrifaction becomes a way of negating the sense of personal engulfment by the mother, but this prevents a separate, creative existence, destroying what can be or has been born. The eyes of others become a psychotic reenactment constantly perpetuating the original failure of impingement with mother. Since in this early

Figure 3.3 When the mother goddess is creative, her body becomes the earth

stage of development mother is the world (see Figure 3.3), and the infant self is not separated in this psychic place, the world becomes full of eyes and vision is everywhere. Others are always staring, invisibly and insistently, at the ineffective, despicable self that the mother had good reason to reject or ignore. The world is populated with the cold, intrusive, envious, hateful, paralyzing, unloving eyes of mother.

The individual sees herself as a spectacle, but does not see her own spectatorship. There is no differentiation between in and out, and what was outside now becomes transferred to the inside. No possibility will be offered of a passage to a deeper, truer inside, and the mother's eyes will internally mirror the self. The symbiotic, me/not me union with the mother has been frozen, so that there is no differentiation of self in the face of those pervasive, all-seeing eyes. Just as in infancy, self and object are all one and the same; the self simply is what the individual believes she sees reflected in the eyes of others, and the full force of dark, bleak shame colors everything. On an inner level, the self, as yet not differentiated from the ego, is subjected to unconscious attacks lived through the eyes of others. What the shamed individual cannot see is how shame distorts and traps one internally in the snare of vision, in mother's madness. The labyrinth is that of one's own perceptions, and one stays caught in the threads of madness spun by the mother's eyes.

In the same way that the infant was unable to master social skills with the mother, the adult finds it difficult to engage socially with others. The aim of shame is disappearance, and object relations are avoided. The shame-afflicted individual lives by building a fortress around herself to keep away an enemy that truly dwells within its insecure walls. In order to survive annihilation, the infant self stays in a state of permanent regression, merged in a "not me space." This manifests in the paralysis experienced in the face of the world and the constant, chronic feelings in shame of wanting to disappear from the face of the earth. Plainly, the ideal would be a self-forgetting, but the shamed individual is never unaware of self, locked in perpetual confrontation with the onlooker who is always gawking. The cycle with this kind of internalized shame was put well by Wurmser:

> Certain ways of being bring rejecting responses from others, which create order not to offend the other, that anticipatory diminishing of the self, that nonbeing, is also experienced as shame. So shame has a dual nature and pertains both to flawed expression and to inhibition of expression, to being wrong and to not being.
>
> (Wurmser, quoted by Miller, 1996: 31)

Maternal impingements that create shame are a painful expulsion from the Garden of Eden, a sudden and violent rupture of a state of blissful oneness. Out of a primary state of symbiosis, the infant is coldly alienated from the mother and becomes an object. Sartre relates shame to the original Fall:

> Shame is the feeling of an original fall not because of the fact that I may have committed this or that particular fault but simply that I have "fallen" into the world in the midst of things and that I need the mediation of others in order to be what I am.
>
> (Sartre, quoted by Broucek, 1991: 39)

A mother's withering, unreflecting eyes prematurely expose her baby to a world of consciousness, suffering, conflict, and uncertainty, creating a sudden and traumatic birth of separateness, alienation, and naked self-consciousness – the hallmarks of shame – defended against by clinging to the staring eyes of the mother. The original sin that produces shame is the mother's failure in holding. Here is the still face of the mother, a cold, hard, depressed, hateful, or envious look seeming to stand off at a distance. She looks at her baby and her sight of the infant's self haunts the space between the two and holds them apart, and, paradoxically, obliterates the space between them. The infant is petrified in exposure and annihilation, alienated from her unifying origins, held in a frozen trance. A holding environment creates a content infant in a state of integration which will eventually add up to a total confidence in people and the world. Maternal failures can throw the infant into a state of disintegration and trap her in the bleakness and alienation of a world of sin. In shame, this is a universe of shriveling, exposing eyes.

The concept of exposure underlines the reality of a premature separation that causes shame. One is exposed and feels exposed. The etymology of the word expose is "to deprive of shelter," to "lay open," "to place in an unsheltered or unprotected position" (Schneider, 1977: 34). "To place out" implies a spatial metaphor that reveals that things have a fit, like a mother and infant. Shame arises when one is deprived of shelter or exposed, when something is out of place and doesn't fit. This implies a separation. The exposure aspect of shame is about an experience of premature separation during what should be a time of symbiotic unity between infant and mother. The infant is separated out from mother through her eyes and left exposed. As the infant develops, this primary, alienating experience results in a profound separation from the world, petrifaction in the eyes of others, and a lack of separation from the all-seeing, condemning eye of mother.

Paradoxically, however, this exposure is a potentially healing element in shame, leading the looker eventually to meet with insight. Exposure contains the truth of one's experience, keeps mother and the world real and constantly present, and holds the only possibility of removing the sting of shame (more about this in Chapter 7). But separation in situations that produce shame is abrupt and premature, so the infant is simply turned to stone and cannot make use of what could otherwise gradually, and only very gradually, occur in healthier circumstances. In shame there is no movement, only exposure linked to paralysis.

Also hidden in the psychotic anxiety of shame is the wish to maintain or restore the good, containing relationship with mother which is necessary for shame's cure. This idea is inherent in the way shame has been described repeatedly in the literature by many authors. Shame is defined as the wish to "sink into the ground" (Thrane, 1979); "wishing to sink through the floor and hide from the penetrating gaze of the other" (Anthony, 1981); a hope that the earth will open and swallow you up (Tomkins, 1963; Wurmser, 1997); a plea "to vanish from the face of the earth" (Morrison, 1996); "a wish that the earth-would-swallow-me-up and hence be covered once again" (Ward, 1972: 62); "gnawing shame makes one wish that the ground would open and swallow one" (Hultberg, 1986: 163); "an impulse to hide one's face or to sink, right then and there, into the ground" (Erikson, 1985); standing "humiliated and long to vanish, to sink into the protective ground, the mother earth with whom we may be reunited, thereby losing our painful self-consciousness" (Pines, 1995: 346); "the feeling of being small, of wanting to hide – to sink right into the ground" (Wallace, 1963). The existential phenomenon depicted in this metaphor of shame portrays a return to the symbiotic union with mother, the desire to return to the womb, a hidden place of safety. Mother is a dark cave, containing everything before consciousness exists. Shame seeks reunion with the "me–not me" state of wholeness with the mother; it seeks to revert back to a painless, blissful time when two were one. This return is to the Garden of Eden, the original place of sin and separation, to one's origins as in the rapture that, according to the Book of Revelations, will bring the shaming, sinful world of man to an end:

> For the divine eye will then look down upon its creation and burn it up in its seven-fold splendour of stars, spirits, angels and vials, while drawing the elect up through the eye in the dome of heaven where there appears a great wonder in heaven, a woman clothed with the sun and with the moon under her feet, and on her head a crown of twelve stars; she was with child and cried out in the pangs of birth, in anguish for delivery.
>
> (Revelations 11: 19)

In this moment the heavenly and good Great Mother is restored in rapturous at-one-ment.

Falling off the face of the earth emphasizes separation and alienation, and hidden in the petrifying moment in the face of those alienating, exposing eyes is the need to hide in the mother. However, since this is not a conscious intention, it simply creates nonexistence for an adult in a regressive state. If the infant is not seen, she cannot exist or have a being. She increasingly feels helpless and ashamed. The adult individual suffering from shame in the core of the self is living in the eye of mother, made insane by the failure situation but unable to separate from the look in mother's eyes.

Shame in the deepest sense, therefore, is a complete symbiotic tie with the negative mother – a pathological symbiosis or parasitic relationship. The individual lands in the devouring underworld, into the deathly womb of the Terrible Mother. Her eyes, too, become a dark womb, with the true self petrified and unable to be born into the world. Clarice Lispector, reflecting on her eye-to-eye experience with a cockroach, articulates both sides of an experience of shame in the face of a mother's impinging psychic content. The following passage relates to being possessed by another through seeing:

But if its eyes didn't see me, its existence existed me: in the primary world that I had entered, beings exist other beings as a way of seeing one another. And in that world I was coming to know, there are various modes that mean to see. One being looking at the other without seeing it, one possessing the other, one eating the other, one simply being in a corner and the other being there too: all that also means to see.

(Lispector, 1964/1994: 68)

The next passage conveys her sense of non-existence:

An eye looked over my life. I probably called that eye sometimes "truth," sometimes morality, sometimes human law, sometimes "God," sometimes "myself." For the most part I lived inside a mirror. Two minutes after I was born I had already lost my beginnings.

(Lispector, 1964/1994: 20)

We have explored how shame develops in the first stage of life and how an adult experiences core shame. But what does the infant's nonexistence look like in mother's face? What is the countenance that can petrify and throw the infant over the brink into these unbearable anxieties? What do the eyes of shame look like? Winnicott answers that such a mother's face will be unreflecting, will reflect her own moods and the rigidity of her own defenses. "They look and they do not see themselves . . . what is seen is the mother's face. Mother's face is not then a mirror" (Winnicott, 1971: 112). Her face conveys what John Ashbery says in *Self-Portrait in a Convex Mirror*:

> But your eyes proclaim
> That everything is surface. The surface is what's there
> And nothing can exist except what's there.
> (Ashbery, 1975: 70)

For Fordham, the infant becomes a visual object to an unempathic or totally passive mother. The infant cannot sustain the mother's psychic content, which leads to disintegration and chronic states of anxiety. "When deintegration is not followed by integration, then the baby's experience becomes persistently persecuting" (Fordham, 1985b: 60). In this disintegrative state, the terrifying archetypal parental images cannot be turned into flesh-and-blood images and will therefore remain in their intensity. It is at the point of separation and the anxieties that are connected with it that the persecuting Terrible Mother comes into play. From this we can surmise that the archetypal bad mother becomes the annihilating universe, a world where one "loses one's beginnings."

When a mother cannot provide the necessary reverie in her mind, her eyes may well feel like the beady little eyes of the cockroach described by Lispector (1964/1994) or like the one depicted in Figure 3.4, a painting by Magritte entitled *The False Mirror*. Magritte

Figure 3.4 Painting by René Magritte entitled *The False Mirror*

deliberately reduced the eye's active, looking function by painting one that reflects no human elements. This eye is isolated from any anatomical reference to a depicted face. The very separation of the eye from the body forfeits the eyes' natural abilities and makes sight meaningless. This eye is false to a self. A distant, cloud-filled sky forms its iris, a boundless expanse that has no limits; the eye seems to extend off the canvas. The pupil is a black disk that floats like an obliterating sun in the center. The eye is dissociated from the real world of human beings, out of contact with what it might perceive, just like a mother's conscious mind that is overtaken by her own unconsciousness that has a rationale all its own. The eye as false mirror ruptures the necessary unity between mother and infant which can lead to a psychosis of shame.

This kind of looking has been explored by several authors (Broucek, 1991; Wright, 1991). Broucek delineates two ways of looking and, hence, two concepts of self. One is the self as subject, the experiencing self who exists prior to this encounter with the Other's view. Then there is the self-as-object, that starkly visual and externally formed image of the self which gets constituted by another's view. Sartre (1956), in his analysis of the gaze, speaks of the destructive, dehumanizing quality of the process of looking at and its capacity to transform the person into a thing.

Shame is a reaction to face-to-face encounters, when one is mainly in visual contact with the observing other upon whom one projects one's self-concept and is instead made to feel like an object. This is best expressed by Sartre (1956), who says "the Other is an indispensable mediator between myself and me. I am ashamed of myself as I appear to the other . . . Shame is by nature recognition. I recognize that I am as the Other sees me" (p. 302). He defines shame as the affect that arises from the look of the other, and goes on to say that shame is "shame of oneself before the Other, these two structures are inseparable" (p. 303).

One could argue that every ordinary mother looks at her child in this way at times – some looks will be cold and distanced, some warm and loving. But the distanced looking that becomes a pattern of impingement creates shame that turns the self of the other into a non-self. This type of looking occurs when mother is out of touch with her baby, lost in her own psychic content for extended periods of time without reparative moments. As Sartre (1956) put it "shame is not originally a phenomenon of reflection" (pp. 301–2).

When the mother does not know instinctually how to adapt to the baby's needs or to reflect the infant through her eyes, it points to a problem within the mother. Of the discrepancy between a good-enough and not good-enough mother, Winnicott states:

> So much difference exists between the beginning of a baby whose mother can perform this function well enough and that of a baby whose mother cannot do this well enough that there is no value whatever in describing babies in the earliest stages except in relation to the mother's functioning.
>
> (Winnicott, 1965a: 57)

Fordham would agree with Winnicott's assessment:

> But a mother does more than act: by holding her baby in mind, by reflecting about him especially in a state of maternal reverie, she relates directly to her baby's protomental life and helps in the transformation . . . It is interactive experiences of this kind that form the basis for the affectively charged mental distinction between good and bad objects, between inside and outside.
>
> (Fordham, 1985b: 57)

I have already described the regressed state in the mother during the first months that could naturally bring her into an adaptive state of primary maternal preoccupation with her infant. When a mother is disturbed, either in her own right or with a particular baby, or with the particular circumstances surrounding an infant's birth, the infant will be deprived and left in a very precarious state. Shame is the result of a particular type of maternal failure, when the baby will subvert her needs for love and reflection to the mood reflected in mother's fixed face and cease to exist in her eyes. The mother's intrapsychic conflicts can be detected easily by the infant through eye contact, and the crying, screaming or cooing baby will not be understood or seen. The mother becomes the one with terrifying eyes on whom the infant depends for all knowledge of self – a self which is turned to stone by the infant's denial of her own existence in order to comply with mother.

Depression is one affect that can make a mother very insecure and distressed, which in turn hinders the establishment of an ongoing relationship with her baby. She may, for example, have a postpartum depression of feeling that in giving birth she has lost a part of her body. Whatever the reasons for depression, the mother's own unresolved anxieties and depressed mood make it difficult for her to bear the similar, primitive ones in her infant. The infant can feel shame as mother's loss and helplessness to have something that is not there impinge on the infant.

The following is an excerpt from an infant observation that Michael Fordham uses to illustrate an infant's distintegrative episode around a separation from his mother who has gone out and left a friend to watch her son. I use it to illustrate how a disintegrative episode can occur around separation when the infant's mother is depressed and this has resulted in the lack of a holding relationship and thwarted eye contact:

> I (the observer) knocked on the door and Pop, an elderly friend of F (the mother), let me in, explaining that F was out . . . I could hear loud cries and sobs from the bedroom and caught a glimpse of N (the baby) in his crib, crying miserably, looking out to where we were standing in the hall . . . His little face was flushed and stained with tears, his eyes were brimming over, and his nose was running. He was too upset to pay much attention to my greeting . . . and after looking at me through his tears, clung to Pop's stomach . . . Finally Pop lifted him up and N stopped crying, although he looked terribly unhappy . . . I was sitting out of his view. Then he suddenly seemed to go to sleep. His eyes shut quickly and he sucks his thumb noisily, using the rest of his fingers to cover his face . . . He stayed like this for a few minutes . . . then he stirred, half sat up with his eyes open, and then fell down asleep again.
>
> (Fordham, 1985a: 6–8)

According to Fordham, the observer had not expected this irreconcilable, catastrophic misery at his mother's going out, as there had been nothing like it before. Brief separations had been witnessed, but it had appeared that N had accumulated good enough inner resources on which he could rely in his mother's absence. What had become clear, states Fordham, was that N's relationship to his mother had become disturbed. However, further on he writes:

> While there were many peaceful and intimate times between mother and baby with good interaction and easy communication, N's sensuous comfort of feeding seemed to be often unrelated to his mother . . . That seemed very well expressed by

his tendency to look away from his mother's face and away from her breast . . . right from two weeks old that behavior was evident . . . N was a baby who used his eyes a great deal, so his tendency not to look at his mother's face nor look at and inspect her breast seemed significant. He inspected some objects with great care . . . Then there was his inspection of F when she was depressed, and sometimes his penetrative looking was accompanied by a possible reflection as if he was experiencing a thought . . . F had periodic depressions in which she felt depleted and developed persecutory fears of cancer. She would say that she "felt like a bit of wallpaper" and seemed to feel she was losing her individuality and was quite out of touch with N. The breast feedings became desultory, N became unresponsive . . . and N could sometimes be seen watching his mother with a look of serious concentration on his face. That observation was made at 10 weeks old.

(Fordham, 1985a: 14)

He ends his commentary on this observation with the speculation that "the [separation] episodes were unexpected and the events must have had something to do with N's development" (p. 15). From my point of view, the "something to do with N's development" was that N had to become the container for the mother's "cancerous" infant self in desperate need of maternal care during the critical phase of holding (evidencing itself in poor eye contact at age two weeks). The mother was very depressed, and her face "wallpaper," an unreflecting surface which pushed N out and created in him a premature experience of separation. The mother's eyes were absent, empty, and flat. The infant would scrutinize the mother's eyes, but she did not see him. N could sense through his penetrating gaze what was really going on with his mother and seemed to know directly that he was not held in her mind, especially during breast-feedings, when her eyes were eight inches away. His mother's depressive preoccupations led to a lack of intimacy and real holding eye contact with him. This lack of containment eventually results in disintegration instead of deintegration. Contrary to Fordham's or the observer's assessment, the catastrophic separation episodes were inevitable given what could be observed through the lack of eye contact and consistent gaze aversion. Since internalization of the good mother did not sufficiently take place, her real physical separations left him without mediating qualities, and in her actual absence he was subject to the annihilating terror of the Terrible Mother. The experience of not being seen will naturally make being seen terribly frightening. Exposure – being looked at and seen – threatens a too vulnerable self, then, with being turned to stone. The image of Echo in the myth of Narcissus is a perfect one for what must occur when the helpless, wordless infant, striving to engage an excessively narcissistic mother who is engrossed in herself and fears being dominated, meets a cold face that cannot reflect or pay attention. The eyes of this kind of mother engulf the baby in a self-centered type of object relationship, which means that the mother cannot relinquish her hold and her baby cannot emerge as a separate, existing self. The following translation of parts of the myth of Narcissus is by Frank Justus Miller. The latter parts of the myth that focus on Narcissus are told briefly since my main concern is with the figure of Echo.

He [Tiresias], famed far and near through all the Boeotian towns, gave answers that none could censure to those who sought his aid. The first to make trial of his truth and assured utterances was the nymph, Liriope, who once the river-god, Cephisus, embraced in his winding stream and ravished while imprisoned in his waters. When her time came the beauteous nymph brought forth a child, whom a nymph might love even as a child, and named him Narcissus. When asked whether this child would live to reach a well-ripened age, the seer replied: "If he ne'er knows himself." Long did the saying of the prophet seem but empty words. But what befell proved its truth – the event, the manner of his death, the strangeness of his infatuation. For Narcissus had reached his sixteenth year and might seem either boy or man. Many youths and many maidens sought his love; but in that slender form was a pride so cold that no youth, no maiden touched his heart. Once as he was driving the frightened deer into his nets, a certain nymph of strange speech beheld him, resounding Echo, who could neither hold her peace when others spoke, nor yet begin to speak till others had addressed her.

Up to this time Echo had form and was not a voice alone; and yet, though talkative, she had no other use of speech than now – only the power out of many words to repeat the last she heard. Juno had made her thus; for often when she might have surprised the nymphs in company with her lord upon the mountainsides, Echo would cunningly hold the goddess in long talk until the nymphs were fled. When Saturnia realized this, she said to her: "That tongue of thine, by which I have been tricked, shall have its power curtailed and enjoy the briefest use of speech." The event confirmed her threat. Nevertheless she does repeat the last phrases of a speech and returns the words she hears. Now when she saw Narcissus wandering through the fields, she was enflamed with love and followed him by stealth; and the more she followed him, the more she burned by a nearer flame; as when quick-burning sulphur, smeared around the tops of torches, catches fire from another fire brought near. Oh, how often does she long to approach him with alluring words and make soft prayers to him! But her nature forbids this, nor does it permit her to begin; but as it allows, she is ready to await the sounds to which she may give back her own words. By chance the boy, separated from his faithful companions, had cried: "Is anyone here?" and "Here!" cried Echo back. Amazed, he looks around in all directions and with loud voice cries "Come!"; and "Come!" she calls him calling. He looks behind him and, seeing no one coming, calls again: "Why do you run from me?" and hears in answer his own words again. He stands still, deceived by the answering voice, and "Here let us meet," he cries. Echo, never to answer another sound more gladly, cried: "Let us meet"; and to help her own words she comes forth from the woods that she may throw her arms around the neck she longs to clasp. But he flees at her approach and, fleeing, says: "Hands off! Embrace me not! May I die before I give you power o'er me!" "I give you power o'er me!" she says, and nothing more. Thus spurned, she lurks in the woods, hides her shamed face among the foliage, and lives from that time on in lonely caves. But still, though spurned, her love remains and grows on grief; the sleepless cares waste away her wretched form; she becomes gaunt and wrinkled and all moisture fades from her body into the air. Only her voice and her bones remain: then, only voice; for they say that her bones were turned to stone. She hides in woods and is seen no more upon the mountainsides; but all may hear her, for voice, and voice alone, still lives in her.

Thus Narcissus mocked her, thus has he mocked other nymphs of the waves or mountains; thus has he mocked the companies of men. At last one of these scorned youth, lifting up his hands to heaven, prayed: "So may he himself love, and not gain the thing he loves!" The goddess Nemesis heard his righteous prayer. There was a clear pool with silvery bright water, to which no shepherds ever came, or she-goats feeding on the mountain side or any other cattle; whose smooth surface neither bird nor beast nor falling bough ever ruffled. Grass grew all around its edge, fed by the water near, and a coppice that would never suffer the sun to warm the spot. Here the youth, worn by the chase and the heat, lies down, attracted thither by the appearance of the place and by the spring.

(Ovid, trans. Miller, 1916/1977: 7–11)

The rest of this tale is well known. Narcissus sees his own beautiful form, "hanging there motionless in the same expression, like a statue carved from parian marble." He "gazes at his eyes, twin stars . . . his smooth cheeks, his ivory neck, the glorious beauty of his face, the blush mingled with snowy white." He unwittingly desires himself, falling in love with his own reflection, vainly attempting to clasp his own fleeting image. After so much pining after himself, he "dropped his weary head on the green grass and death sealed the eyes that marveled at their master's beauty. And even when he had been received into the infernal abodes, he kept on gazing at this image in the Stygian pool" (p. 12).

Echo is like a newborn child, learning, echoing movements and facial expressions in a process of learning mother's face, the beginning of all object relations. Immediately after birth the baby is able to imitate facial expressions. She seeks to imitate them as a point of engagement, as if to say, "look at me, see what I can do!" Schilder (quoted in Hart, 1949: 1) notes that imitative movements seem to be connected to visual presentation. When one person moves, is it apt to evoke a similar movement in our own body?

Just as Echo gropes after Narcissus to notice her, the infant looks eagerly into the mother's face, looking for signs of her own appearance in her face, a nuanced response, a sense of self. Later, this will form into a self-concept of how the person appears in the world, what kind of person one is or can be. This process is barely perceptible and largely unconscious for most people, but for the individual who suffers unbearable amounts of shame, it is an omnipresent fact. A narcissistic mother has no capacity to send back sight of the other. She can only see herself reflected just like Narcissus, enthralled with himself in the mirror-like water (albeit a fatal stupefaction before his own image), or only hearing his own voice echoed. In such instances, the infant turns to stone.

And what about the circumstances under which Echo was reduced to an echo in the first place? The possessive Hera, a mother figure known for her envy and evil eyes, was responsible for robbing Echo of her own true voice. This bit of history shows how Echo was reduced in her existence under the power of the negative mother even before meeting Narcissus. Meeting Narcissus was simply a repetition of her original injury. Not being made visible by Narcissus who only has eyes for himself, and is hence completely unattainable, Echo withdraws in unbearable shame and is seen no more. She "lurks in the woods, hides her shamed face among the foliage, and lives from that time on in lonely caverns." Echo enters the woods, that archetypal place of desertion and exile, never to be seen again by human eyes in the world. Thus spurned and caught by her own negative narcissism, she chooses to remain invisible to the eyes of others. Her hiding and isolation commence a process of petrifaction that eventually transform her into a pile of bones that turn to dust. The myth vividly depicts the way one can be turned to stone when shame takes full possession: "the sleepless cares waste away her wretched form; she becomes gaunt and wrinkled and all moisture fades from her body into the air. Only her voice and her bones remain: then, only voice; for they say that her bones were turned to stone." This is metaphorically the same process that can occur for an infant who can be made nonexistent and petrified by mother's eyes.

The myth of Narcissus presents a shaming experience, and the process of petrifaction that occurs more through the mother's narcissistic neglect and preoccupation with herself. Echo is like the infant who cannot contribute anything of herself to which a mother can relate, a helpless reactor who stays trapped in invisibility and unrequited love. The mother cannot see her baby outside of her own projections. Such a mother is described well by Rose Selavy:

> Many a time the mirror imprisons them and holds them firmly. Fascinated they stand in front. They are absorbed, separated from reality and alone with their dearest vice, vanity . . . There they stand and stare at the landscape which is themselves, the mountains of their noses, the humps and folds of their shoulders, hands and skin, to which the years have already so accustomed them that they no longer know how they evolved; and the

multiple primeval forests of their hair. They meditate, they are content, they try to take themselves in as whole.

(Selavy, quoted by Duchamp, 1958: 95)

Another kind of mirroring experience is depicted in the fairy tale of "Snow White." Here we see a beautiful but narcissistic queen stepmother, "imprisoned in a mirror that holds her firmly" to suffer the same fate as Narcissus. This time, however, she is filled with hatred and envy, obsessed with her vision of her stepdaughter for whom she harbors death wishes. With such a perfectionistic mother as this, there is no chance to be seen and exist. Sylvia Plath (1965: 74) writes:

Perfection is terrible, it cannot have children. Cold as snow breath, it tamps the womb

As the story of Snow White is told (paraphrased from Brothers Grimm, translated by Lucy Crane, 1963, p. 213–21), this Queen has a magic mirror which she gazes into and asks "Looking-glass upon the wall, who is fairest of us all?" and the mirror answers, "You are fairest of them all." Then she is content because the looking-glass always tells the truth. But by the time Snow White is 7 years old, she is even more beautiful, and the mirror replies, "Queen, you are full fair, 'tis true, but Snow White fairer is than you." The Queen shudders and turns yellow and green, inflamed with so much envy and hate for the girl that her heart throbs. Envy grows in her heart like ill weeds until she has no peace day or night. At last, she requests a hunter to go into the forest and bring back Snow White's vital organs, her heart and liver, as proof of the deed, saying, "I never want to lay eyes on her again." Like most fairy tales, of course the huntsman does not kill her. Snow White is left alone and petrified in the forest, "running through strange staring eyes and over the sharp stones." She eventually makes her way out of the woods and into the home of the Seven Dwarfs. She tells them the story of how her stepmother wanted her heart cut out and they agree to keep her as long as she tends their home, to which Snow White agrees "with all her heart."

The Queen naturally asks her faithful mirror again who is the fairest, and this time it responds "Queen, thou art of beauty rare, But Snow White living in the glen, with seven little men, is a thousand times more fair." The Queen is horrified, knowing that the huntsman must have deceived her, and she begins to plot ways to kill Snow White herself. She paints her face so that no one will recognize her, dresses up like an old hag, and makes her way to where Snow White lives. She tries twice to kill her – once by lacing her up so tightly that she loses her breath and once with a poisoned comb. Yet each time the Queen is told by her mirror that Snow White is still the fairest. At her wits' end the Queen exclaims, "Snow White shall die though it should cost me my own life!" She makes a poison apple (the same object that induced shame in the story of the Garden of Eden). Snow White takes a bite and instantly falls down stone dead. The Queen's envious heart has peace. The Seven Dwarfs come home in the evening and find Snow White lying on the ground dead. They lay her on a bier and, grief-stricken, lament for three days. Then they say, "We cannot hide her away in the black ground" (black is the color of shame). Instead, the dwarfs put her in a transparent glass coffin out upon the mountain so that she can "be seen from all sides," and put her name on it. One of the dwarfs always remained to watch it.

Many years later it happens that a prince comes to the forest, and upon seeing her falls in love and asks to take the coffin, for, he says, "I can't go on living without being able to see Snow White." The good dwarfs feel pity and give the coffin to him, but as they are moving it the bit of poisoned apple is dislodged from Snow White's throat. It is not long before she opens her eyes and sits up alive and well. She and the prince return to his castle to marry and live happily ever after. The Queen is invited to the wedding and feels that she must see the bride. She recognizes her as Snow White and becomes "so petrified with fright that she cannot budge." They have red-hot iron slippers heating over a fire in which she has to dance until she falls down dead.

For a mother to feel such hatred is not at all an uncommon phenomenon. When a woman conceives a child, her life changes in many ways, and she may resent this long-term interference. Babies are, undeniably, a lot of trouble. Winnicott (1992a) states that "the mother hates the baby before the baby hates the mother, and before the baby can know his mother hates him . . . the mother hates her infant from the word go (pp. 200–201). He gives a list of 16 reasons why this is so, which includes ideas like "he is ruthless, treats her as scum, an unpaid servant, a slave" or "the baby at first must dominate . . . life must unfold at the baby's rate and all this needs his mother's continuous and detailed study . . . she must not be anxious when holding him . . . Or if she fails him at the start she knows he will pay her out for ever" (p. 201). This hatred is, he points out, hidden in the nursery rhymes that mothers sing to their babies:

> Rockabye Baby, on the tree top,
> When the wind blows the cradle will rock,
> When the bough breaks the cradle will fall,
> And down will come baby, cradle and all.
>
> (Winnicott, 1992a: 201)

When mental health prevails, the good enough mother does a remarkable thing. She is able to "be hurt so much by her baby and to hate so much without paying the child out" (Winnicott, 1992a: 202). The mentally sick mother, however, can be caught in infanticidal impulses and cause the infant mental death through a mere glance. This point is brought home in the following dream of a patient. It is a dream, I believe, that speaks for itself, and it is remarkable how well its meaning is amplified by the tale of Snow White:

> Mother and I are talking about Robert Frost – we both enjoy his poetry – mother was sitting on a piano bench in front of the piano – facing away from the piano. I said, "Wasn't it tragic that Frost never had a wife who would live with him or understood him – what was that tragedy about his wife, do you know? It always seemed to me that a man with Frost's ability and perspective on life deserved a wife who understood his poetry. What was wrong with his wife, do you know?' As soon as I said that, my mother turned her face rapidly away from me and would not let me see her – she covered her eyes with her hands – the light dimmed and I could not see what she was really like. I said, "But I didn't do anything terrible to her! I didn't even know her!" (I had this feeling that she thought I was responsible for this tragedy.) Then I said, "What's the matter, mother? Did I say the wrong thing? Did I do something wrong?" Very slowly the light grew brighter and I realized as I kept looking at her that there was something terribly wrong with my mother's face but I did not know what. Finally I saw her quite clearly and she slowly turned to face me. I saw her head almost like a skull, there was an atmosphere of death about her but she still would not uncover her eyes. Suddenly as I watched she removed her hands from her eyes; her eyes were black and staring with a terrible hate and she said, "You took my place!" I was suddenly

paralyzed, I could not move or scream for help but I knew she wanted to kill me. I wanted to call my father to help me but there was a wall between him and me, he could not hear me.

And what about the envy in those eyes? The envious mother destroys. The word envy is derived etymologically from *videre*, to see. Evil, envious eyes stare to destroy. When mother is so unconscious of her envy, her eyes gaze fatally, and fatality at the earliest stage of infant development means premature separation and mental death. This phenomenon is pointed out by Lacan (quoted by Berressem, 1995), who writes that the "eye carries with it the fatal function of being in itself endowed with a power to separate . . . the eye made desperate by the gaze" (p. 175).

The stepmother's blood-thirsty, envious eyes have an insatiable appetite for attention and her own self-reflection. Snow White, an innocent, virtuous child, is going to be devoured and sacrificed to those eyes; she attempts to feed on Snow White by eating her lungs and liver, and poisonously freezing her movements in death. This story, however, has a much happier ending than the one that met poor Echo. Like Echo, Snow White also enters the woods petrified. But unlike Echo, she does not get devoured by the Queen's gluttonous psychic content which allows shame to fully take hold. Snow White keeps her head; she runs, keeps moving, and finds protection in a new world at the home of the Seven Dwarfs. She stays connected with others to meet her needs for love and reflection, and they in turn reflect her true nature and inner beauty. She continues to live visibly in the eyes of others. Even when she is pursued by the Queen's hatred and envy, and falls down hard as a rock, stone dead, she is placed in a transparent glass coffin so that she continues to be seen by the loving eyes of others. This leads to a restoration of Snow White's life, with the result that the Queen is made to suffer her own psychic content, her own hatred, envy, and its underlying shame and fears.

Invited to Snow White's wedding, the Queen dresses in beautiful clothing and then seeks reflection once more from her magic mirror, which says, "You, my Queen, may have a beauty quite rare, but Snow White is a thousand times more fair." The evil Queen "utters a loud curse and becomes so terribly afraid that she doesn't know what to do." This time the Queen gets caught in her own reflection. The mirror finally reveals the unconscious life of her own soul, the face she only once (as a hag) showed the world, and discloses to the Queen the truth about herself. This is unbearable; she no longer wants to go to the wedding, but resisting what she sees and unable to withdraw her projections, she is at the same time compelled to lay eyes on Snow White. Upon seeing her, the Queen is "so petrified with fright that she cannot budge. Iron slippers had been heated over a fire, and they are brought to her with tongs. Finally, she puts on the red-hot slippers and dances until she falls down dead." In other words, the Queen is made to step into her own shoes (if the shoe fits, wear it) and be subjected to the effects of her own inflamed, searing hot envy and hatred. The psychic content that could not kill Snow White causes the Queen's own death.

Conclusion

So far we have talked about intense dependency needs during a time when babies are indistinguishable from their mothers and liable to the most severe anxieties that can be imagined. Shame is a deep-seated fact of environmental failure during the earliest stage of development, a time long before the infant could possibly be prepared to deal with the separation and loss of mother. It was established that psychotic anxieties could result from "the look" in mother's eyes. The eyes of shame are a concrete, unsymbolized representation of a sensory experience of the bad mother. In order to hold on to a sense of predictability, the infant introjects the look in mother's eyes, a look that lacks reflective capacity due to the mother's own mental disturbances. Shame at this level is generated through the cumulative effect of "still faces" which form the core of the self and all future object relations, and underlies all sense of identity which gradually unfolds over time. The infant is particularly subject to mother's psychic content due to her already precarious psychological state at this level of development, the level of intimacy in mother–infant eye contact, as well as the fact that this look has the power to intensify the anxieties which the infant is already suffering, and does not serve to transform them. It is also during this time that the infant is internally subject to the absolute dimension of the archetypes which are getting stimulated by affect-driven instinctual discharges. The bad mother, then, takes on archetypal proportion in the psyche of the infant dominated by collective energies. It is the recurring presence of these collective images that surface when the boundaries of ego are lost which led Jung to postulate the existence of primordial images or archetypes in what he called the collective unconscious. In the next chapter, we will examine these emotionally charged collective images of the Great Mother's eyes. These symbols and images, evolving out of and tied to human nature, will provide important keys to understanding the mythology of the eyes of shame.

Chapter 4

The Evil Eye and the Great Mother

What does one fear? – the human eye.

(Woolf)

In these eyes of mine, I have the power to reduce an entire city to rubble!
Look out for me!

(Pirandello, 1867–1936)

A snake's small eye blinks dull and shy,
And the lady's eyes they shrunk in her head,
Each shrunk up to a serpent's eye,
And with somewhat of malice, and more of dread,
At Christabel she looked askance!
One moment and the sight was fled!
But Christabel in dizzy trance
Stumbling on the unsteady ground
Shuddered aloud, with a hissing sound.

(Coleridge, *Christabel*, 1816)

She who fascina (bewitches you by means of the Evil Eye)
has gazed upon you,
has wounded your heart;
with her eyes and mind has gazed upon you;
pass through afascina, begone and do no harm.

(Zia Mimma)

The eye, more than any other part of the body, has long been the subject of curious beliefs. On the physical level, the absolute minimum that can be said about eyes is that they function to see; that the eye opens and registers light. However, there are many kinds of eyes – real eyes, fake eyes, poetic eyes, metaphorical eyes. Verbal expressions reveal the intimidating nature of eyes. Eyes can "burn holes through you," "look daggers," or be "sharp, penetrating, keen and deadly." That the eye has powers of intention beyond that of sight is an idea that spans a far-reaching spectrum, from the animal world of insects, birds, spiders, and reptiles, to the human world of superstition and mental disorders, to the world of the gods and goddesses in all religions, both past and present, and lastly, to the world of the heavenly bodies, the sun and the moon, planets and the stars.

To account for all the reasons for this is beyond the scope of this work. Suffice it to say that eyes are objects of profound archetypal significance with meanings both positive and negative. In a nutshell, the seat of the soul and the power of evil are both qualities possessed by the eye. St. Matthew (6:22–23), expressing the thoughts of Jesus, put it this way: "The light of the body is the eye: if therefore thine eye be single (that is, sound), thy whole body shall be full of light. But if thine eye be evil, thy whole body shall be full of darkness." The eye can stand for spiritual and mental vision, and intelligence. In this dimension it is frequently connected with the sun as the all-seeing eye that watches the world. In the Vedas, for example, Brahma is given the name "Person in the Eye" and it is said that "The eyes opened, from them a luminous ray, from it the sun was made – the sun, becoming seen, penetrated the eyes" (quoted in Huxley, 1990: 23).

These more positive aspects of eye symbolism will be explored further in Chapter 7 when we turn to the transformative, consciousness-raising dimensions of shame. This chapter, however, is an effort to document historically and cross-culturally the connection between shame, visibility, the mother's eyes, and looking, in order to establish the eye as an archetypal symbol for shame. This examination will reveal the petrifying effects of eye contact that can transform a human being into a stone, dust, raw piece of meat, or other such things – in other words, a dehumanized object of shame.

The Evil Eye

Looking into the archetypal dimension of the eyes of shame brings the power of the Evil Eye sharply into focus; by far the most ancient, universal, and persistent emblem of terror that expresses the link between the mind and the eye. An evil mind must be behind an Evil Eye. The Evil Eye is a highly charged symbolic configuration of belief in the power of the eye to project the malignity of its owner and of inflicting an injury wherever its gaze falls that has lived in the collective unconscious of peoples for at least 5000 years (Gifford, 1958). The Evil Eye is the result of an enormous power of negativity that produces feelings of agony. Merely by looking, an individual sends out emanations from her eye, internalized evil power derivative of intense emotional states, that can influence the mental state or damage the physical state of another. Misfortune, weakness, illness, and even death can be caused through a mere glance. The expression "if looks could kill" contains an echo of this very primitive and ancient fear of being watched, perhaps unaware, by an enemy. Its enduring presence symbolizes the eternal anxieties produced by the very human fact of being visible and exposed. The perennial credence in the Evil Eye reveals that it may be as contagious and deep as the affect of shame.

The Evil Eye has received considerable scholarly attention from varied perspectives, and this has produced a number of explanations for its enduring presence and functions. I would like to take particular note of one of the most common psychosocial explanations – that is the attempt to understand the Evil Eye within the broader context of envy, an underlying sense of fear, insecurity, and relative vulnerability to powerful, hostile forces in the environment. It has been found that envy is aroused when one is perceived as having more of what is desired than another in a society where resources are limited. In fact, the idea of envy is such an integral part of the belief system of the Evil Eye that in some places, especially in Africa and the Middle East, the Evil Eye is otherwise known as the Eye of Envy. Envy is considered a directed emotion: without a target, or victim, it cannot occur, almost in the same way that shame cannot occur without the presence of eyes. Victims of the Evil Eye become paranoid, diagnosed on the basis that they see plots everywhere and suspect the worst, constantly ascribing evil motives to others. Similarly, cultures where the Evil Eye is strong have also been called paranoiac, in that even an innocent look may be suspected of wishing harm, the more so if accompanied by a compliment.

However, one can speak of the Evil Eye without speaking of envy and paranoia. Before the Evil Eye took on all the connotations connected to envy, its effect was petrifying, caused by envy perhaps, but the result is shame. Therefore, my intention is to concentrate on the Evil Eye as a feature of sight and staring, as the fear of being trapped in someone's visual field and mental content (i.e., projections), and to link the phenomenon of sight with the social construction of self.

When the Evil Eye is understood in this context, it is linked to the deeper affect of shame, not envy, and, depending upon the individual, this kind of "evil" vision leads to petrifaction instead of paranoia. It is important to note, however, that the fear of being stared at is not limited solely to pathological psychology. The healthy individual can also fear the measuring glances of other human beings, and we need not suffer core shame in order to wish that another's glance be focussed on anything other than ourselves.

Paranoia, like petrifaction, is an affect of terror that can be psychotic in nature, but the experience of eyes and the processes that result in one or the other are quite different. In paranoia, the individual maintains her human characteristics while suffering delusions of persecution and suspiciousness, or grandeur and an exaggerated sense of her own importance. Etymologically, paranoia is made up of the Latin *para*, meaning beyond, and *nous*, meaning *mind* (*The American Heritage Dictionary*, 1980: 951). This is to say that paranoia is the result of being beyond one's mind, implying that it is an unrelated affect that occurs beyond the boundaries of normal thinking. The word petrified, on the other hand, means to "convert (organic matter) into a stony replica by structural impregnation with dissolved materials; to cause to become stiff or stonelike; deaden; daze; to stun or paralyze with terror" (p. 981). This definition reveals that petrifaction is a very related affect of terror, directly connected to an object and its nature. Its definition provides a wordplay to define the sense of exactly what happens in the process of shaming (remember Echo in the myth of Narcissus), either to an adult caught in a deeply shaming experience or to an infant in the earliest stage of life in the face of mother's disturbances conveyed through eye contact. The infant becomes a thing, a stony replica (or mirror when the mother should be mirroring) of the mother when impregnated, through their intimate eye contact, by her disintegrative, unmetabolized psychic matter, resulting in an annihilating terror and sense of nonbeing. Also of note on this point is that etymological relations indicate an archetypal connection between petrifaction and face. The word petrify is made up of two Latin roots: *petra*, meaning stone; and *facere*, meaning to make, form, hence, to form (something) into stone (*The American Heritage Dictionary*, 1980: 981). Interestingly, *facere* is also the root for the word face (p. 468). The origins of this etymological unity will also be illuminated when the Evil Eye is placed back into the cultural and historical context in which it originated, to be accomplished through an exploration of the prehistoric origins of the Great Mother, the gradual appearance of her face and eyes, and their evolution into the Evil Eye.

Before the evolutionary origins of the Evil Eye are explored, let us examine the broad spectrum of eyes mentioned initially in order to delineate to what extent the Evil Eye riddles life on earth, define what it is, and elucidate how it functions. The world of animals is a place where nature has played with the seeing power of eyes. Animals instinctually engage in looking as the usual introduction to all engagements. Even animals know the difference between an uninterested look, an attracting look, a submissive appeal or a dominating glare that is all power and intention.

Nature's strategies to escape capture or death are all precision engineered and can mimic anthropomorphic qualities. Eye spots – pairs of concentric pupils resembling converging vertebrate eyes – on certain types of insects, fish, and birds (even flowers, like daisies) direct attention to specific parts of the creatures' bodies so as to become a deterrent against predators. The African owl, for example, makes real the saying "eyes on the back of the head," with eye spots on the back of its head so an oncomer can't tell which way those real penetrating eyes are looking. Coral fish have eye spots on their tails to attract a predator to the wrong end while the fish darts in another direction. The wings of moths and butterflies (Figure 4.1) sport fake eyes at the edge of their wings that may serve to both attract a mate, threaten, and defend against attack. Caterpillars show flashing eye spots as they squiggle across a branch. There are also spiders who have eyes and faces on their bodies that serve no other function than to ward off attacks and frighten. Take, for example, a trapdoor spider (Figure 4.2) that possesses a special rear armor, a tailplate with a facelike design that plugs a retreat hole as the spider burrows to hide. This tailplate resembles a many-eyed Aztec sun god who is always victorious over death.

The last mention of the eyes in the animal world are those nestled in a peacock's feathers. Peacocks' tails are covered with eye spots, row after row of mesmerizing, colorful eyes which make an otherwise ugly bird quite beautiful. These fake eyes, however, have a lethal reputation. Charles Darwin, in his attempt to explain their evolution, wrote to a friend that the eye on the tail of a peacock feather made him feel sick. Many people hold the peacock feather in superstitious horror because it is believed that the feathers have the nefarious ability to cast the Evil Eye. Today they are still considered unlucky and many would not allow a peacock feather in the house, perhaps

Figure 4.1 Eye spots on moths' wings to ward off predators

Figure 4.2 Rear view of a cyclocosmid trapdoor spider

for fear of exciting the anger of Hera for plucking the feathers of her bird, or even her jealousy due to the belief that a house with peacock feathers will invite no suitors (Elworthy, 1958: 120). Mythologically, the eyes on the tail of the peacock are reminiscent of the jealous eyes of Hera, who due to this quality is thought herself to have Evil Eyes (Gifford, 1958). After the death of the hundred-eyed Argus (Figure 2.11), Hera's watchman, she placed his eyes in the peacock's feathers to keep a perpetual watch over her husband's amours. This is how the peacock's eye spots came to be associated with the Evil Eye. Yet the power of the Evil Eye is not confined to peacocks. It is thought to be contained by any number of creatures, including birds, lions, tigers, jaguars, panthers, hyenas, wolves, horses, sheep, dogs, cats, ostriches, eagles, falcons, owls, and crows.

The concept of the Evil Eye is historically and geographically widespread. Evidence indicates that the Evil Eye has had a long history within the Mediterranean region. DiStasi (1981) suggests that a prototype for the phenomenon can be traced back to the Paleolithic period. Because the belief in the evil power of the eye is found in the oldest of written human documents, anthropologists have imagined that the Evil Eye was a well-known belief with early Stone Age people. It may, in fact, have been cultivated as a protection against shame, as a means of saving face, which can be construed from the following passage:

> The Paleolithic hunter, climbing up some rocky mountainside, found himself looking into the beady eye of a rattlesnake and was paralyzed with terror, or he rounded a turn in the forest path to confront the baleful glare of a saber-toothed tiger and was frozen in his steps. If our hunter survived the encounter, his own

pride, or any one of his friends who might have been present, demanded an explanation of this unheroic conduct. Naturally, a confession of fear would never do. There must have been some strange power in the animal, some invisible emanation from those wicked eyes which reached out to grasp the hunter and to render him helpless. The beast had the Evil Eye.

(Gifford, 1958: 4)

Whatever the origins of these fears that reach far back into the recesses of time, such ideas are hardly confined to primitive societies. From the idea that the eyes of frightening animals had the power to harm developed the terrifying belief that the human eye could emit a ray which under certain circumstances could be highly dangerous to the person on whom it was focussed. This idea was even given scientific support long after its inception by the Greek philosophers, who taught that visual rays in the form of energy originating in the observer were thrown out by the eyes to strike external objects, from which the rays were then reflected back to the originating eyes. Ideas that vision was a form of energy at the disposal of an observer persisted until the beginning of the 17th century (Gifford, 1958).

The Evil Eye takes two forms: the one voluntary, moral Evil Eye inspired by malice; the other involuntary, the natural Evil Eye, a feature over which the unfortunate possessor has no control. One can also consciously or unconsciously cast an evil spell without discrimination. For the most part, when not a deliberate attack, the Evil Eye is regarded as an unconscious expression of dangerous emotions like envy, covetousness, greed, anger, or even overadmiration. In particular, situations that inspire such attacks are the birth of a child or those rare occasions when someone seems to have at least temporarily overcome the surrounding hostile forces – evidence, perhaps, of the anxiety produced by the tension between human beings and our right to peace and happiness.

A straight, hard glance is always thought to be dangerous, but a fascinating glance cast obliquely would appear to be the most lethal. Francis Bacon (quoted in Gifford, 1958: 14) wrote that the Evil Eye is of the greatest force when the cast of the eye is oblique. When a nature-loving poet named Horace (65–8 BC) wrote to his farm manager he said, "In the place where you live, no one spoils the edge of my enjoyments with sidelong glances or poisons them with the tooth of secret hate" (quoted in Gifford, p. 14). In general, any condition of the eyes which appears abnormal or unusual may awaken the fear of the fascinator with an Evil Eye. Into this category fall sorcerers, those with crossed, diverging, or otherwise abnormal eyes, the blind, and even hunchbacks and dwarfs. Drooping upper eyelids, eyes set at markedly different eye levels, inflamed eyes, dark lowering eyebrows or eyebrows that meet over the nose, all these types of eye conditions are to be feared. Someone who is troubled by a negative identity or discongruent self-image may, in an almost delusional way, experience his eyes as disfigured. Even glittering, brilliant or prominent eyes – or the color of the eyes – can cause alarm. Interestingly, the glance of a woman when pregnant or in her menses was equally dangerous.

One of my patients who suffers from deep shame vividly remembers her mother's eyes and their eerie effect. She describes them as eyes with heavy eyelids and many folds (for which her mother eventually sought surgery) that were hidden behind thick glasses. Countless other patients complain of their mother's look that bristled with uncanniness, looks that everyone in their families knew well and formally named "mom's Evil Eyes." One patient's most shaming psychosomatic disturbance when she is extremely distressed includes eyes that puff up. During these times she thinks of her mother's look, known also in her family as Evil Eyes. Another patient complains of the opaque quality in her mother's eyes, for which she had three operations that replaced the lens of her eyes.

The Evil Eye is a terror of antiquity that haunts people to this day and still permeates modern society around the world. The Evil Eye is called *malocchio* in Italy, *aojo* in Spain, *vaskani* in Greece, *mauvais oeil* in France, *böse Blick* in Germany, *buda* in Ethiopia, and in Judaism it is called *ayn-hara*. One day I was talking to my South American neighbor and noticed her wearing an attractive gold bracelet with what appeared to be eyes. I commented on it, which prompted her to show me an eye pendant, ring, and earrings as well. While showing me these objects she said simply, "I'm covered."

Fear of the Evil Eye is prevalent among individuals afflicted with strong emotional disturbances. Psychologically, wherever shame and guilt are aroused, the Evil Eye follows. The Evil Eye appears in the delusions of the mentally insane. Dr. Phyllis Greenacre (1926) reported several cases of schizophrenics: one believed he could kill with a look; another, a 16-year-old girl, kept her eyes covered and begged the nurses, "Don't look. You mustn't look in my eyes. If you do you will go insane." Tourney and Plazak (1954) report on a man who mumbled incoherently about eyes staring at him, and about the Evil Eye. Another woman complained that her male employer concentrated his eyes first on her left eye, then on her right and finally on both together as a means of extracting her brain. A 32-year-old woman described a "private eye", by which she meant an actual eye and not a private detective, watching and directing her. She saw this frightening eye in people about her, in cats, and in the radio.

In instances of shame, the Evil Eye could express the terror of being very bad, and the need for self-punishment. In very simple terms, a terror of the Evil Eye may indicate a bad self that will be exposed and cast one into hell. Hart (1949: 4–5) gives several clinical examples of this. A boy with anxiety and shame over masturbating cannot look at himself in the mirror. A woman with concentric constriction of vision has the obsessive impulse to stare at every man's penis. A little girl at the sight of the penis showed a restriction of vision to that object. A man of 23 who masturbated, and bored a hole in the bathroom to see his aunt, avoided looking in people's eyes, and saw eyes, which were his own, in three different places. An unmarried woman of 59 with photophobia felt that light was causing crazy feelings through her head and wore dark glasses.

St. Matthew (5:32) said: "If thy right eye offend thee, pluck it out and cast it from thee; for it is profitable for thee that one of thy members should perish, and not that thy whole body should be cast into hell." Lucy of Syracuse, patron saint of eye diseases, took this admonition very seriously indeed. She had such lovely eyes that she captivated a young man, but had such a fear that her chastity would be lost that she plucked out her beautiful eyes and sent them to the young man on a salver. In Deuteronomy (30:17) one finds that "the eye that mocks a father, and scorns to obey a mother, will be picked out by the ravens of the valley, and eaten by the vultures." The wicked people of Sodom were struck blind because of their sins (Genesis 19:11).

Deities and semi-divine beings are often depicted with several eyes to mark their all-seeing, omniscient vision and power. In ancient times, man had not only to fear the gaze of his mortal enemies and animals, but also the watchfulness of the gods, who might be envious. To primitive man, nature is capricious, filled with vengeful and above all jealous gods who perpetually seek to regain from the hunter or farmer the riches so hardly won from the earth. Even the deserts were once assumed to be populated by hostile dragon demons whose devastating looks could, quite literally, kill. According to Pliny, Libya was once the domain of the basilisk whose eyes possessed such lethal power that it would itself die if it saw its own reflection in a mirror (Gifford, 1958). To the poetic imagination, the stars are the eyes of the night or the souls of the dead (remember Figure 1.1), and the night sky is full of eye demons. The rays of Luna, goddess of the moon, have long been acknowledged as the cause of lunacy (hence the word). Luna's eyes penetrate with an energy, and Roger Bacon (quoted in Gifford, 1958: 14), believed that "many have died from not protecting themselves from the rays of the moon." There once existed the curious belief that if the Evil Eye of the moon were cast upon a pregnant woman, she would give birth to a monster. Mothers of modern Greece are careful during the first 8 days, or even the first 40 days, after the birth of a child to be at home and shut up in a room lest the light from a star cause the death of both mother and child.

Regardless of being animal, god, heavenly body or human, past or present, the consequences to the victim of the Evil Eye are ruin, sickness, or death. The immediate effect of a blast from the Evil Eye upon the victim involves not only misfortunes of every kind but the infliction of the worst diseases, often leading to death. The Evil Eye causes the most terror when it is thought likely to cause the greatest disaster.

Now that the reader has been given a broad outline of the Evil Eye and its basic operations, the remainder of this chapter and the next will be devoted to narrowing this ambiguous and vast subject by tracing its distant origins in recorded human history, and its connection specifically to the emergence of the terrible aspects of the Great Mother. Delving back into the origins of the Evil Eye clearly delineates its connection to the petrifying aspects of shame. This is in part evidenced in the prominent link between the Evil Eye, mothers, pregnancy and childbirth, and children. The most vulnerable to the baneful influence of the Evil Eye, of course, are infants and young children. They are susceptible because of their inherent weaknesses, as they have not yet developed the internal strength to prevent and defend against suffering. In other words, an infant's ego consciousness is weak or undeveloped. As stated in the previous chapter, an infant lives in a state of total dependence, unable to gain control over what mother does well or poorly, only to be taken care of or suffer disturbance. Children are also considered the Achilles heel, so to speak, of an adult, so what better way to make a mother suffer.

Women, in fact, have a special role in Evil Eye beliefs, especially as repositories for all knowledge about it. First, they are considered the most active practitioners of fascination because they are the chief exponents of witchcraft. In particular, menstruating women and women in childbirth, being ritualistically unclean in many cultures, are considered very dangerous indeed. However, the mother can herself be a victim of the Evil Eye, which may charm the milk away from the breast so that the mother can no longer feed her child. During pregnancy, the Evil Eye may seek out a woman to cause death, abortion, birthmarks on the child, congenital defects, or the birth of monstrosities. The Evil Eye can even close wombs and all life stands still (a clinical example of this is provided by Barbara in Chapter 6). The danger increases as pregnancy advances and becomes more apparent. After the birth of the baby, it is important to avert the Evil Eye away from a beautiful child, by speaking disparagingly of it to the parents. In Ancient Egypt, when an infant was being hushed to sleep, her mother sang a ditty to scare away the ghosts of dead men wrapped in mummy bandages with decaying cheeks, flat noses, and eyes of horror who entered rooms with averted faces. The following is a rendering of one of the old "sleepy songs:"

> Oh, avaunt! ye ghosts of night,
> Nor do my baby harm;
> Ye may come with steps so light
> But I'll thwart you with my charm.
> For my baby you must not kiss,
> Nor rock if she should cry-
> Oh! if you did aught amiss,
> My own, my dear, would die.
> (Mackenzie, 1978: 177)

It is also women who relay the folklore associated with the Evil Eye and transmit it from one generation to the next. Women are both the generators and healers of the ills brought about by the Evil Eye.

The Great Mother

Chapter 3 presented the importance of mother's eyes to the infant and the role they play in the baby's development of sight, attachment, social skills, and healthy psychological growth. The good, personal mother can provide for the stability and creative development of one's inherited potentials and true self. In a similar vein, this chapter presents the Great Mother and an exploration of her positive aspects specifically related to her face and eyes, and the role that these features have played in her collective, life-giving functions. Then, just as the last chapter presented how the good mother can turn bad, and this will be evident in her unreflecting eyes that can petrify and throw an infant into states of unthinkable anxieties, the subsequent section entitled "The Eyes of the Great Mother" will reconstruct this same story through an exploration of the collective deathly aspects of the Terrible Mother, the focus of which will be her Evil Eyes. When speaking of either pole of the archetype of the Great Mother, I am referring not to any concrete image existing in space and time, but to an inward image at work in the human psyche.

Ivory or stone statuettes of the Great Mother have been discerned as early as 30,000 BC, symbols of the earth's fertility and the life principle, the creative force in all of nature, the mother of all things, responsible particularly for the periodic renewal of life. The Great Mother reigned supreme as the author and giver of the productive powers in nature. Marija Gimbutas, writing about the evolution of Mother Goddess figures, states:

> It was the sovereign mystery and creative power of the female as the source of life that developed into the first religious experiences. The Great Mother Goddess who gives birth to all creation out of the holy darkness of her womb became the metaphor for nature herself.
>
> (Gimbutas, 1993: 222)

This comment is in sharp contrast to God's statement to Adam: "You shall gain your bread by the sweat of your brow until you return to the ground; for from it you were taken. Dust you are, to dust you shall return" (Genesis 3:19). Worship of the Great Goddess reaches back to the dawn of human existence and must indeed be one of the oldest and longest surviving religions of the ancient world, where she has been worshipped under many names and attributes. It is believed that the goddess presided over the rituals in the caves of Paleolithic sites from Siberia to the Pyrenees. Her presence continued into the Neolithic period and even intensified. The Great Mother was a dominant figure in ancient Middle Eastern religions, Greece, Rome, and Western Asia. In Phrygia and Lydia she was known as Cybele; among the Babylonians and Assyrians she was identified as Ishtar; in Syria and Palestine she appeared as Asharte; among Egyptians she was called Isis; in Greece she was variously worshipped as Gaea, Hera, Rhea, Aphrodite, and Demeter; and in Rome she was identified as Maia, Ops, Tellus and Ceres (James, 1959). Many attributes of the Virgin Mary make her the Christian equivalent of the Great Mother, particularly in her great beneficence, in her double image as virgin and mother, and her son who is god, dies and is resurrected.

Woman, with her inexplicable natural powers of menstruation, pregnancy, childbirth, and lactation, was a mysterious person. She called forth a deeply felt numinous reaction permeated with religious sentiments, rendering her at once sacred and taboo. The Great Goddess, being the mother of the race, was essentially the life producer, and in that capacity played a critical role in the production of offspring. Mother Goddess cults sprung up to celebrate the awe-inspiring, mysterious processes of birth and generation. She held enhanced status in society and in the pantheon of gods, taking on importance with the necessity of the mother and infant relationship – that an infant is an offspring of its mother is never doubted. The Great Mother was regarded as the sole source of family, kinship, and the parental instinct. Because of these qualities, she became the personification of the principle of life, embodying all the vital forces responsible for the various manifestations of life, maternity, and existence. As in the procreation of children, so in the origin of all things, the fertilizing female principle was the operative cause. All sources of abundance and generative power in nature and in mankind were the universal mother, and the sprouting of new life through her was a symbol of her immortality. She was the fertile earth, the womb from which all life was born.

Since the Great Mother was the personification of fecundity who brings forth all life from herself, the carvings of her figure, found on many Paleolithic sites extending over a wide area from France and Italy to South Russia and Siberia, were impregnated with her creative, fertile qualities. Behind her figure lay the realization of the complex rhythms of birth and growth, epitomized in the miracle of woman in her bearing of children. The earliest figures, so widely worshipped later in the Ancient World, are known technically as Venus figures. They have pendulous breasts, broad hips, rotund buttocks, excessive corpulency, and protruding stomachs suggestive of pregnancy. Overall, they are characterized by an emphasis upon the sexual or maternal features of the body. These parts of her body are not physical organs, but numinous symbols of life. In his book on the Great Mother, Erich Neumann (1974) states that "the goddess of fertility who was looked upon throughout the world as goddess of pregnancy and childbearing, and who, as a cult object not only of women, but also of men, represents the archetypal symbol of fertility" (p. 96).

The most remarkable feature of these figurines, however, is the complete absence of any facial features, a deliberate intention on the part of the artist. For example, sometimes the head is merely a knob, as on the Venus of Menton (Figure 2.9). On the statue known as the Venus of Willendorf (Figure 2.8), the whole head is elaborately carved with what appears to be a horizontal thick layer of curls, yet she is faceless. Figure 4.3 is an extraordinary ivory sculpture with breast and buttocks appearing like eggs, yet again without a mark on her face. It has been thought that this strange differentiation of the face and emphasis on body parts was some reluctance, probably inspired by magical considerations, of depicting the face, which certainly speaks to the potency contained in a face and primitive beliefs about its effects – evidence of belief in the powers of eyes. Emphasis on sexual or maternal body parts also concentrates exclusively upon the female in her creative capacities as the source of new life. So, then, what would carving in her face symbolize?

In the evolution of the Great Mother Goddess, attention was first focussed on the feminine and maternal aspects of the process of generation, their primary function to promote fecundity and guard the sacred portal through which life entered the world. This belief was held during a time when Paleolithic man was mainly concerned with the struggle for existence and survival that lasted for millennia. As the years passed and humanity developed, new cultural patterns evolved. Food gathering gave way to food production, and hunting to a more settled way of life. Mother Earth became the womb in which crops were sown and from which they were brought forth in due season. Mother's fertility came to symbolize the renewal of life as well as the delivery of the earth from the blight of sterility and death. "A strong link was forged connecting women as the cultivators of grain, to grain as the bounty of the Goddess, and to bread as the staff of life. Ovens, grain storage bins, and grinding stones became essential ritual furnishings of Goddess shrines" (Gadon, 1989: 22). This connection between fertility and ovens must lie behind the reference to pregnant women, when it is said that they have "something cooking in the oven."

To this additional function in the cycle of the planting and reaping of crops, the care and revivification of the dead was added. The great

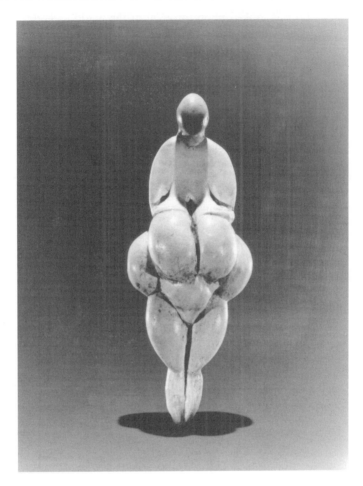

Figure 4.3 Venus of Lespugue, ivory sculpture, Deux Rideaux, at Lespugue, Haute Garonne, France, 23,000 BC

Mother symbolized the mystery of birth and death, not only human but all life on earth. Her basic functions included Giver of Life as well as Wielder of Death. In a profound way life and birth are always bound up with death and destruction. It came to be believed that growth and life can only be achieved and consummated after the perennial struggle between the two opposing forces in nature, those of fecundity and barrenness. To be productive, there must be a conquest of the forces of death, accomplished, for example, when someone has been rescued from the land of the dead, upon the restoration of the resurrected child following a primeval battle. Only then can the revival of new life spring forth upon the earth.

As the Mother Goddess cult developed, intensified, and reflected these collective cultural and psychological changes, so did the carvings of her figure. Dramatically, with the addition of the mother's functions in relation to death and barrenness, emphasis on facial features and eyes began to emerge. Facial features seem to be the vehicle for depicting these destructive, deathly aspects which must be tied to an actual, intimate human experience. For example, small figures have been found in graves in the Nile valley with the nose and eyes clearly marked. Female statuettes at Ur are of nude women holding their breasts with large hips and slender waists, their rounded faces inhabited by almond eyes. Sometimes, however, the head is not so petite but is monstrous, with a snout and gashes in strips of clay for the eyes. Still others are small and devoid of features, except for a large nose. The eyes on other statues are represented by cutting across an applied pellet of clay with a horizontal gash, and the eyebrows by applied strips nicked to show hair. Others have rounded faces with deep eyes and ridged eyebrows, and bodies with the prominent breasts of the Venus figures (James, 1959). Still others emphasize the facial features, with perhaps only a head forming the entire torso, chin forming a vagina, and then legs.

The eyes of the Great Mother

With the establishment of husbandry and domestication of the flocks, and as the physiological facts concerning paternity were more clearly understood and recognized, the function of the male in the process of generation became more apparent and vital (James, 1959). The Mother Goddess was then assigned a male partner, either in the capacity of her son and lover, or as brother and husband. Later Neolithic forms of her cult involve the ownership of a male deity, known variously as Adonis, Attis, and Osiris, whose death and resurrection symbolize the regenerative powers of earth, usurping the power of the great Mother on the life principle.

Meanwhile, humankind continued to evolve, and increasing levels of civilization were attained as early as the seventh millennium. At first the Goddess continued to be present as an all-powerful and all-encompassing presence, for here too the female form predominates. Sculpted women, seated or standing, are frequently seen with feline breasts, holding and fondling young animals. However, by the third millennium BC, when a patriarchal form of society began to rule, the religion of the Goddess began to suffer a decline. For the first time city-states emerged, with a kingship and priesthood organizing the populace for large-scale public works such as irrigation and the construction of temples, palaces, city walls and government buildings. These first had to be visualized in detail and then put into effect by a hierarchy of power, or bureaucracy. The fertility and prosperity of the land are closely bound up with the physical health of the king. Power and rules predominated over feelings, and with this shift the Goddess is relegated to become the wife or mother of the ruling male. Slowly but surely "The Mother Goddess . . . who once was mother of the gods and soil as plants, fruit and golden grain, gradually became identified with the negative principle" (Baring and Cashford, 1991: 114). The Terrible Mother began to reign wherever the patriarchal world developed.

These dramatic changes are reflected simultaneously in the carving of the figure of the Great Mother (as well as the myths of the times, which are related in the next chapter). It is in ancient Mesopotamia (3000 BC), in the temples of Ishtar-Inanna now called the Eye Temple of Brak, that we see some of the earliest manifestations of the Great Mother now simply as an eye. The eye appears to depict her identification with "the negative principle." Archaeologists discovered thousands of eye idols in the temple, made of black and white alabaster on whose faces the eyes had been engraved and colored with black or dark green paint, but without a nose, mouth or ears. The Great Mother's body no longer symbolizes fertility and the life principle. This strange and remarkable collection of female figurines has a general form of a thin biscuit-like body surmounted by a pair of eyes. This feature has caused them to be given the name "spectacle idols." On some of these figurines a smaller image was superimposed as if to suggest mother and child (Figure 2.10). A number of heads were wide enough for two pairs of eyes and seemed to represent two individuals. A few had three pairs of eyes. Some have crowns or caps upon the head-knob. Eventually, the eyes of the Great Mother migrated westwards, mostly connected with megalithic cultures, through Anatolia, Cyprus, Crete, Greece, Sicily, Malta, Italy, Spain, Brittany, Ireland, and Britain (James, 1959).

A central eye forms the main feature of the Eye Temple itself. According to Johnson, it is:

crowded with countless figures of the Eye Goddess. High on the walls of the dramatic interior, great eye-faces alternate with symbols of the gate guarded by Inanna's reed bundles. Her special role was evidently to stare back an attacker at the gate. Punctuating the design are rosettes, vorticles of petals that look like eyes with lashes. The design, which displays three symbols with similar meaning, is repeated around all the walls. The shrine overflows with hundreds of variations of the eye figure, each apparently a votive presentation. Alone on an altar is an enormous pair of hypnotically staring eyes that resembles nothing so much as a pair of opera glasses.

(Johnson, 1988: 70–1)

Why the mother goddess should have been represented by a pair of eyes is unknown to archaeologists. That these figures had some cultic significance is obvious. The Eye Goddess has been found throughout the ancient world as the guardian of mortuary urns and megalithic tombs (again emphasizing her connection to death), whose construction will have required powers of organization like those needed in Mesopotamia and Egypt. The symbol also appears on a great variety of objects, including crudely anthropoid images, pots, standing stones, and rocks. They have been interpreted as an all-seeing goddess who watched over the inhabitants of the city, or as votive offerings to her. For example, records show that in Egypt a powerful eye goddess presided over the courts and the administration of justice as Maat, the "All Seeing Eye of Ancient Egypt," whose attribute of the powerful eye was eventually transferred to a male god as the Eye of Horus (Walker, 1985). Archaeologists have speculated that it is possible that the Eye Goddess was considered a mighty healer of eye disease and received images as thank offerings from those who had been cured. However, it is only from the written records of later peoples that we can be sure that the gods were expected to cure diseased eyes. The suggestion that they depict a goddess seems to be the best supported, and the goddess concerned has been identified with Ninhursag, the Sumerian goddess of childbirth. An eye idol has been found engraved with the form of a stag and a bird on its back, a symbol of this goddess.

If this identification with Ninhursag is sound, this association of the Sumerian mother goddess with the symbol of a pair of eyes represents the earliest phase of a long tradition of such eye symbolism, and is connected with the first written reference to an Eye of

Death whose look could kill – the first definitive evidence of the presence of a belief in the Evil Eye. We may assume that the Eye Goddess was the Great Mother in whose embrace life and death changed places, and that she was also the giver of revelations. But these eyes are not necessarily benevolent. One feels the power of the eyes as they stare the supplicant into submission.

The attribution of many eyes to deities, doubtless to symbolize their all-seeing power, has been widespread. I wonder, however, about this omnipotent eye in conjunction with the waning of the Mother Goddess cult. The Great Mother, originally a one-sided symbol of fertility, the life-giving force of nature that ensures the survival of humanity and the family, takes on duality in the process of her evolution. She assumes the power that can damage or kill the very life she is meant to foster. In relation to the Evil Eye and its prominence among mothers and children, this is the power to destroy the infant that perpetuates and ensures the survival of the human species. Could it be that the female, maternal spirit was diabolized through these eye images to represent her power over life and death, the power to decide if the infant, hence the human race, would live or die. Perhaps in her form as Eye Goddess, the power of the Great Mother merges with the magical power to kill. This idea is supported by the emergence of Eye Goddess figures in conjunction with the Eye of Death.

Conclusion

In this chapter, we have investigated the collective symbolic dimensions of the archetypal eyes of the Terrible Mother, identified as the Evil Eye, that recall the earliest days of human history and the chthonic dawn of our evolutionary beginnings. The face and eye in the natural world of insects and animals was explored to demonstrate the instinctual basis of the eye and its imaginal operations. The image of the maternal eye was then traced in human history, from its absence in the faces of the Paleolithic Great Mother figurines to its compelling emergence in the Neolithic Eye Goddesses of ancient Mesopotamia. The Great Mother is connected to both life and death. Love and hate, creation and destruction, death and resurrection – all lay within her domain. On an evolutionary, collective scale, however, as the Great Mother's fertile, life-giving qualities and cult following waned in favor of the patriarchal gods, her face and staring eyes emerged and were held to be malevolent.

It is significant that in her evolution the Great Mother as a force of death lost her human shape and became only one eye, two eyes, or simply a face. This manifestation points to two issues. First, her potency was distilled and condensed into a nonhuman form (psychotic) without the possibility of mediation, the "ugly bogey-Erinys side of the Great Mother . . . a potent goddess . . . not to be slain by heroes" (Harrison, 1922: 194). What this means on a psychological level is that the Terrible Mother in her form as Evil Eye does not function in a way that can be easily integrated into human life. This is a critical concept to keep in mind when attempting to humanize the eyes of shame.

Chapter 5

The eyes of the Terrible Mother

I am ashamed before earth;
I am ashamed before heavens;
I am ashamed before dawn;
I am ashamed before evening twilight;
I am ashamed before blue sky;
I am ashamed before darkness;
I am ashamed before sun;
I am ashamed before that standing within me which speaks
    with me.
Some of these things are always looking at me.
I am never out of sight.
Therefore I must tell the truth.
I hold my word tight to my breast.

(Navajo chant)

Over the millennia, the Great Mother as giver of life and symbol of fecundity was transformed into a frightening image of death. As an image of death, the Great Mother loses her fertile body, and her sculptures become dominated by eyes. With this change, humankind swings fully into the negative pole of the archetype of the mother, known as the Terrible Mother. This occurrence coincides with the belief in the possibility of injury by vision – in other words, the Evil Eye.

The Eye of Death

The evil eye first appears in the earliest written records that archaeologists have yet unearthed. A popular myth of the advanced civilization of the land of Sumer (Tigris-Euphrates valley of modern

Iraq, home of the Eye Temple), and one of the oldest known myths that relates the idea of an eye that can kill, is translated from cuneiform inscriptions in clay tablets which date back to the third millennium BC. This myth gave Ereshkigal, whose name means Lady of the Great Place Below, the power to kill Inanna, goddess of love, with a deadly eye. In the story (Kramer, 1944: 86–93), Inanna abandons heaven and earth, and her office as holy priestess, to descend to the underworld.

> From the "great above" she set her mind toward the "great below,"
> The goddess, from the "great above" she set her mind toward the "great below,"
> Inanna, from the "great above" she set her mind toward the "great below."

> My lady abandoned heaven, abandoned earth,
> To the nether world she descended,
> Inanna abandoned heaven, abandoned earth,
> To the nether world she descended,
> Abandoned lordship, abandoned ladyship,
> To the nether world she descended.

As part of her preparations she arrays herself in all her regalia, and fastens seven divine decrees to her belt. She falsely announces the death of Ereshkigal's husband in order to finally gain admittance to the grim underworld. Progressively, through a series of seven gates, she is stripped naked. Inanna is starkly exposed and ashamed as she moves through the underworld, or the ground that has opened and swallowed her up. The following passages depict the process of her exposure:

> Upon her entering the first gate
> The shugurra, the "crown of the plain" of her head was removed.
> "What, pray, is this?"
> "Extraordinarily, O Inanna, have the decrees of the nether world been perfected,
> O Inanna, do not question the rites of the nether world."

> Upon entering the second gate,
> The rod of lapus lazuli was removed.
> "What, pray, is this?"

"Extraordinarily, O Inanna, have the decrees of the nether world
   been perfected,
Oh, Inanna, do not question the rites of the nether world."

Upon her entering the third gate,
The small lapis lazuli stones of her neck were removed.
"What, pray, is this?"
Extraordinarily, O Inanna, have the decrees of the nether world
   been perfected,
O Inanna, do not question the rites of the nether world.

Upon her entering the fourth gate,
The sparkling stones of her breast were removed.
"What, pray, is this?"
Extraordinarily, O Inanna, have the decrees of the nether world
   been perfected,
O Inanna, do not question the rites of the nether world.

Upon her entering the fifth gate,
The gold ring of her hand was removed.
"What, pray, is this?"
Extraordinarily, O Inanna, have the decrees of the nether world
   been perfected,
O Inanna, do not question the rites of the nether world.

Upon her entering the sixth gate,
The breastplate of her breast was removed.
"What, pray, is this?"
Extraordinarily, O Inanna, have the decrees of the nether world
   been perfected,
O Inanna, do not question the rites of the nether world.

Upon entering the seventh gate,
All the garments of ladyship of her body were removed.
"What, pray, is this?"
Extraordinarily, O Inanna, have the decrees of the nether world
   been perfected,
O Inanna, do not question the rites of the nether world.

Stark naked, she is brought before the throne. She bowed low. The
Annunaki, judges of the underworld, surround Inanna and pass
judgment on her by fastening their eyes upon her – Eyes of Death:

At their word, the word which tortures the spirit,
The sick woman was turned into a corpse,
The corpse was hung from a stake.

On the fourth day, Ninshubur follows his instructions, and Enki, the water god of wisdom, devises a plan to restore her life. Fashioning two sexless creatures, he sends them to the nether regions with the "food of life" and the "water of life" to sprinkle on her corpse. This they did and she revives. Accompanied by some of its shades, she leaves the land of the dead and ascends to the earth, where with her ghostly companions she wanders from city to city in Sumer.

This myth depicts the unification of the loving Mother Goddess, Innana, with her dark aspects, Ereshkigal, who possesses an Eye of Death. This process entails a stripping of the false self in order to be revealed as a true self and all the powers this contact provides. In this process, the unconscious forces which come from the "Great Place Below" have the power to kill off the good, loving mother. These primitive forces that inhabit the Eye of Death appear driven by Ereshkigal's narcissism, domination and self-centered ideas of her own perfection, articulated in her comment that "the ways of the underworld are perfect. They may not be questioned." Yet what the myth seems also to say is that only after the good mother integrates her dark aspects can she be resurrected with her life-giving functions restored; after which she must stay in touch with her darkness, her Eye of Death. This is expressed in the line "ascends to the earth with her ghostly companions."

The Eye of Death is a pitiless, judgmental eye that does not care in any personal way at all as it callously performs an act of murder. It is a petrifying, raw, and objectifying glare that transforms being into non-being, or a raw piece of meat. Possessed like the Queen in "Snow White" of her narcissism and rage, Ereshkigal's face is said to turn yellow with primal madness, her lips are black, and she bites herself. Imagine a nursing infant looking into such a mother's glaring eyes, a victim to the archetypal hate, greed, raw sadism, and rage at the center of her mother's wound (Perera, 1981: 31). Yet just like Snow White, Innana is held in mind (i.e., the reverie of the good mother), remembered by her faithful servant Ninshubur, who laments to restore her life.

The Eye of Death can also be the eyes of depression, which make all things appear or feel "dead" or "raw." Depression can become eyes that petrify life and carry the projection of our shame, an affect that seizes an idea about oneself, viewed through the eyes of others, and makes it concrete and static. Since ideas about self are in direct conflict with the reality of oneself, rigor mortis sets in. Such eyes have the potential to create the core of shame and bring psychosis. In fact, we see these kinds of eyes in individuals suffering from psychotic states of being, captives of the underworld who have lost touch with external reality.

From the ruins of the library of the Assyrian King Ashurbanipal (668–626 BC) at Nineveh in northern Mesopotamia, other cuneiform tablets in the Akkadian (not the Sumerian) language have preserved the beliefs of the Babylonians and Assyrians. There is an Akkadian story that follows very closely the tale of Inanna. It is called the "descent of Ishtar to the Nether Regions" (James, 1959). This tablet makes it clear that Inanna was essentially the Sumerian counterpart to the Akkadian Ishtar, and in this capacity stood for the embodiment of the creative powers of spring and the personification of the autumnal decline in the seasonal cycle, a time of desolation and death on the earth.

It is also known from the Sumerian tablets that in the first millennium BC men feared a class of demons called utukku, who could injure by a single glance. This type of looking was regarded as being etiological for most diseases. From a series of 12 tablets in the king's library, a collection of adventure stories about a Sumerian hero named Gilgamesh have been translated. In the course of this Assyrian epic, Gilgamesh, on a quest for Eternal Life, encounters a special kind of devil called scorpion-men, guardians of the gate whose glance was death (Gifford, 1958: 5).

Overall, the Assyrians and Babylonians in the first millenium BC had a preponderance of female witches over male wizards who possessed an evil eye as part of their professional equipment, connecting the evil eye more to women than men. I have found it intriguing that, despite the profusion of Sumerian sculpture depicting various figures from the myths of Inanna and other important deities, nowhere was I able to find a depiction of the Eye of Death that Ereshkigal uses to kill Inanna. My guess is that the ancients believed it was dangerous to create images of this eye, for no one could look directly upon it without suffering its effects. The psychological result of this blindness is that content around the eye is relegated to the unconscious, pushed into its primordial layers until it becomes an archetypal image of the Terrible Mother. This idea is supported by the following passage from the Epic of Gilgamesh:

Nobody sees Death,
Nobody sees the Face of Death,
Nobody hears the Voice of Death.
Savage Death just cuts mankind down . . .
Sometimes there is hostility in [the land],
But then the river rises and brings flood-water.
Dragonflies drift on the river,
Their faces look upon the face of the Sun,
(but then) suddenly there is nothing.
The sleeping and the dead are just like each other,
Death's picture cannot be drawn.

(Dalley, 1989: 108–9)

The Eye of the Terrible Mother in Ancient Egypt

About 3000 BC Egypt became the first great nation state with a system of picture writing that marks the beginning of history. The religion of Ancient Egypt, the myths of which were recorded in documents known as the Pyramid and Coffin Texts, was the heart of the civilization, penetrating and informing every aspect of life. The gods were everywhere. The ruling pharoah was priest and all acts of life were played out against a background of divine patterns which grew directly out of prehistoric customs connected to the main cult of the Great Mother Goddess, which blossomed in the great expansion of the Isis mysteries in the second and third centuries AD (Clark, 1959: 28).

The Eye, which presides over all, is the key to the Egyptian religion, and the complex of eye symbolism is all woven around the Egyptian Mother Goddess whose roots lay in the Great Mother of Neolithic times. "One fact does stand out – the Egyptian Eye was always a symbol for the Great Goddess, whatever name she may have in any particular instance" (Clark, 1959: 218). Clark surmises that the widespread popularity of the eye symbol must have been based on the common experience or sensitivity to the power and vitality which seems to reside in the eye. The Egyptians, however, felt this so much that they exalted their feelings to cosmic dimensions.

The Eye begins to play its significant role in Egyptian cosmogony according to Heliopolitan myth. There is no standard creation myth, but according to one version, the first event is the manifestation of the primal divinity Atum, who rests in the Primeval Waters of the Abyss. He is at first alone in the universe, representing God and all things to come. Then the world begins to be created, much of which takes place through Atum's face and the Eye, illustrative of the potency of the emanations from the eye. This Eye, in particular, was the medium for creation on at least two occasions: when he is alone in the waters and produces a brood of creatures, and then later, when mankind springs from his tears. Here are Atum's omnipotent words:

> But I created some of them while I was still in the Primeval
> Waters in a state of inertness, without anywhere to stand.
> It occurred to my heart, I devised with my face
> that I should make every form, while I was still alone . . .
> before another had come into being that he might create with
>   me.
>
> (Clark, 1959: 91)

At one point, this Eye seems to be the equivalent of the Word through which things come into being:

> An eye of Atum appeared on the Babet Tree
> an eye of Atum appeared on the Date Palm
> . . . and that was his appearance at the beginning.
>
> (Clark, 1959: 76)

Atum, "he who came into being by himself," is figured as a man although embodying both sexes, "that great He/She." At this point in creation, the Eye is symbolic of his feminine, emotional, and creative aspects. He is thus said to couple with himself by putting his hand, sign of his female half, upon his phallus. Shooting out of himself there emerge the first creatures, male and female, brother and sister, called "eye twins." Shu, lord of air and space, and Tefnut, lady of moisture, of life and the world order, are created, but they all lay locked together, embraced in one body. Eventually Shu and Tefnut are separated and lost in the waters of the immense abyss, so Atum, who initially has only one Eye which can mysteriously be separated from his person, dispatches it to find them. The task of the Eye is to rescue the formless, indeterminate creations of Atum from the sight-less negativities of the Abyss. "The Eye becomes the power of life to defend itself inviolate against dissolution and the spirits of non-being" (Clark, 1959: 94). These mythological concepts give collective dimension to, and underscore the psychological idea, that the eye is the infant's first self-object and means by which she comes solidly into her own existence. Without mother's eyes – her reflection and reverie – the infant will not be able to defend herself against "dissolution and the spirits of non-being." In other words, the infant will be unable to protect herself against shame.

Meanwhile, aeons pass until the Eye has caught up with Shu and Tefnut and brings them back to be cherished by Atum. Atum weeps over them, and man comes into being from the tears of his Eye. This is partly a pun on the Egyptian words for men and tears, but possibly also contains lingering traces of the old connection between eyes and the Great Goddess, the mother of all living things: the Eye is the Mother Goddess because all mankind has come from the tears of the Eye. While the Eye searches for his lost companions, Atum replaces the Eye with one brighter than the original Eye. Upon return to its creator, the Eye is furious with rage when it finds that another has taken its place in the god's face. To pacify it, Atum places the Eye on the front of his face, binding it to his forehead, with the promise that this Eye, now and forever, would rule the entire world. Atum says:

> My Eye followed them for many ages,
> . . . and they brought back my Eye with them
> Whereupon I rejoined my limbs. I wept over them
> and thus mankind came into existence from the tears that sprang
>   from my Eye.
> Then it became enraged against me, when it returned and
> saw that I had put another in its place,
> replacing it with a brighter one;
> so I promoted it to the front of my face
> so that it could rule the whole world.
>
> (Clark, 1959: 91)

This act precipitates a turning point in the universe: the creative, life-giving and emotional maternal aspect of Atum, as well as the image of the Mother Goddess, becomes terrible in the fight against dis-solution. Feeling, consciousness, and relatedness are replaced by dominating, unconscious, envious power never to be fully or per-manently appeased. This movement reflects the historical moment when worship of the Great Mother diminished in the service of civilization and masculinity. This neglect and fear of non-being enrages the Great Mother to the point that she becomes possessed by her negativity.

The original Eye thus becomes the Uraeus serpent, the rearing, swollen-necked cobra placed at the front of the royal crown of Egypt to ward off enemies. On a cosmic plane, the Eye became the ruling sun in the sky and, on a terrestrial plane, it became Pharaoh, the human sun, on earth. "The Eye is personified might," says R. T. Rundle Clark (1959: 93), "the essential violence that is used to protect gods and kings against disintegration in the waters or spirit enemies in the created world." The Uraeus is also clearly a form of the Great Mother Goddess in her terribleness, made obvious when it is celebrated as "she whose appearance strikes terror," as "Lady of Slaughter, Mighty One of Frightfulness," and "most ancient female of the world and conductress of the One Lord" (p. 221). The Mother Goddess adorns Pharaoh's brow and is his dominating mother at the same time.

In a country where the sun's blasting and withering heat beats down daily, the sovereign aspects of the Eye may well seem more terrible than majestic, confirming the Eye (hence Mother Goddess) in its symbolic role as an annihilating force. The following are the words Atum speaks to the Eye as he installs it in his face, words that underscore the power of the Eye to destroy – a power given while the Eye was still in the dark and in her primordial condition (in other words, unconscious):

> Great will be your majesty and mighty your influence,
> great will be your power and mighty your magic over the bodies
>   of your enemies;
> they will fall howling on their faces,
> all mankind will cringe beneath you and your might,
> they will respect you when they behold you in that vigorous
>   form . . .
> . . . I am – yes – I am a burning flame, but also
> the boon companion, the darling of Re . . .
> I have seized the gods, there is no opposition to me–
> as Master of the Primeval Place declared.
> "And when did this god come?"
> "It was before the shadows were separated
> or the outlines of the gods were visible."
>
> (Clark, 1959: 221–2)

The Eye merges with the image of an enraged, rearing cobra with a poisonous bite, inspired by its unconscious, possessive and narcissistic rage at being replaced by another. It loses its fertile, lifegiving functions and thereby becomes a symbol of power-driven, destructive forces – blinding light, fire, and the most powerful of hostile emotions, namely anger, aggressiveness, uncontrollable fury, hate, and envy. Clark (1959) identifies what he calls the fundamental equation of Egyptian symbolism: eye = flame = destructive goddess = cobra = crown. Thus, "the power of the High God is the Great Goddess of the universe in her terrible aspect" (p. 220).

At the same time that Atum promotes the Eye to the front of his face as a cobra, he creates all the serpents in every form. Serpents are notorious for their lidless, unwinking eyes with which they are said to fascinate their prey. The word fascination, in fact, comes from the Greek *vaskania*, whose primary meaning is "Evil Eye" to signify its seductive capacity to bewitch, enchant, and charm. The power to fascinate can be the power of control over another. The force takes many forms, including jealousy, coveting, anger, and destruction, all of which are attributes of the Eye. Thus, the power of the serpent is the terrible power of the Mother and her evil eye.

The Eye, then, is the striking power of the High God in all his manifestations, although it is important always to keep in mind that the origin of these many manifestations is the one Eye which is the Great Goddess in her terrible aspect. Its incarnations include the Eye of Atum, Eye of Horus, Eye of Osiris, and Eye of Ra – all symbolic of deity. In every aspect, the Eye assumed three functions: seat of the soul; creation of good; and creation of evil. The Eye of Atum has been discussed at length, so let me delineate the remaining three in their evil aspects in order to demonstrate their connection to the Great Terrible Mother.

There were, in particular, two sacred eyes in Ancient Egypt. So far we have been considering the Eye of Atum, the *iret* (feminine noun for eye in Egyptian), which is the Eye of the Sun and the Eye of the Primeval Water. There was, in addition to the Eye of the High God, the sacred Eye of Horus, son of Isis, which in mythology the evil god Seth tore out of Horus's face during the great quarrel (Horus got Seth's testicles in just retribution). These two eyes, however, are actually one, since this eye is a symbol of the divine spirit as victor, and its aggressiveness is derived from the High God, whose real hostility is derived from the Eye. Again, crown and cobra and Mother Goddess are one, as can be seen in the following passage:

> The "Great Matter" has born you,
> the great Cobra has born you . . .
> for you are Horus who fought in defense of his Eye.
> (Clark, 1959: 226)

The Eye of Horus is also the eye of the moon, a symbol of the Mother and her cycles. Seth flung Horus's eye away beyond the edge of the world, and the god Thoth, the moon's genius and guardian, went and found it lying in pieces in the outer darkness. He brought them back and assembled them again to form the full moon that becomes the Wedjat Eye (Eye of Horus). Thoth says:

> I came seeking the Eye of Horus,
> that I might bring it back and count it.
> I found it (and now it is complete), counted and sound,
> so that it can flame up to the sky
> and blow above and below . . .
> I am he who returns the Wedjat Eye,
> I am he who abolished its dimness, when its brightness was
>   damaged . . .
> I am the returner of the Wedjat Eye
> when it is saved from its misfortune . . .
> [so that all is now well] in the House of the Moon.
>
> (Clark, 1959: 225)

Egyptian religion also has much to do with Osiris, whose name means either "the place of the eye" or "the one enthroned" – enthroned on Isis his sister-wife, whose name means throne. His story is simultaneously that of the rise and fall of the Nile and of the immortality of the soul. The Eye of Osiris converges with the Eye of Horus, for both are important in the death-resurrection theme which dominates Egyptian religion. When Horus went to look for his dismembered dead father, Osiris, he took the Eye with him to restore him to life and presented it to Osiris. As soon as Osiris was given the Eye, he became a soul or received new life in the after world. This is how the eye of Horus became a symbol of the funeral rites which a son should provide for his dead father. For example, twin eyes frequently keep watch from the sides of Egyptian coffins, protecting the dead from harm. On his death, Horus becomes Osiris, who rescues the eye from Seth and recreates himself as Horus. This all-powerful, ever-living god brings peace to mankind when his eye is intact in his body. Loss of the eye disturbs the social order of man. To explain how the soul of the dead Osiris hides in the eye of the living Horus, it is said: "In the eye there is a pupil, the reflection of a child. The Great God himself becomes a child again, he enters the womb to renew himself" (Clark, 1959: 226).

In addition to the role it plays in death, the Eye of Osiris is also an instrument of anger that carries with it destruction. When angry, Osiris could destroy with a glance. Plutarch informs us that Osiris killed a small boy by looking at him in anger. One of the judges of the dead, who sat with Osiris, was Artifemtex, whose name means "eyes like flint knives."

So far, all the deities discussed are masculine. For example, the High God of the Primeval Water has been considered bisexual, and is referred to as Atum, a masculine figure. In Egypt it is the Pharoh, rather than the Mother Goddess, who is predominant, because he is the incarnation of the Sun God and the living son of Osiris (James, 1959). There was, however, a provincial tradition about a Mother Goddess, and this brings us shortly to a story about the Eye of Ra. The Primeval Ocean was imagined as a "great flood," worshipped in several places as a cow whose star-speckled belly formed the sky. The following passage alludes to the origin of the Eye in the Primordial Ocean which is now called the "Father of the Gods":

> Behold me, O Men and Gods! that is how I became the burning
>   Eye of Horus . . .
> the Flood, the parent of the gods, it was that clothed me,
> creating therefrom the eye for his body.
>
> (Clark, 1959: 222)

The most attractive form of the Great Goddess for the Egyptians was Hathor, the face of the sky, the deep and the lady who dwells in the grove at the end of the world. The sun emerges from the sky beyond the world, and the sky is a cow form of the Mother Goddess who is also the Eye. Hathor is also known as Nut or Isis, who together make up the three great forms of the Mother Goddess. The Hathor aspect of the Great Mother is the protector of eyes. In the following story, Hathor is the feminine, undeveloped and terrible Eye of Ra, the goddess "coming out of the distant land, the virgin who is in the left eye as the pupil" (Pope, 1968: 9).

Before 2000 BC a famous myth had developed that at one point mankind began to speak disparagingly of the Great Sun God Ra, who proclaims of himself: "I am Ra. I am the Master of Eternity. I am Master of the Great Crown. I am he who is throned in the Divine Eye" (p. 9). Knowledge of the evil words spoken about him reached his ears, filling his heart with a fierce anger and wish utterly to destroy mankind. He said to one of his followers: "Call my Eye and Shu and Tefnut, Keb and Nut, and the Fathers and the Mothers who were together with me in the waters of Nun" (p. 9). Then Ra said to Nun: "Thou oldest god, out of whom I came, and ye ancestor gods, look at mankind, born out of my eye; the people have thought thoughts against me. Tell me what to do" (p. 9). Nun said: "People fear you, even if you only direct your Eye against the malefactors!" (p. 10). His advisors counseled him further, saying to "let thine Eye go forth against those who are rebels in the kingdom and it shall destroy them utterly. When it cometh down from heaven in the form of Hathor, no human eye can be raised against it" (p. 10). The goddess Hathor, in the form of the Eye of Ra, vengefully slaughtered men in droves and would have exterminated mankind altogether if the Sun God, now repenting, had not distracted her. Ra said: "I will protect mankind from her . . . and carry the beer to that place where she intends to kill them!" (p. 10). The beer was poured out until the fields were flooded four spans high. In the morning the goddess went forth and found everything flooded. Looking closely at this flood of beer, she discovered her face mirrored in beauty. She drank of it, and it tasted good. She returned home drunk and no longer recognized mankind. Thus, Hathor is stopped only when the beer, acting as mirror, restores her connection to her beauty, and she is able to withdraw her terrible blood-thirstiness. This is to say that the Terrible Mother seeks to restore her own goodness through the reflecting eyes of humankind.

The petrifying face of Medusa

The petrifying gaze of Medusa undoubtedly belongs to the province of the Terrible Mother. With her power to slay by a malign effluence coming from her eyes, it is also clear that the Medusa is an incarnate evil eye. She is the epitome of the arresting archetypal fascinator with a face that depicts hatred and terror as the source of evil. On a personal level, Medusa (whose name means "queen") is the unempathic, unreflecting mother personified, a woman who petrifies the life of feeling by having no concern for another's subjective experience. She is the mother who holds her baby at a distance and makes no approach to warmly comfort, hold, or touch her. This mother looks at, and never into, her children during a time when their lives are entirely dependent upon her.

Greece, like the rest of the Mediterranean, has a long oral and documented history of the evil eye and Medusa, but the tradition is older than the Greeks. The first representations of the Gorgon are found in Greece in the 8th to 7th centuries BC, but they inherited the images from the Etruscans, where she was originally depicted as a parturient (squatting birth position) woman (Gravel, 1995: 12). This image of the Gorgon is distorted only in that her face depicts the grimace of the pain of childbirth, meaning that at this point in time the Gorgon was still a symbol of fertility. The later hideous images of drooping tongue and funny grin that strike terror at the soul are, at their roots, symbols of the critical moment of delivery.

In Greece, she was eventually reduced to a head and mask with petrifying eyes and an alarming face, similar to the way the Great Mother lost her fertile body and was gradually reduced to eyes in Mesopotamia or Egypt, despite her original connection to birth, productivity, and labor. The essence of Medusa became her head and nothing more. She is a cursed mask with a body later appended (Harrison, 1922: 187), and even when furnished with a body, the mask-head is still dominant.

On a side note, the basis of the disembodied eye or face is as cult or ritual objects that comprise part of the tools of a religion of terror. According to Harrison (1922), "the ritual object comes first; then the monster is begotten to account for it; then the hero is supplied to account for the slaying of the monster" (p. 187). Masks are natural agents of "riddance," and so form a part of the appliances of most primitive cults. The purpose of such masks is to make a permanent ugly face at you if you are doing wrong in some way (in other words, to shame you), not unlike the gargoyles on our Christian churches. If you are doing good, these masks serve as protection.

It is in her destructive capacity that the eyes of Medusa, profoundly horrible eyes that can turn everything freely living to stone, reflect the birth of shame. Medusa has been held in reverence as the "Eye of Judgment," with eyes that radiate "divine judgment which fixes the sinner for eternity, with no further possibility of redemption, in the place which life has prepared for him" (Barnes, 1974: 54) – a vivid description of the experience of shame and condemnation. We find in Goethe's *Faust* the same idea; the head of Medusa signifies the Eye which appraises conduct, condemns, and shames. In fact, one hears in these ideas a precise description of how shame functions intrapsychically as an all-seeing judge. Like God in the Garden of Eden, Medusa casts the sinner into a dark, condemned place of no redemption. Mimicking the power of God, one has to both admire and fear her ability to transmute the spirit of that which lives into immortal rock.

Just as the Great Mother has been revered for her transformative powers of life and death, many are held in awe of both Medusa's maternal, death-dealing glance as well as her prophylactic face that promotes magical healing. Medusa is both beautiful and horrible, as can be see in the following poem by Willoughby Weaving entitled "Medusa Awake":

Elf-locks? Serpents! writhing hair
Features lovely – fell and cold
From the black pool's mirror shine
Beauty – horror – both divine!
(Weaving, 1916: 53)

In this section, I will be looking at Medusa as an image of the archetype of the Terrible Mother with a face containing the evil eye that shames, a hideous visage contorted with rage and threatening, hissing eyes. Later in Chapter 7 we will look at how this image is also a figure of transformation, and that in her decapitation Medusa functions as a talisman for empowerment and protection.

To the modern mind, the Gorgons are three horrific sisters with locks of serpents, tusks of wild boars, and golden wings fixed to their shoulders. The most evil of the three, Medusa, had a lovely, terrible face with the power to turn whoever dared to look into it instantly to stone. Yet according to many classical legends, she was once the most seductive of women with beauty unsurpassed, and her two young sisters were also beautiful. Medusa became the epitome of evil and ugliness after she was raped in Athene's temple by Poseidon, a viola-tion which could not go unpunished by the imperious goddess, who "turned away, hid her eyes," and cursed the outrage by changing Medusa's once beautiful face into a monstrous one. Thomas Gordon Hake captures the horrible transformation of her beauty, infantile features, and childlike state in the words of his poem entitled "The Infant Medusa":

I loved Medusa when she was a child
Her rich brown tresses heaped in crispy curl
Where now those locks with reptile passion whirl,
By hate into disheveled serpents coiled.

I loved Medusa when her eyes were mild,
Whose glances, narrowed now, perdition hurl,
As her self-tangled hairs their mass unfurl,
Bristling the way she turns with hissings wild.

(Hake, 1894: 28)

The face of the Goddess of Death (from the fifth millennium BC) is depicted with large open mouth and dangling, flickering tongue, fearsome, glaring eyes and writhing snakes in her hair. The images of snakes suggestive of a connection to the Snake Goddesses (symbols of protection), the staring eye, and the severed head are similar to the archetype of the Terrible Mother at the heart of Egyptian religion, but the emotions that can create such a face are those that belong to terror and rage rather than envy and possessiveness. Medusa's face became "a visage contorted into the hideous to combine the horror, outrage and all the malevolence of vengeance into a portrait of fear itself" (Huxley, 1990: 56).

In the most popular version of the Medusa myth, Perseus eventually undertakes the murderous quest of killing Medusa, but only after taking elaborate precautions to avoid being turned into stone himself. According to Ovid (1955: 106), Perseus is guided to the Gorgon by the aged daughters of Phorcys – who shared one eye between them, passing it from one sister to another – and passed through lands filled with the rigid shapes of animals and men who had looked upon Medusa's face and been turned to stone. Athene, herself the product of an absent mother who has never been a child, plays the role of the good mother who protects Perseus from the look of Medusa. She advises Perseus on precautions to take, which include making himself invisible by wearing her helmet and using Athene's bright bronze shield as a mirror so as not to have to look directly into Medusa's face. Apollodorus gives this version of the beheading: "While Athene guided his hand and he looked with averted gaze on a bronze shield, in which he beheld the image of the Gorgon, he beheaded her." Note the averted gaze, as if only in knowing his shame could Perseus kill the Gorgon.

The myth also implies Perseus's fear of the evil eye as the explanation for this curious manner of execution. The shield as magic mirror becomes a necessary supplement to the sword, reflecting back to Medusa her own fascinating face, doubling her own force against her. In this way, Medusa, like Narcissus, dies of her own glance (Siebers, 1983). Anyone with such a mother is shamed just as was

Echo, and the only way to survive initially is to become her mirror, to fuse with mother in order to become whatever she feels.

The antithetical figures of Athene and Medusa become two expressions made by the same face, together creating an interplay of good and bad mother. The queen of Athens and the queen of hell occupy two poles, one of birth and one of death, the fertile mother and the destroying mother. This polarity is expressed in the history they share, dramatically stressed by the fact that Athene's birth presents the mirror image of Medusa's death (Siebers, 1983). Zeus made Wisdom (Metis) his first wife, but swallowed her before she could give birth to Athene so that none but he could be her parent (hence the absent mother of the patriarchy). Later, Athene springs forth fully armed and grown from an open wound inflicted by an axe in Zeus's head. Medusa dies from the sword blow, while Athena is born of a blow from an axe. Athene, a goddess born of an absented mother, must overcome Medusa to establish her own identity, which speaks to the psychological fact that without facing the dark mother an individual cannot come into her own, independent existence.

Both Athene and Medusa pass through the same transitions, which bring a transformation from destructive goddess to benevolent guardian. "Athene and Medusa merge, confounding impiety and piety, savageness and civilization, monstrosity and divinity" (Siebers, 1983: 15). In their resolution, the differences between the grotesque and the divine disappear. Once beheaded, Athene affixes the face of Medusa to her breastplate, "metal vipers to serve as awful warnings of her vengeance," and a symbol of the integrated good and bad mother. This, in turn, lifts the curse upon Medusa, whose beneficent potency begins when her head is severed. Her face becomes a protective charm against the evil eye. For Medusa, her beheading becomes her own rebirth, gradually revealing traces of the human face behind her mask, and from her severed head are born fully grown the winged horse Pegasus and his warrior brother Chrysaor. In her death, Medusa grows more human instead of more monstrous. She becomes a symbol of birth, which is an apt metaphor for shame when it is exposed, reflected, and suffers humanity. When the curse from her face is dropped, Medusa becomes more recognizably human.

The fiery eyes of the Baba Yaga

Both the gifts and the curses of the Mother of Death are also to be found in the character of the Baba Yaga, the old Russian Wild Hag, otherwise known as the Life/Death Mother. In keeping with the theme of this chapter, however, my focus will be on her fearsome aspect known as "The Great Destroyer." In this capacity, she manifests as a skull with burning eyes that can turn whomever her gaze captures into a pile of ashes – again, an image of disintegration and petrifaction. She appears in this form in a fairy tale entitled "The Beautiful Wassilissa", a story about a girl who meets the powers of the evil eye face to face but astutely finds her way out of trouble. Evidence of this story's archetypal roots date back to at least the old horse-goddess cults of the Baltic countries which predate classical Greek culture (Estes, 1992: 75). The version is the one presented by Marie Louis von Franz in her book entitled *The Feminine in Fairy Tales*:

> In an empire in a faraway country there once lived a merchant and his wife and their one beautiful daughter called Wassilissa. When the child was eight years old, the wife suddenly became very ill. She called Wassilissa to her deathbed, gave her a doll, and said, "Listen, my dear child, these are my last words and don't forget them. I am dying and leave you my blessing and this doll. Keep it always with you, show it to nobody, and whenever you are in any trouble ask it for advice." Then she kissed her daughter for the last time and died.
>
> The merchant mourned his wife for a long time, but then decided to marry again and chose a widow with two daughters. But for his daughter Wassilissa, the marriage was a disappointment for the new wife was a real stepmother who gave her all the hard work to do, hoping that the sun and wind would spoil her beauty and that she would begin to look like a peasant girl. But Wassilissa . . . got more beautiful every day . . . The doll, however, always comforted Wassilissa and did a lot of the work for her.
>
> A year passed this way, but Wassilissa, though much sought after, was forbidden to marry before her stepsisters, whom nobody looked at. Then the merchant had to go away to another country. In his absence the stepmother moved to a house at the edge of a great forest . . . in which the Baba Yaga lived. The Baba

Yaga permitted nobody to approach, and anyone who did she ate up. The stepmother, for whose plans the new house stood in exactly the right place, always sent Wassilissa into the wood, but she always returned safely, thanks to the doll.

One autumn evening the stepmother . . . [told her] she must go to the Baba Yaga to fetch fire . . . The doll told her not to be afraid, but to take her with her and nothing bad would happen.

Although terrified, Wassilissa put the doll in her pocket, crossed herself and went into the wood. Suddenly a man in white rode by on a white horse, and day came. Farther on, a man in red rode by on a red horse, and the sun rose. All through the night and the next day Wassilissa walked through the wood and in the evening came to a hut surrounded by a hedge made of human bones with skulls stuck on the posts. The doors were made of bones, the bolt to the door of a human arm, and in place of the lock there was a mouth with grinning teeth. Wassilissa was almost senseless with horror and stood rooted to the spot. Then suddenly another rider came by, this time all in black and sitting on a black horse. He jumped off and opened the door and disappeared as though swallowed up by the ground, and it was black as night. But soon all the eyes in the skulls that made the hedge began to twinkle, and it was as light as day in the clearing. Wassilissa trembled with fear, but didn't know where to go and stood still.

Then the trees began to rustle and the Baba Yaga appeared sitting in a mortar, steering with a pestle, and wiping out her tracks with a broom. When she reached the door she sniffed and cried out that it smelled like Russians and asked who was there. "I am, Grandmother. My stepsisters sent me to you to fetch the fire." "Good," said the Baba Yaga, "I know you. Stay with me for a bit and then you shall have the fire."

So they went in together and the Baba Yaga lay down and told Wassilissa to bring her everything that was in the oven to eat. There was enough there for ten, but the Baba Yaga ate everything up and left only a crust of bread and a little soup for Wassilissa. Then she said, "Tomorrow when I go out you must sweep up the yard, sweep out the hut, cook the midday meal, do the washing, then go to the cornshed and sort out all the mildewed corn from the good seed. Everything must be done by the time I get home, for otherwise I shall eat you."

When the Baba Yaga had gone, Wassilissa was left quite alone and troubled as to which work she should begin, but it was all done, and the doll was just removing the last seeds of the mildewed corn. Wassilissa called the doll her savior, saying it had saved her from great misfortune, and the doll told her that now she only had to cook the dinner.

When evening came, Wassilissa laid the table and waited, and when the Baba Yaga came she asked if everything was done. "Look yourself, Grandmother," said Wassilissa. The Baba Yaga looked at everything and was furious not to be able to find any fault, but she only said, "Yes, it's all right," and then called on her faithful servants to grind her corn. Thereupon three pairs of hands appeared and began to grind. The Baba Yaga ate just as much as the evening before and then told Wassilissa she should do the same work the next day, but in addition, she should sort the poppy seeds in the granary and clean the dirt away.

When the old woman came home she looked everything over and then again called to her faithful servants. The three pairs of hands came and removed the poppy seeds and pressed out the oil. While the Baba Yaga was eating her meal Wassilissa stood silently beside her. "What are you staring at without speaking a word?" asked the Baba Yaga. "Are you dumb?" "If you will allow me to do so, I would like to ask some questions," said Wassilissa. "Ask," said the Baba Yaga, "but remember that not all questions are wise; much knowledge makes one old." Wassilissa said she would only like to ask about the riders. The Baba Yaga told her that the first was her day, the red her sun, and the black her night. Then Wassilissa thought of the three pairs of hands, but didn't dare to ask and kept silent. "Why don't you ask more?" said the Baba Yaga. "That's enough," said Wassilissa. "You said yourself, that too much knowledge made people old." The Baba Yaga then said that she was wise only to ask about what she saw outside the hut, but that now she would like to ask her questions, and she asked how Wassilissa had managed all the work? Wassilissa said that her mother's blessing helped her. "Is that so?" said the Baba Yaga, "then get out of here, I don't want any blessing in my house." And she pushed Wassilissa out of the room and out of the door and took a skull from the hedge with the burning eyes in it and put it on a pole and gave it to Wassilissa, saying, "Here is your fire for your stepsisters. Take it home with you."

So Wassilissa hurried away and by the evening of the next day arrived home and thought she would throw the skull away, but a voice came from it saying she should not do so but should take it to her stepmother. And because Wassilissa saw no light in the house, she did just that. For the first time the stepmother and her stepsisters came to meet her in a friendly way and told her they had had no fire since she left, that they had not been able to light any fire and what they fetched from the neighbor was extinguished as soon as it got to their room. "Perhaps your fire won't go out," said the stepmother. She took the skull into the living room, but the glowing eyes stared unceasingly into hers and her daughters' eyes, right down into their souls. They tried to hide but the eyes followed them everywhere, and by the morning they were burnt to ashes. When day came Wassilissa buried the skull, shut up the house, went into the town and asked a lonely old woman to let her stay with her until her father came home.

(von Franz, 1986: 143–7)

This fairy tale, like most, ends when the beautiful Wassilissa meets the king, they fall in love, and live happily every after.

   The overall task for Wassilissa is to withstand the terrible demonic power of the Great Mother, to come head on with her fearsome face and eyes without wavering. This process is ignited by the loss of the good mother, with whose death, or absence, one is necessarily faced with the negative mother. In this fairy tale the Terrible Mother is depicted as both an envious, malicious stepmother bent on infanticide (the stepmother is often depicted as the evil side of the good mother, and is made so in relation to father's absence), or, on a deeper and more primitive level, the devouring Baba Yaga who possesses skulls with eyes that can incinerate the child. The reward of dealing with this psychic place is to transform the negative form of a skull with fiery eyes – the bad mother – into a face of great power – the good mother.

   I want to focus on the part of the tale that tells of Wassilissa meeting the Great Destroyer face to face in order to find out what it may say about shame. This confrontation occurs at the house of the Baba Yaga deep in the woods, a very primitive and wounded spot of loss and confusion. The Baba Yaga's hut is a petrified place, represented by the skulls and bones. But strangely, this inanimate place is alive. Skeleton hands dispense corn, the skull's eyes burn. In this petrified but alive place is contained the paradox of shame: this

Figure 5.1 The house of Baba Yaga

affect can both annihilate self and spark consciousness – depending on the dose.

The key image of that which induces shame in the other (or that which defends against shame by projecting it into the other) is the skull with the fiery eyes, posted on the fence that sets the boundaries of the Baba Yaga's house, or delineates this internal psychic space. The skull is a vessel of death, a symbol for the killing side of a life-giving mother, yet it points to a specific kind of death, the same kind of death that afflicted Echo in the woods. This is not a moist, messy death, but a rigid death by terror which transforms living, soft flesh into dry, skinless bone. It seems almost as if all the Baba Yaga's power that is contained in the skull is the very shame she dreads.

Wassilissa's fourth question, which she resists asking, refers to what she saw inside the hut, the three pairs of skeleton hands that fly through the air. The Baba Yaga tells her that "it is good that [she] didn't ask about the inside things, because one should not carry the dirt out of the hut." In other words, she is warning Wassilissa not to become curious about her shame, not to expose her dirt, and that her soul is not to be "peered into unceasingly." If shame were not involved, she wouldn't care if questioned about things inside her house. That shame is inside the hut is also depicted by the image of the rider on the black horse who opens the door to go inside and "disappeared as though swallowed up by the ground." The Old Hag contains enough goodness, just enough, to make her ashamed.

Like any ordinary human being, the Baba Yaga is capable of experiencing the sting of shame, revealing a secret humanitarian side. In her being as a goddess and as the Great Destroyer, however, she would have shamed Wassilissa right there on the spot, annihilated the good mother and wiped her existence off the face of the earth, had her own shame been touched. It is at this point that the Baba Yaga will destroy to defend herself, to keep from being destroyed, just as, on a more personal level, the mother, whose infant can see into her soul from their intimate eye contact, can disintegrate her when exposed and shamed.

Although they have much in common, the Baba Yaga is different from, for example, Ereshkigal or the Eye in Ancient Egypt. The latter start out with humanity and become evil, while Baba Yaga has a reputation for being totally evil but actually has a human side. Whichever side puts its face forward first, this dichotomy illuminates an interesting aspect of the archetypal nature of shame. It is the missing human, related, and reflecting component that creates shame's petrifying qualities, and its restoration is needed for its transformation.

Conclusion

Mankind's stories are repositories for images that reflect individual and collective historical patterns, which make them, in essence, containers for persisting patterns from early infancy. In other words, hidden in these collective images are aspects of the actual psychic, intimate, eternally human and earliest experiences of the infant with mother. Fordham describes the infant's psychic life as follows:

Mainly controlled by the play of archetypal energies which derive from the self by deintegration. They are natural, ruthless, absolute in the ebb and flow of their need to discharge themselves, and so the infant, we might say, seeks means to represent them. Verbal images are not available, but visual impressions, sensations, noises are at hand. The characteristics of the archetypes become attached to them and at the same time begin organizing the infant's experience We have to add that because the infant's ego is so weak, they are felt to be omnipotent.

(Fordham, 1965: 98)

Children perceive the world mythologically, experiencing it predominantly through archetypal images that get projected upon it. The creation of meaning, then, is always both objective and subjective, made up not only of reality but also of what is contributed to the object by the self. What is projected depends upon the individual's state of being at the time of perception. For example, the infant's first wonderful experiences of mother will be as a manifestation of the Great Mother, an all-powerful, life-giving, and numinous woman on whom she is dependent for all things. This is a quite different perception from the objective reality of her personal mother, an historical, actual human being whom she will be viewed as later in development. Bad experiences of the mother can develop into, and be amplified by, fantastically destructive images that do not originate in the outside world but are fed by the archetypes of the collective unconscious.

In this chapter, we have focussed on the primordial images of the evil eye specifically as they relate to the archetypal Terrible Mother and the experience of shame in early infancy. The Great Mother's eyes represent a specific form of the negative mother that has been overlooked in the psychological literature. These images originate in and are derived from an actual experience of catastrophic anxiety, absence of reflection and reverie, and fear of annihilation with mother. When an infant is overpowered by the affect of shame, it will manifest as a negative psychic reaction called the Terrible Mother, which will be expressed through eye images. In the grips of shame, the infant endows mother with unrealistic, chimerical features, seeing her in many ways that are almost impossible for adults to conceive (except when observing an infant or watching an adult patient in a process of psychotherapy). In fact, the extraordinary vitality of the archetype of the Terrible Mother's eyes is embodied in the affect of shame, which can engender figures full of penetrating, omnipotent eyes that manifest the black side of life and the human psyche. The Great Mother who generates life and all living things on earth is the same woman who is capable of petrifying and ensnaring a human infant in stone simply through eye contact. The reality of painful, unreflecting, shameful experiences combines with infantile, catastrophic anxieties to form the archetypal images of the Great Mother's petrifying eyes.

The myths and fairy tales presented in this chapter depict both the generation and shaming effects of the evil eye and provide means for its redemption. They reveal that the look comes from and penetrates the depths of the psyche. It is consistently referenced as residing in the underworld, the world of the deeply unconscious, and is connected to petrifaction: the Eye Goddesses were found mainly in tombs; Ereshkigal is queen of the underworld with an Eye of Death that can turn Inanna into a piece of raw meat; Medusa as a Gorgon is connected to the nameless horror of the "underworld bogeys" with eyes that turn men to stone; the Creator Eye in the ancient Egyptian religion lives in the "sightless negativities of the abysmal waters" and turns her energies to an all-seeing power and killing rages; and the shaming power of the Baba Yaga is contained in a skull "which stares unceasingly." All of these images afflict the unsuspecting and innocent with a terror of petrifaction.

Archetypal images of the Terrible Mother's eyes unconsciously determine human behavior in accordance with what the individual's experience has been, and are always accompanied by strong emotional components that decisively influence the mood, feelings, and varying propensities of a given personality. In this respect, the shamed individual projects her own unconscious expectation of pathetic failures into the eyes of those who might be envious, narcissistic, or depressed, then fails or loses and blames the other for her shame. When core shame develops, this repetitive, persisting trend from infancy is a fear of eyes, and being visible is always the reason for things gone bad.

This very repetition, however, is not without a purpose. In his essay entitled "The Psychology of the Child Archetype," Jung states:

> Humanity, too, probably always comes into conflict with its childhood conditions, that is, with its original, unconscious, and instinctive state, and that the danger of the kind of conflict which induces vision of the "child" actually exists. Religious

observances, i.e. the retelling and ritual repetitions of the mythical event serve the purpose of bringing the image of childhood,
and everything connected with it, again and again before the
eyes of the conscious mind so that the link with the original
condition may not be broken.

(Jung, 1959: 162)

When shame gets structured into the psyche at its core, eyes act
with an autonomous force that actually determine the situation and
prompt psychotic anxieties. Only in the course of psychotherapy can
the adult learn to de-animate the catastrophic power of eyes. Within
this container, shame can be transformed through the reviving of the
good mother and the experience of bringing life to that which has
been annihilated. Going through petrifaction is a necessary transition toward rebirth and new fertility, for when confronted and integrated eyes become things of great power. "The look" has all the
makings of a symbol, and in the next chapter we will examine
the therapeutic work that needs to be undertaken in order to turn the
instinctual, primal and unmetabolized eyes of shame into symbols
of the self.

Chapter 6

The look

My face is a mask I order to say
nothing
About the fragile feelings hiding
in my soul.
(Mohawk poem)

In the darkest eyes the brightest eyes have secluded themselves.
(Paul Éluard, 1895–1952)

I too am become a cunning eye
Seeking you past your time-gnawed surface.
(Amy Lowell, 1925)

A cave of pain a howling mouth
it is dark
the emptied self
Striking my head on the rock my mother.
(Rachal Blau DuPlessis, *Medusa*, 1980)

At the beginning of this chapter, I have little in the way of preliminary remarks to make. This is because after the theoretical material presented in prior chapters these four remarkable, deeply moving case histories will vividly reveal the story of the eyes of shame for themselves, and so need little clinical introduction. The words, images, and therapeutic processes depict clearly both the archetypal and personal roots of shame, as well as its evolution and core solidification in a personality structure. Each story uniquely depicts how in infancy the mother–infant relationship got reversed, so that in the absence of maternal reverie, each individual had the terrible, dim awareness of being a container for the mother's disturbances. This led to a life filled with shame, a fusion with the mother's conscious or unconscious disgust in one form or another, and their collusion to deny a true self. Each person whose story is told developed, very early on, a highly functional false self through mental activity. Although protecting a fragile self, this defense created unfulfilled lives. Shame finds its roots only by coming face to face with the mother's internalized unconscious. Inevitably, this leads to the need to regress back to birth to recapture what has been petrified. Each patient whose story is told in the following pages goes back to her birth and the earliest days of life. There, each one finds madness and fragmentation, comes close to the edge of utter destruction, and grows to live without pathological shame. This process is depicted through multiple eye and stone images, as well as reactions to facial expressions.

Many of us will never have to regress back to the level of fragmentation that these patients needed to negotiate. For the psychotherapist, however, these case histories offer essential insights into the type of corresponding regression that will inevitably occur and needs to be undertaken by the therapist if this material is to be contained and healed. Regarding his work with Margaret Little, one of the patients presented in this chapter, Winnicott said:

> I have therefore had a unique experience even for an analyst. I cannot help being different from what I was before this analysis started . . . It has tested psychoanalysis in a special way, and has taught me a great deal . . . I had to make personal growth in the course of this treatment which was painful and which I would have gladly avoided. In particular I have had to learn to examine my own technique whenever difficulties arose, and it has always turned out in the dozen or so resistance phases that the cause was in a countertransference phenomenon which necessitated further self-analysis in the analyst.
>
> (Winnicott, 1992b: 280)

The regressions depicted in these four stories will teach the psychotherapist about primitive emotional processes, specifically in relation to eyes and shame; clearly show the inner object images and symbolized affects that will manifest when traumas stemming from mother's eye have created a personal experience of shame; and delineate the deepest dimensions of their own psyches which may need to be explored in the process of a cure.

These cases are simply told with little analysis or clinical interpretation. I do this for two reasons. First, psychological jargon tends to
dehumanize (hence, shame) patients' most painful material and
remove the psychotherapist from what needs to be felt and received
fully in the moment. Second, I have found that when dealing with the
earliest developmental layers, the unconscious speaks clearly. I have
never ceased to marvel at the clarity of transactions between conscious and unconscious in the deepest strata of the human mind,
especially when working with the image of the eye, which has the
peculiar ability to render what is invisible, visibly clear. When dealing
with core shame, it is above all important to follow the patient's own
course, and allow him or her to stay at their own pace. The healing
process needs to be derived from the psyche of the patient, which
will speak with for itself. The last two women whose stories are
told (or retold) are very popular in psychoanalytic literature: Marie
Cardinal's autobiographical account of her analysis in *The Words to
Say It* (1975/1996), and Margaret Little's (1990) story of her analysis
with D. W. Winnicott in *Psychotic Anxieties and Their Containment*.
They were chosen due to the remarkable clarity of eye images, non-
existence, their connection to birth and early infancy, a disturbed
relationship to mother and the prominence of shame. This single
thread has been teased out of these otherwise complex analyses to
make the reader aware of the presence of shame in their psychoses,
and to show how, despite how well known their stories are, this affect
has gone unnoticed in psychoanalytic literature.

A countertransference psychosis: The stone womb

As Barbara began to talk, I found myself sitting in a room filled with
apprehension, struggling to listen to her in the face of a compelling
experience of our eye contact. I felt glued to her eyes; I was pulled
into them as if there was no space between us, and felt they possessed
a power to draw out my life energy. This adhesive grasp that reached
deep inside of me defended against any inkling of separateness. This
feeling quickly disappeared when the polar opposite occurred; I felt
miles away from her despite the five feet between us, a total separation without any sense of connectedness. Our liminal space was
eerie and electric, and I simply knew that she desperately needed
something to hold on to. Through her presence, I was immediately
drawn into a world of shame and the terror of losing the life-saving

mother. I was deeply shaken by the immediacy of these intense countertransference feelings, wondering if I would be enough for her to
cling to given the autistic nature of her grasp.

Barbara came for her second session, and this time I noticed the
strange hunger in her eyes, a craving for recognition colored by a
feeling of being ignored. Again the same terrible sensations
occurred. I imagined that this rhythmical feeling of being drawn in
and then blown apart through eye contact was her experience of
seeing and being seen. To see meant to manifest devastating power,
and to be seen meant to be engulfed. Both possessed a magical power
to suck the life energy out of anything. There was no space in which
two people could exist – one person's life is always at the expense of
the other.

She was verbal in the same way her eyes met mine, without separation as she worked so hard at engaging and holding onto mother.
Or, paradoxically, she was working at blocking mother out, as there
was little space for me to respond. Her thoughts were clear and her
words fitted together perfectly with little space in between. She
seemed to know exactly what she wanted to say. I ceased to try and
focus on her words, instead directing my attention to the dimensions of these terrible feelings and our eye contact. Her glibness
enabled me to attend to this stultifying experience without much
disruption.

I felt completely dominated and helplessly immobilized, converted
into a stony substance through a projection from her internal world –
that of a merciless, inattentive, but omnipresent mother. I only
vaguely heard her immediate reason for entering therapy, a recent
separation from her husband and the beginning of a new relationship. She also told me that she had only a year for therapy (perhaps
the reason why my experience of her was so immediate) because she
had already committed to return to school in another state. This
move would entail a separation from her 5-year-old son, who would
stay with his father.

Her third visit prompted the same countertransference experience,
but this time I was able to feel, think, and verbalize her intense need
for my maternal eyes to hold onto her. This spoken feeling opened a
door, and she began to reveal the presence of a tyrannical, dissociated masculine voice that told her she was very bad, that she
deserved to die and that she should begin planning her suicide
immediately. She could be feeling fine one minute, and in a flash
overcome with the insane thought of driving to her parents' home in

another state to get their gun and kill herself. She continually cursed herself for being "beyond tragic."

Following her revelation of this voice, she is bombarded with dreams of ice caps breaking up, breast milk flowing in floods, and space aliens taking over. Thoughts swirl around and will not be pinned down. Things can make her feel a panic and sadness that prevent her from keeping civil conversation going. Nausea and dread dominate somatically. She is scared all the time about the depth and complexity of her emotions, and full of unbearable despair. She complains that the ground beneath her feet is fragmented. She has no relief, and dreams of having to go to the bathroom, but it is a horrifying mess because everything is covered in shit.

Barbara connected these dream images to the onslaught of her murderous voice, which accompanied a postpartum depression that left her feeling numb, cold, and dead inside. Five years before, she and her husband began to think about having a child. She really wasn't ready, feeling that her husband procrastinated and couldn't really get things done – how could she handle it all and rely on him? He really wanted a child and insisted upon his wishes, so they went ahead and got pregnant. Conception and pregnancy put her in a bad place, but her labor was the most terrible, lasting 36 hours without any pain relief. She just wasn't having contractions. The midwives gave her castor oil and pitocin. Either her body just didn't want to let him go, or the baby just didn't want to come out. In the counter-transference I, too, had the experience of enduring a difficult pregnancy. Interpretations were hard to form in my mind, indicating that her infant self experienced a fall from mother's mind. Her infant self's experience of this fall was triggered by the birth of her own son.

Three days after the birth of her son, when her husband returned to work and her mother went home, she became immobilized by a crippling depression. She struggled daily by the minute to stay alive, and then each morning would wake up to that voice that had regathered its strength. Despite the fact that this petrifying depression descended every day for four years, she never told anyone. This murderous aspect alienated her from friends and family, and this absence of people confirmed her view of herself as a dirty, disgusting individual, undeserving of contact with anyone. This psychotic part reeked of shame.

In the midst of relating this most painful experience, she uttered one sentence that made sense of what I was feeling: "Giving birth to my 13-pound son was like giving birth to a boulder." Internally what she was giving birth to was the experience of a container without transformative potentials, her earliest experiences of mother. There was no chance for human connection when the only other element was stone. We would spend the rest of our time together examining the meaning of this comment.

Barbara suffered from a strong feeling that her mother never wanted her to be born and that she was ashamed of her because she was such a peculiar baby. She amplified this feeling with a tale that her mother shared when she was in kindergarten of a pregnancy just prior to Barbara's own birth. As the story goes, her four months pregnant mother was out to eat one night with her father. At one point in the conversation they got into a fight because of her father's jealousies. In an instant she felt her womb turn "hard as a rock," and said that from that moment on she was no longer pregnant. The terror that such a story would strike into the heart of a 4-year-old child is unimaginable. I myself, upon hearing this story, was so disturbed by it that I inquired further, and learned that while it is a phenomenon in the animal world known as spontaneous abortion, this was an unknown phenomenon in the human world. On a psychological level, however, it indicated that the omnipotent Terrible Mother ruled, and there was no room for reflection and containment in the face of such an indestructible element – any chance of this must not feel possible in the face of such stone.

Throughout her life, the fight to keep a place in mother's mind and the fear of being done away with split her. On the surface, Barbara was an extremely bright, entrepreneurial spirit doing whatever she applied herself to with seeming ease. She could spend all day alone taking care of her son, and then work to earn a living while her husband flitted about exploring his options for a PhD. She worked with sheep and dogs, farmed land, had her own writing business, and was being pursued by a prestigious university to attend their PhD program.

Simultaneously, she lived terrified by the thought that everyone would discover her shamed self lurking underneath. In her journal she writes that she "feels she has permanently damaged so many things, so many things that are irreparable" and "I think about killing myself . . . My life has changed for the better in so many ways and yet this remains as a constant . . . I am scared all the time, I am afraid that I will never go along normally, without constant fears and worries." In order to escape this trap she withdrew, and turned any feelings into impenetrable stone, just as her mother had turned her to stone. True self is lost as the experience of a rock is substituted. As the gap between her outer and inner worlds widened, she couldn't tolerate the tension. It was ripping her apart. Any sense of self was obliterated in the rupture. The murderous voice would then take hold of its opportunity, becoming louder and more insistent. I always found the disparity between these two aspects of her unfathomable. A very functional part progressed rapidly, her self-preservation system fully intact, while she struggled by the minute in a persecutory inner world.

Entering her psychosis in therapy, I too found myself in a dark stone womb. Her dreams revealed the picture of a petrified, dissociated infant self frozen out of the ice queen's castle, constantly in search of something to hold onto. My eyes were the only living thing the infant part of her had to hold onto in the face of a mother whose womb could turn a little budding life to stone, yet these same eyes contained the cold terror which could obliterate her existence.

In fact, death pervaded her mother. Her mother's worst nightmare (and shame) was that the family would realize that she was insane and commit her to an asylum. She kept hoards of pills on hand so that in case this happened she could kill herself. Barbara made a connection between her brother's close bond with his mother and his accident proneness, which eventually ended in his accidental death a few years before.

Barbara was beginning to realize that she lived at the mercy of a withholding mother, a critical observing eye always looking, watching, just waiting for her to make a mistake and reveal her as selfish. Putting these feelings of being engulfed in a black hole into words brought her to memories of her frugal mother going over her father's accounting records with her every week in order to show her just how much her father spent on her expensive hobbies. Her mother had no feelings in the face of facts, and one fact she always faced was retirement, a reality many years off. So despite her father's lucrative profession, they never lived according to their means. In the face of this withholding, Barbara built up a character defense to avoid any possibility of exposure. She would hide shame beneath the rules of her mother's dominance.

Barbara always felt that she should have been a boy because her mother hated women. She pursued her mother for answers, and in a letter to her daughter explaining her fears about having a girl, her mother wrote about her reactions to certain "female behavior habitually exhibited in her youth by myriad . . . females ranging from self-fooling to fakery to manipulation, always with cover-up." She stated that over the centuries women "prissily pretend" while they cultivate a power to manipulate men. She said she is full of her own "corrosive, unreleased anger" that she made no attempt to hide so as not to become one of these women. She signed her letter "mom (ster)."

Barbara's mother didn't want her daughter to be tied down to the masculine-dominated femininity that she accepted. She did not want her to be one of those "manipulative, posing, whiny, backbiting, false, pretentious and cruel" women who competed for men. Barbara was to take the world as her oyster all in her own good time and not rely on any man. So three days after the birth of her son, stuck at home, Barbara entered this stone place.

All these realizations culminated in a dream of a rushing river. Waves begin to wash up over her face, and as the water recedes, the foamy part of the wave forms a crust on her face. With each wave, her face gradually turns to stone. This dream image calls up Alexandra Grilikhes's inspirational poem of a daughter's reconciliation with her stone mother entitled "Medusa, Smiling".

To you
great lady
I dedicate the storm
ing flower
writhing in my wits while
brazen pride and
fear, bronze
in all their harshness
move and move
in the tomb
of my hands for you Medusa
always for you
    oh, when
    was it
    that the eyes
    of the sun
    were on me
    and I turned
    gold on the branch
    my tongue singing
    praises other than these?

> Fond
> mother, stone
> mother, with me now
> in weariness, in
> dark
> water I see you now Medusa
> see your face at last
> with my face
> in your eyes, gleaming.
>
> (Grilikhes, 1981: 72–3)

This facial image made a powerful connection to the self that had hardened over in order to defend against the lack of maternal containment. It is as though time had slowly pressed out her feelings, and this pressure builds into stone. This dream confirmed for Barbara the understanding to which she was coming. She was learning how her mother had projected her own insanity into her through their early eye contact, turning her to stone. Her mother, deprived of her own feminine, life-giving functions, became possessed by the rage of Medusa and couldn't help but petrify her only infant daughter.

Barbara came to feel deeply moved and calmed by these insights. They made sense of her implacable madness. This was how eye contact had become a snare, capable of piercing her to the very core of her being. She then remembers childhood dreams that for her confirmed our analysis of her mother's eyes. One terrifying, repetitive childhood dream occurred so often, and felt so real, that she was afraid to go to sleep at night. She would dream that she is asleep in her bed and wakes up to see the yellow eyes of wolves staring at her through her bedroom window. She'd wake up scared to death. It is of note that the evil eye has been detected in many animals, including the wolf. In the *Dictionary of Symbols and Imagery* (de Vries, 1984), the wolf is in general evil, the chaotic, destructive element, and sacred to the Great Goddess (p. 505).

Over time she revealed a hobby of photographing eyes, something she started doing at the time her son was conceived, and had over the last five years compiled a vast collection of eye photos. In addition to giving me a photo of her mother's cold, lidless eye (see Figure 2.4), she gave me the following poem entitled "I Am a Photo," written during the onset of her postpartum depression:

In the midst of conversation
I glance at my mother.
She is gazing at me with a bemused expression,
lips curved into a smile, distant,
as if she was holding
my browned, curled baby photos.
The rest of my sentence falls away in my mind.
I feel I have become as abstract,
as untouchable to her
as my ancient baby self.
She watches me like a film.

A desperate longing to be seen and recognized persisted, and kept her alive, for it is imperative to exist in someone else's eyes in order to feel in existence. Upon reading this poem I realized that she had fallen away in her mother's mind, and our work together entailed holding her in my mind through our eye contact in order to forge a maternal connection to her shamed "ancient baby self." I had to suffer on her behalf the sensation of being drawn in and then blown away that I felt with my entire being, and verbally construct its meaning. This meant intense concentration and the hard labor of pushing to bring her to the petrifying emotional experiences hidden in her shame.

With awareness of her own thoughts, the world now had a new feeling to it. We had entered her mother's stone womb and matching eyes in order to satisfy her needs to feel visible and received. A fragile part of herself had been blocked behind a wall of separation. With only a year of work together our accomplishments would be limited. During our time together, Barbara found an important piece of her self, the rock that needed to continue to be the object of sight. On an external level she returned to complete her PhD. Her dissertation would focus on determining the type of rock in the earth that enabled continents to float upon it. She brought me a prehistoric, crystallized salt rock shaped like an outstretched hand that she dug up in a creek bed. She also became preoccupied with encouraging her son to tell her when she hurt him, and asked often how he felt. No one in her childhood could accept the fact that they were actually wrong, and so she felt soothed and relieved to know that her son wasn't going to be building up painful shame experiences that could deform his character.

As Barbara and I proceeded to our own separation, her inner life presented numerous dreams that contained the image of the stone she would need to continue to examine. One dream presented three boxes with a stone in each. She is to pick one. She selects one that contains mica (a mirror-like black rock that splits into flexible sheets), but a voice warns her that due to our ending she is not ready to dream about that rock yet. The image of mica is connected to a daughter's quest to transcend her mother's disturbance in a poem written by Rachel Blau DuPlessis entitled "Medusa":

> What is this thing
> This ancient middenstead?
> All stark.
> It is a stone.
> Its lips are stone.
> Its eyes are mica mirrors.
>   (DuPlessis, 1980: 48)

Another dream tells her that she will be making new rocks, indicating that her treatment had transformed a potentially psychotic, malignant regression into a healthy, benign one. Fordham has said that unanalyzed infant material

> will augment the shadow and often render it unmanageable. By assimilating its value, the "primary truth" found there helps us to understand not only how the present state was reached, but also reveals the primary affective patterns for management of the shadow. Through them regression can turn into progression.
>   (Fordham, 1965: 97)

Remarkably, the dissociated voice intent on murder had been transformed into a narrator in the dreams that sought to bring her to a deeper knowledge of this black rock. Black is the color of shame, and a quote from Shakespeare states well why: "I am black because I come from the earth's inside." Shame connects us to our earthiest substance, since it begins in the primal earth and mother's dark depths. Shame is the depressed, inexplicably hopeless, and sinful – the result of being swallowed up by the earth.

At our ending, deintegration had started through a painful linking of shame to awareness. We had partly succeeded in turning her rigid stone self into a solid but penetrable possibility for containment in analysis, and the development of mature insight. The petrified rock that made movement impossible had become the bedrock of her search for true self-expression.

A psychotic transference: The petrifying eyes

The psychic world of infancy can also be reflected directly in preverbal manifestations acted in the transference. This patient, whom I will call Alexandra, hit moments of annihilation catalyzed by subtle shifts in my facial expressions. Reality adaptation appeared to be maintained in all parts of her life. However, psychotic anxieties emerged through our eye contact, making her primitive disturbance readily available for therapeutic work. In fact, if not for this manifestation, the psychosis would probably have gone unrecognized.

Alexandra needed to know that I could survive and function despite her own struggle with the most unacceptable parts of herself. In this way, my presence to her existence became the singlemost, important curative factor. Her dream process, which continually guided our course, clearly depicts the value of simply being present to the patient's experience, and supports what John Perry (1976) understands about psychosis. He interprets the symbolism of psychosis as the autonomous self-representation of a spontaneous healing process that occurs within the individual. Indeed, so thoroughly is this healing process "within" that although "the therapist must be receptive and attentive to the psychic process . . . the psyche does the work of healing" (p. 22). In keeping with this thought, Alexandra's story will be told plainly through a series of dreams with multiple eyes and faces, as well as interpretations of the transference which manifested in reaction to my face.

In the introduction to this chapter, Winnicott was quoted as saying that he had to make painful personal growth in the course of treatment with a regressed patient which he would have gladly avoided. The same is true for my therapeutic work with Alexandra, and I cannot help being different from what I was before my work with her started. My experience speaks to the intersubjective element essential in psychotherapy, and the need for the other as container. It forced me to reexamine the earliest aspects of my relationship with my own absent mother, and this came to me in a most powerful way. I was driving away from my office as Alexandra arrived for her first appointment. I spotted her in my rearview mirror (a shadow area), and, feeling deeply confused, realized that I had forgotten she was coming. I put the car in reverse and sped up the hill to find a bewildered Alexandra coming out of my home office (strangely I had left the door unlocked). I wondered what it meant that she was in my empty house when I wasn't there. At the end of our session, she said of our beginning moment, "You will have to believe that I don't exist."

Alexandra's unconscious immediately offered dreams that laid out the foundation for the work that needed to be undertaken, and eventually, through work on the transference, brought into vivid relief the image of her "autonomous self-representation," the eye and face. Throughout this phase of our work, Alexandra's dream material served as a container for her most primitive affects as well as a form of therapeutic mirroring. Through them she could relive her life events and emotions. She could safely react to and explore their images. They were unsurpassed as a focus of our shared attention, and this gradually built up her capacity for a relationship that could open the way for her existence and creativity to come forth.

Soon after beginning, Alexandra dreams about being shot, and the bullet is going to explode inside. This is going to cause a great deal of pain. This image prefaces a search that she needs to undertake to find her watch (what eyes do). Her quest leads her to a small town, the center of which is a movie theater named "Quanta de Sol" [how much soul/sun]. She is so excited to find that *She* has been made into a movie and is playing there. She knows that she must see it. This dream promised that Alexandra was going to find the source of her pain, the seat of her nonexistence, once the bullet penetrates and explodes. She would find what she must "watch;" seeing *She* will show her "how much soul" she possesses. This movie in the dream refers to "Ayesha," otherwise known as "She-who-must-be-obeyed," a succubus in H. Rider Haggard's book entitled *She*. She is a mysterious white queen who rules over a tribe of black savages deep in the heart of the Africa, where "the river is a great rock carven like the head of an Ethiopian" (Haggard, 1957: 36). She guards the Pillar of Life which lies hidden deep down in a tremendous rocky cavern, so that among the many magical powers she possesses is a power over life and death. She has herself stepped into the pillar of fire, which clothed her in immortality and godlike beauty. Simultaneously, enraged with a man for spurning her love, she incinerates him with a single glance from her eyes. The novel picks up at the point that Ayesha has been alive 2000 years, waiting for her beloved to reincarnate back into life so that they can marry, and he is preparing to make a trip to find her.

A leitmotif of the tale is her face, so beautiful that she must keep it under a veil lest anyone see it. Its poetic description in the following passage captures beauty and terribleness, two aspects of the mother of childhood. The first face strengthens the infant's sense of being, whereas the second arrests any continuity of being:

> I gazed upon her face and shrank back blinded and amazed. I have heard of the beauty of celestial beings, now I saw it; only this beauty, with all its awful loveliness and purity, was evil . . . Never before had I guessed what beauty made sublime could be – and yet, the sublimity was a dark one – the glory was not all of heaven . . . Though the face before me was that of a young woman of certainly not more than thirty years . . . yet it had stamped upon it a look of unutterable experience, and of deep acquaintance with grief and passion. It shone even in the light of the glorious eyes . . . and it seemed to say: "Behold me, lovely as no woman was or is, undying and half divine; memory haunts me from age to age, and passion leads me by the hand – evil have I done . . . and from age to age evil I shall do."
>
> (Haggard, 1957: 179–80)

Her countenance turned rigid as stone when inhabited by her malevolence and fascinated terror:

> Suddenly she paused, and through my fingers I saw an awful change come over her face. Her great eyes suddenly fixed themselves into an expression in which horror seemed to struggle with some tremendous hope arising through the depths of her dark soul. The lovely face grew rigid, and her gracious, willowy form seemed to erect itself.
>
> (Haggard, 1957: 181)

She finally meets up with her lost lover, and in an attempt to unite them once again, she steps into the Pillar of Life. But suddenly:

> A kind of change came over her face, a change which I could not define or explain . . . The smile vanished, and in its place there came a dry, hard look; the rounded face seemed to grow pinched, as though some great anxiety were leaving its impress upon it. The glorious eyes, too, lost their light, and, as I thought, the form its perfect shape and erectness.
>
> (Haggard, 1957: 334)

Her face instantaneously begins to take on the age of 2000 years and reflects the atrocity of her evil deeds. It shrivels up into mummified stone, hideous beyond words. Her dying words are "Forget me not, Kallikrates. Have pity on my shame" (p. 336) (the same turning to stone suffered by poor Echo in her shame). The face of She-who-must-be-obeyed, a face that held life and death so close together, provided a key to what Alexandra would come to understand about her mother's face and her birth.

The next night a dream is narrated, a story being told about a woman dressed like She:

> I am at an older woman's house. She is preparing to go to an O.T.O. Lodge Ritual. She is getting dressed in a white gauze gown. She has pulled her hair back with an ancient gold hair piece. Her face is revealed. I see her hairpiece clearly, since my view is from behind, watching her view herself in the mirror as she puts on the last finishing touches. Then the woman goes to her sister's house – she is also going to the ritual. Her sister is an older woman with white, short hair. I am facing her sister, and as I write this dream its seems like the narration stops and I am more in the picture, the sister herself.

This dream prompted a deep and prolonged exploration of the problematic relationship between her mother, her sister and herself. She ached to belong to her mother, whom she felt was inaccessible and never really mindful of her. Her mother always considered her to be different, and so Alexandra went along in what she called her bubble of laughter and naivety, reaching for nothing. In the core of a big ball of love for her mother, Alexandra held enormous shame. Mother meant a stone wall of separation. She did not yet know that it was not she but her mother who was deeply disturbed.

Her sister, Lucy, was sheltered by her mother. She had always been envious and hateful towards her more adorable little sister. Lucy complained that Alexandra had a better name, prettier hair, a cuter doll. At night she would torment Alexandra with threats that she was going to kill her so that "she would wake up dead." Alexandra was instructed by her mother to be nice, to share, to put up with whatever Lucy dished out. She was forced to include her when she played with her friends. Lucy, after all, was simply more delicate. Her mother's blindness and passivity led to Lucy's excessive impingement on Alexandra with unmitigated envy, so that she didn't dare exist. She lived at the mercy of the evil eye and her mother's envy.

The perspective from behind that Alexandra has of the woman's hairpiece made me think of my own point of view the time I spotted her in my rearview mirror. Our discussion of this material precipitated a profound disturbance in the transference. My face became the movie screen playing *She*, displaying what she needed to see. Alexandra began to experience unexpected moments when she perceived a certain shadow or darkening cross my face and eyes. This look devastated her. In a flash she would curdle, losing her ability to speak or think. She lost internal connection to herself and felt externally severed from the world. She would indeed cease to exist.

We spent the next three years analyzing this barely perceptible millisecond into which her existence could disappear. As the transference around my face developed, Alexandra has a dream about a birthmark that appears on my face. She writes:

> Mary is getting visibly sick. She has a flu or something, but I also notice a large bluish black mark on her left cheek near her mouth that extends almost to her ear. It looks like a birthmark, and I wonder that I never noticed that before. As I get closer to her I begin to notice her face getting even uglier. Her skin has thickened and gotten very porous, especially her nose. I feel compassion and say "you might think about calling in when you feel sick."

Like the character She, my face is beginning to change and unmask hidden, ugly feelings that can no longer be denied because they are what makes her sick. All her inner badness and destructiveness is visually exposed on my skin. These feelings have their roots in her birth and earliest days of life when all she had to hold onto was mother's eyes. Her compassion in the dream towards me reflects her receptivity. These feelings are showing themselves through veins, rising to the surface of my skin. They can no longer be hidden. Her shame, like the mark of Cain, is revealed, and she must look on my face. The porousness of the skin forms minute surface openings or passageways that will let out the thing that makes her sick, her black shame. The image of my nose is accentuated, seeming to say that she needs to know what she knows.

A woman veiled like She, whose face also needs to be revealed, shows up in another dream. Alexandra dreams that she is looking at her sister and thinks that she looks very different from the last time she saw her. She realizes that she has hair all the way from below her eyes to her chin. She associates this veiled face to another queen, Orual, the envious, monopolistic sister of Psyche in C.S. Lewis's retelling of the myth of Amor and Psyche, *Till We Have Faces*.

Orual is ashamed of putting the idea into Psyche's mind that her husband, Eros, is a monster whose face must be exposed. Psyche is caught in this act and sent into exile and misery. Following a cryptic proclamation by Eros that Orual "shall know herself and her work. She also shall be Psyche," Orual comes to a resolution:

> Hitherto, like all my countrywomen, I had gone bareface; on those two journeys up the Mountain I had worn a veil because I wished to be secret. I now determined that I would go always veiled. I have kept this rule, within doors and without, ever since. It is a sort of treaty made with my ugliness.
>
> (Lewis, 1956: 174)

Her face is veiled in order to keep her secrets which make her feel so ugly and despicable. Shame is symbolized as a veil, a covering for that which is threatened by exposure. Dirty, disgusting people need to veil themselves in order to approach the powerful. Orual's veil, however, led the people she ruled to fantasize many things about her face:

> My second strength lay in my veil. I could never have believed, till I had proof of it, what it would do for me. From the very first . . . as soon as my face was invisible, people began to discover all manner of beauties in my voice . . . No one believed it was anything so common as the face of an ugly woman. Some said . . . that it was frightful beyond endurance; a pig's, bear's, cat's or elephant's face. The best story was that I had no face at all; if you stripped off my veil you'd find emptiness. But another sort said that I wore a veil because I was of a beauty so dazzling that if I let it be seen all men in the world would run mad . . . The upshot of all this nonsense was that I became something very mysterious and awful.
>
> (Lewis, 1956: 229)

Orual, with consciousness of her envy and possessiveness of Psyche slowly dawning, begins to dream that she had walled up, and "gagged with stone," Psyche herself. Her insights lead to a new thought about her veil:

> My veil was no longer a means to be unknown. It revealed me; all men knew the veiled Queen. My disguise now would be to go barefaced . . . I showed that face which many had said was too dreadful to be seen. It would shame me no more.
>
> (Lewis, 1956: 278)

Through years of suffering, Orual had lost her fear of the ugly, and that loss did her great good. She would no longer suffer such deep shame.

In connecting the two images of veiled faces with the mother–sister transference, the image of the black facial birthmark comes prominently into view. In one she is sitting with a new client, a woman with a large birthmark on her face that makes her face half white and half black. The skin on the black side is thick and porous. In another she is sitting behind the wheel of a car with a deep black mudpack on her face. Another dream reveals a big family secret: her mother is really black. As this material was beginning to be metabolized, she dreams that the birthmark appears on her face. She looks in the mirror and sees her dark, bluish black face. Her dream consciousness zeros in on the skin, which is now transparent and smooth, appearing this color because of her pulsing veins. Feeling the pain was bringing movement to what had been petrified. Her life's blood was beginning to flood her veins.

It emerged after a time that her suffering was intensified by the intrusive glances of others. She talked about how she sheltered herself from contact with people; the look haunted the space between she and others. Alexandra often saw the devastating look that she saw on my face on the faces of others, which prompted, of course, the same petrified reaction. Blocked by shame, she felt unable to learn, to explore, to be social, even to think. She lived so cautiously in the eyes of others, whose words and faces inhabited her, lived in her, tortured her, never left her. Looking out from this place at the world made any other form of life seem preferable.

Her unconscious takes up images of the world, revealing that ego consciousness is solidifying in relation to her shame. In one dream she is screaming at her family, telling them that they always needed someone to shame, and she would no longer carry it. Then she is showing me a map of the United States that she is outlining in yellow. She is coloring in the lines to create the different states. In other words, she is separating and differentiating her own self in the family complex, and this creates a unity out of chaotic states.

Alexandra begins to comprehend the source for her feelings that she should never have been born. Her sister, born two years earlier, nearly died of pneumonia at age 11 days. She was read the last rites three times. This was a traumatic experience for both Lucy and her mother, resulting in a special life-and-death bond. Alexandra's birth became an intrusion into their relationship, hence, mother's absence with Alexandra and her sister's envy and aggression, triggered by their own fears of death. Alexandra's birth triggered an immediately prior traumatic birth experience in her mother so that she could not attach. This led to her premature exposure in a world inhabited by her sister who, threatened by the feeling that Alexandra could steal mother's love, felt that she could kill her. I imagine also that Lucy's anticipated death served to constellate the Terrible Mother for Alexandra's mother, and so when the trauma was re-experienced it catalyzed the Death Mother as well. This was the reality that my face triggered.

This insight opened up a longing for real, empathic human contact. This lack is re-experienced in the course of therapy in the exquisite pain that became almost constant. She dreams that she and I are painstakingly trying to place an order for a new original birth certificate. She must first undergo an initiation into a primitive African cult. This ritual takes place in my office on the mother goddess Yemaya's holy day (New Year's day). Two women adorned with cowry shell masks with black hollow eyes guard the doorway through which she must pass. As she crosses the threshold the women thrust their faces into her face, and she must remain fearless. She makes the transition, and presently meets up with a woman who works for a defense contractor. The woman is trying to get her a job, but Alexandra tells her she is not interested, that she "must live under her own light."

The dream in some ways speaks for itself. The work being undertaken in analysis was to be reborn, which is synonomous with undergoing an initiation. This entails dealing with the terrible faces. Her initiation takes place on Yemaya's holy day. Yemaya is a white goddess in the Yoruba religion symbolizing womanhood and maternity (Gonzalez-Wippler, 1994: 57). She is a particularly interesting goddess in relation to the transformation of the Terrible Mother. Myth has it that she was at one time a dark goddess who owned a cemetery.

Through trickery, she traded residences with the sea goddess, which made Yemaya an ocean deity with life-giving powers. The presence of the good mother will allow Alexandra to get through her rigid defenses, get her new original birth certificate, and live "under her own light."

With this shift, her dream images begin to zero in specifically on eyes. She is feeling that she doesn't want to open her eyes, she doesn't want to see anymore. She dreams that she sees a young girl sitting on a chair. Her eyes are mangled and slit just below the lower eyelashes. Alexandra struggles with her reluctance to look into my eyes, for what she sees there is mangling. She believed that I meant her harm. This was not an idle, irrelevant thought, but the feeling root of her shame that needed amplification. She would catch me in my thinking look, a moment I had abandoned her to my own thoughts. This became for her "you loathe and despise me. I am alone. I don't exist." For many months her reactions blocked any means of restoring a trusting bond. Her experience of separateness produced a loss of psychological existence.

On the other hand, she felt her eyes and the power of looking could mangle too. If she became the one seeing she wanted to expose what was covered, and realized that her desire to invade and destroy others with her considerable gift of intuition was self-destructive. In this way looking had become too damaging, and then she would have to hide her face. The following dream depicts the infant self trapped in stone but looking out:

> I am in the vestibule at St. Andrews church with some unknown people. I am looking at a rack, and two items catch my attention: on the lower rung is an orange geode, the outside shaped like a baby swaddled in clothing, everything but its face wrapped. The opening of the geode is formed like a baby's open mouth through which you could see the crystalline formations sparkling. The other object is hanging on the hook right above it, an amber Paleolithic sculpture of the Great Mother on a key chain. It is large enough to fill the palm of my hand and is cold, but warms to the touch. Then I am outside the church with a group of people. It is dusk, and suddenly there are these extraordinary lightening bolts and I stare gasping. A spectacular bolt spreads across the sky and leaves an imprint of the deepest cavernous darkness in the shape of the lightening bolt, opening the sky. The light begins to float down to the ground, bouncing among

the crowd who begin to panic. I run for cover and see an older woman who has fallen on her face. She has a gray complexion and is dying, moaning on the sidewalk. Lightning particles flick around her.

She was the infant swaddled in a rock, but something is happening inside the stone. There is fire. Consciousness is getting closer. The cold and petrified stone is getting warm, and the same is true for the mother, who warms to the touch. With the emergence of the Great Mother, the dream presents an image of her shame: a woman with ashen face, publicly exposed, being singled out of the crowd and falling flat on her face. Lightning particles flit about her head, connecting the woman with the infant geode with sparkling crystals. Alexandra, in seeking to avert psychic fusion with her biological mother, hopes for rebirth in the Great Goddess archetype, to be empowered by her energy. These sparks of light, or consciousness, will have to be collected into an ordered, centered unity. Venus of Willendorf, however fertile she may be, is still a stone mother, an idealized, archetypal image that could not humanly soothe, nourish, and cuddle her infant self.

One can only face what is inanimate inside when there is some goodness and reliability for support. Alexandra could only move deeper into the poison of shame as images of the archetypal Great Mother were constellated. She dreams of being in a junkyard where toxic chemicals have been stored, and sees a barrel with a skull and crossbones on it. Alexandra continues to regress more deeply into her psychosis. She dreams:

> I am led into an ancient underground ruin unearthed in the basement of my house in the process of laying the foundation. While a smiling baby sits outside my door in a basket, I enter this cave to find, among other treasures, a black skull and cross-bones plaque on a rock hewn wall with an inscription that reads "Baba Yaga."

With the newly born, healthy infant self imaged as a smiling baby outside, she enters the stone womb that lays at the foundation of her being to find the black skull and crossbones of Baba Yaga, the symbol of the Mother of Death herself. Just as Wassilissa could only face the Baba Yaga with the blessings of the doll, the good mother, in her pocket, Alexandra could not face the abyss of nothingness in her being until the Great Good Mother emerged as a means of separating from mother. The meeting with Baba Yaga points to the fact that something is going to be integrated.

This dream encapsulated her petrifaction and brought her into the core of her psychosis. During the day she suffers enormous agitation, while her nights are dark and disturbed. She feels incapable of working, but works incessantly. In sessions she forces thoughts into some kind of order, struggling to articulate words. She is crushed by her sense of shame. She dreams of eyes and hideous human faces looking at her small, weak, worthless, nobody self. All of her social and therapeutic interaction is conducted under the thick pall of shame and exposure. One night she has a lucid dream:

> I am awake in the dream world. I know that I am in relation to my psychotic part and begin to get frantic. I know what it feels like to live in madness, to live in hell, it is very alarming. I see people who ignore me while looking at me, they won't go away, I can't get myself out of this hell.

At this point her process mobilized to reveal the murderous roots of her shame. These are expressed in an eye dream that strikes horror:

> I have to go pick up my Mobile One rebate from an office in LA. I am escorted into a back office where detectives are at work on a case. I see pictures of a mangled woman's heart-shaped face. She had been tortured and then murdered. The girl had to gouge her own eyes out, and cut them into hundreds of tiny pieces. Then each eye part was put on the ceiling. With her own eyes cut out, she had to paint the remaining parts of each eye to depict a complete eye. The ceiling was then covered with painted eyes, each containing a real piece of her own plucked out eyes.

Her shame was a universe of murdered eyes, and this dream facilitated an integration of her projections onto the eyes of others. She was no longer chained to their thoughts, at the mercy of their eyes. She no longer felt plagued by people, but came to exercise full power over what had previously terrorized her. She was a normal human being with a story of her own, and she now felt that she could allow her life to impact the world. She truly existed, with feelings and thoughts of her own.

With the resolution of the transference psychosis, Alexandra's entire life began to change. This eye dream marked the ending of her first marriage of 17 years, almost to the day. Over the next two years she would undergo significant upheavals, until all the details of her life were different. Her main focus was reorienting herself towards becoming part of a whole. She reconnected to her family with whom she had been alienated for many years. At one time her identity rested in her considerable ability to function in her profession and advancement, and she was childless. She remarried, conceived a child, and changed her focus to raising a family which included two stepchildren.

Remarkably, the same week Alexandra learned she was pregnant, her mother was diagnosed with liver cancer. Birth and death would come together again, but this time her mother would have to deal with her unmetabolized (or failing liver), killing dimensions, while Alexandra would bring a life into the world and become a mother in her own right. This would prove to be a tremendously validating and healing experience for Alexandra. Over the course of her illness, Alexandra's mother was forced to deal with her own toxic poisons, and this opened the way for Alexandra to enjoy a different relationship with her. The following poem echoed her new awareness of mother:

> But I have peeled away your anger
> down to the core of love
> and look mother
> I am
> a dark temple where your true spirit rises
> beautiful
> and tough as chestnut
> stanchion against your nightmare of weakness
> and if my eyes conceal
> a squadron of conflicting rebellions
> I learned from you
> to define myself
> through your denials.
>
> (Lorde, 1973: 68)

Alexandra had the rare opportunity to witness, through her mother's life-threatening cancer, the now bodily disturbance that had made her psychotic. She realized the source of terror as the early experience of the death (through abandonment) of her good mother, and hence the natural progression to the experience of the Terrible Mother who possessed a skull with burning eyes that had the power to annihilate. In the course of our work together, Alexandra and I came to humanize what was petrified, namely the primordial baby swaddled in an orange geode and the offspring of the Great Stone Age Mother Goddess, Venus of Willendorf (see Figure 2.8). Fully entering the microsecond of petrifaction culminated a regression that revealed and connected her to her shamed, ancient baby self. This connection moved her into the age of concern, a time when love and hate could come together, and the recognition of dependence dawned (Winnicott, 1992b: 279).

The words to say it

" 'Doctor, I have been ill for a long time. I ran away from a private sanatorium to come to see you. I can't go on living this way.' He showed me with his eyes that he listened attentively, that I could continue" (Cardinal, 1975/1996: 3). This was the beginning of an analysis Marie Cardinal would undergo for seven years to cure her madness – and later wrote about in an autobiographical novel entitled *The Words to Say It*.

Feelings of deep shame plagued Marie's existence. She describes herself as just garbage, a person who allowed herself to be overrun with terror because of her evil nature. Like Barbara, she was afraid of everything, and these fears had relegated her to the alienated of the world. No one should see. No one should know. Merely existing felt so extremely dangerous that on some level she preferred to hide herself, to "close off all orifices" so that her body concretized into the wall of shame that would prevent the putridness from coming out. Since shame is the wall of separation, this isolation forced her to withdraw into the horrid depths of her own universe, a sewer filled with decomposing matter.

She developed a false self in order to appear normal, to "stop the fear behind a glance." To others she seemed fine, yet she did not experience herself as successful in this endeavor. She feared that her disturbance would inevitably reveal itself, "hunched between her shoulders, sad, at once absorbed by the growing agitation within and by the armor descending over her eyes, so nothing could be seen" (Cardinal, 1975/1996: 4). This madness shrunk the world, smaller and smaller, blacker and blacker, until eventually the space she could move in her house was so limited. She could only hide between the bidet and the bathtub. This is because since the age of 27, the same age that her mother was when she gave birth to Marie, her menstrual blood had not stopped flowing. Marie was literally bleeding to death. And as the flow of blood persisted, her eyesight grew weaker. She knew that the bleeding was only a mask for what she felt was preventing her from living with others. On the rare day that she didn't bleed she was "able to move about, to see, to get out of herself" (Cardinal, 1975/1996: 5). Then she imagines that if she doesn't "make even the smallest possible movement, it is going to stop completely." She lies motionless: her petrified state of being holds the hope that she can be normal again like others, and stop bleeding.

As if this symptom were not enough, there was her main preoccupation – the Thing. It had a life of its own that she didn't dare tell anyone about, and had to keep it hidden at all costs. It kept her prisoner, for surely this Thing would force her back to the insane asylum. This Thing was polarized against a nothingness that she otherwise felt, dull and sweet. She was so taken up with trying to control the Thing that her vision was warped. She feared that she was going blind, and navigated by radar to avoid colliding into people and things. Marie said of the Thing: "the presence of a living eye, looking at me, really there, but existing only for me (that I knew), seemed to me the evidence of genuine insanity" (p. 11).

This eye that looked over her life, the Thing that terrorized her every waking moment, was at the core of disturbance (Cardinal, 1975/1996: 46–7): "I had less of a desire to move about, to express myself, to throw myself into an action or thought . . . I became heavy, slow, dense, with moments of agitation . . . The sluggishness, the viscosity, and the absurdity of existence became fixed in my mind, before becoming the Thing". In vain she tried to hide it, but shame inevitably entails exposure, and the Thing knew very well how to reveal itself through the veins and skin (just like Alexandra's dreams), and her shaking, shivering anxieties. With the Thing danger lurked everywhere. What she says of the Thing also expresses nicely what it means not to exist: "I had to figure out a way to see without seeing, hear without hearing, feel without feeling" (p. 38). Like that which plagued Cain, she imagines a mark on her forehead, a "scar which invades the letters engraved in stone on an old tomb" (p. 78), a stigma visible to everyone.

From the moment he agreed to take her on for analysis the doctor insisted that all medication stop. The next day, at the appointed hour, she arrived for her first session diapered up like a baby after having bled all night. "Doctor, I am bled dry." The doctor answered, "Those are psychosomatic disorders. That doesn't interest me. Speak about something else."

> The words that this man had just uttered were a slap in the face. Never had I encountered such violence. Right in the face! My blood didn't interest him! If that was so, then everything was destroyed! ... But of what else did he want me to speak? What *else*? Apart from my blood there was only fear, nothing else, and I could no more speak of it than think about it. I broke down and cried – I who had been unable to cry for so long . . . now at last they flowed freely.
>
> (Cardinal, 1975/1996: 32)

This analytic move made her have to begin to face the Thing, the madwoman who accused her of bad deeds, of sinking herself into evil, the imperfect, the indecent, or unseemly, "a skull with rotten teeth and vacant eyes, shinbones yellow with age and dried blood" (p. 35). Like Wassilissa, she had to enter the woods, the nothingness the Thing was polarized against, to reclaim herself through a face-to-face encounter with the Baba Yaga, whose image comes to the fore in her description of the "filthy hag whose two enormous buttocks were the lobes of my brain. Sometimes she propped up her big ass in my skull. . . and was able to find some clear dark place to curl up like a fetus" (p. 38).

Marie had always harbored inklings that her suffering was connected to her parents' divorce. She was born in the middle of their divorce proceedings, and her parents fought over her until her father's death of tuberculosis when she was still young. As a child, she obediently paid hated visits to her father to collect the alimony, hated because her mother would fill her with a terror of his germs. She listened to their incessant quarreling over her, and her mother's insistence that she needed more money to raise Marie, who was too expensive.

Tubercular meningitis claimed the life of her mother's firstborn daughter, for whom she had never stopped grieving. Marie would hear her mother nightly lamenting her sister's loss, on her bed unwrapping relics of the dead child: slippers, locks of hair, baby clothes. Marie could never replace this dead sister, could never be loved like her – how could anyone compete with the perfection of the one who is dead? When she and her mother visited the gravesite, she yearned to be the big white marble slab that her mother hugged, and, by extension, the dead daughter. Only then could she be loved – and now she was bleeding to death, perhaps in some attempt to be loved? Despite these profound rejections, she nevertheless knowingly protected her mother. She had tried so hard her whole life to win her mother's affection and love, had waited so long for just one look from those lovely green eyes. She thought she knew all about them, but what she needed was to know what she didn't know – the precise point of manipulation that her insidious mother, who was incapable of loving maternally, employed to subvert her birthright to grow up as a person in her own right. On some level, Marie knew that the remedy to the Thing lay in separating from the grip her mother had on her: she must strip away her mother's mask to reveal her true face – her impenetrable narcissism that wanted only her own reflection, martyred self-absorption, and infanticidal impulses that created Marie's womb of shame. Over the years, Marie

> explored the very depths of her being, as though she were a cavern. Thus did I make the acquaintance of the woman she wanted me to be. Day after day I had to weigh the extent of her desperation to create what in her opinion was a perfect being. I had to measure the force of her will to distort body and mind, to make them take the path she decided upon. It was between the woman she had wanted to bring into the world and myself that the Thing had lodged itself. My mother had led me astray to such a point that I was no longer conscious of what she had done so profoundly and so well, nor did I understand.
>
> (Cardinal, 1975/1996: 67)

This filled her with horror. It was either reveal her mother or spend the rest of her days in a pitch black asylum. In order to resolve her shame, she had to come to see that her mother had conferred death upon her at conception, that the bond between them was one of annihilation. Words, and the analyst bearing witness to her words, become the only thing that keeps her moving, her only weapon against the Thing. "Talk, say whatever comes into your head . . . Everything is important, every word" (Cardinal, 1975/1996: 65). This is the only remedy her analyst gave her, that and reading his eyes which at times made her want to kill herself. She had to lay on the couch and keep her eyes shut tight in order to touch and retain her hold on the little girl who could see into the vacancy in mother's eyes; who knew that she had internalized her mother's death wishes and had the words to say the catastrophically unthinkable. In these blind wanderings, memories came. Palpitating, alive memories rushed in and awakened a terrible shame she couldn't explain. She recalled how she would fill her pockets with pebbles that were perhaps diamonds, emeralds, or rubies. She ran home to surprise her mother, sure that her face would relax, that she would be kissed and loved. Instead, her mother said severely, "Don't drag such filth into the house" (Cardinal, 1975/1996: 69). What a horrible response. For her mother, who loved only "priceless things," Marie's love was not the right thing. All of Marie's fruitless efforts made her reject herself, despise herself. Only in a secret hiding place could she make up who she was for herself alone. Like Inanna, she had to make the descent into the petrifying underworld of memories – her mother's perfection – where she would be hung from a hook like a raw piece of meat:

> I had begun to speak of my mother, and of how difficult it was to make her love me. I poured out memories which were a little sad and recited the catalogue of attentions . . . of which I had been the object . . . Unconsciously, so as to protect myself and not be so much raw meat on display, I pushed aside the essential element . . . Was it my fear, once expressed, would destroy me? Or as if my fear, once expressed, would take away my importance? Or when it was revealed, would it show itself not as fear but as a shameful sickness? At the time, I was not capable of answering these questions . . . I was a hunted animal; I understood nothing about people.
>
> (Cardinal, 1975/1996: 93–4)

Through this retrieval process, she came to understand that the Thing took root in her when she was unable to please her mother or to make her love her, and by her own complete conviction that she was ugly and bad. As she put these memories into words, plunging into the waves of filth, unworthiness, horror, the altogether unendurable that lived inside her, she found that she was able to protect herself from the eyes that could rob her of existence. She caught glimmerings of her own nascent self, and knew this was the means to free herself from her small, walled world. With this realization she confronted her doctor for the first time, questioning his power as a person just like a child with her mother is unable to do (and in a way she attempted to gain some control over those shaming, leering faces): "You shouldn't keep that gargoyle in your office, it is hideous. There is already enough horror and fear in the minds of the people who come in here, no need to provide any more of it" (p. 103).

After this, she was able to talk about her mother's beastly villainy instead of her martyrdom and saintliness. Looking at her from this perspective, mother had a dangerous personality when the features of her otherwise expressionless face would grow agitated and drawn back as if by claws, her eyes even greener than usual, wide with terror. This is the raging face of Inanna's sister, the deadly Ereshkigal. By her mother's own admission, this face was connected to her own shame of having a daughter who died, "it was such a scandal" (p. 124), and divorcing her father when pregnant with Marie. Divorce just wasn't done in her family. Her mother told her all this on a street, without containment, as though it meant nothing. Marie searched for the merest change in her expression to derive what she was getting at. Then her mother dealt the most terrible shock. She confessed that she had attempted to abort Marie by all possible means:

> There exist evil women and evil doctors who can do away with a baby in a woman's womb. It's a monstrous sin . . . It's one of the worst things a person can do. It is possible, however, to lose the baby naturally . . . Then it is no longer a sin, it's nothing, it's an accident, that's all . . . But it isn't easy . . . when a baby has taken hold there's nothing you can do to dislodge it. Do you see how one can get trapped? . . . After more than 6 months of treat-ment, I had to resign myself to the obvious . . . At last you were born, for it was you whom I was expecting . . . You were born with your whole face forward, instead of presenting only the base of your skull.
>
> (Cardinal, 1975/1996: 136–7)

After her mother's admission, Marie fell into the depths of her shame, "that fissure in the earth that had just opened up. Alone, face-to-face, we experienced this encounter" (p. 137). She was left in pro-found self-disgust: she could not be loved, could not be pleasing, she shouldn't have lived and could only be rejected. Everything was bound to be experienced as abandonment, since she was a failure and failed at everything. The best she could hope for was that the fissure that had just opened up would swallow her. Simultaneously, however, she also realized in this encounter that her mother had discharged her madness into her in the form of infanticidal intent. Marie was the sacrifice, the failed abortion, the thing that never should have been. Defeated, powerless, resigned, her mother let the "little girl turd" come slowly, face forward, staring up at her mother, into the world. Her mother must have felt exposed and shamed by that face staring up at her at the opening to her womb. Her mother's intentions that she never be born had been internalized as a self-disgust that blossomed into madness. Marie wondered if her mother knew the consequences that the projection of her hatred and her weak, wretched attempts to murder her, as well as her current attempts to start it up again by telling her 14 years later casually on the street.

This epiphany brought an important turning point in Marie's life, a point that commenced a process of separation from and under-standing of her mother. Realizing that her own insanity was her mother's facilitated a full revelation of the Thing. Four years into treatment, she was now strong enough to reveal what she had alluded to in the first few months. "You know, doctor, every once in a while, something strange happens: I see an eye looking at me" (Cardinal, 1975/1996: 145). I want to quote at length the dialogue around the analytic moment when she reveals the core of her shame, as it describes so essentially the eye of shame and its psychotic anxieties:

I settled down. Stretched out, my arms and legs extended, I wanted to be sure first I had access to my material: my mother, the red earth of the farm, all the shadows and the outlines, the odors and the lights, the noises, and above all the little girl who had so much to tell: Every once in a while, something strange happens. It never comes during a crisis, but it brings on a crisis every time because it makes me so afraid. It can come on whether I'm alone or with another person or a number of people. Now that I think about it, it happens mostly when I'm with someone. With my left eye I see the person facing me and the decor of a room down to the smallest details, and with my right eye I see a tube just as clearly which advances to fit gently over my socket. When it's in place I see an eye looking at me from the other end of the tube. The tube and the eye are as alive as what I see with my left eye. This could only be taking place in the real world. It is on the exact same plane as what I am living through. The light is the same. The atmosphere is the same. What I see through my left eye has no less objective validity as what I see through my right eye. Except that the one reveals what is a normal situation while the other terrorizes me. I am never able to find the equilibrium between these two realities; I lose my balance, I sweat, I want to run away. It's unbearable.

The eye looking at me is not like mine pressing against the tube. If it were, it would be dark inside the tube, very clearly defined, and very watchful. The eye makes me sweat because the look it fixes on me is severe, though it is not really provoking. It is a cold severity, with shades of contempt and indifference. It never leaves me for a second. It scrutinizes me intensely, never softening. Its expression never changes. If I close my eyes, it doesn't help at all: the eye is there, evil, cruel and icy. It can go on for a long time, several minutes even, and then it disappears as suddenly as it came. After I start to tremble I have an attack. I experience an enormous feeling of shame. I suffer more shame from the eye than from all the other manifestations of my illness.

(Cardinal, 1975/1996: 145–7)

In exposing the core of her shame, she found that she had nothing to fear (remember the eye depicted in the tube in Figure 2.3). It helped her to realize that "her mother's eye, which she confused with the eye of God (and unconsciously with the eye of the movie camera), was always there, looking at her, assessing the way she moved, the way she thought even, never letting anything slip by unnoticed" (p. 160). The hallucination had been unmasked, and it moved to a distance. She now wanted people to look at her, and felt for the first time her own existence in the thought "I am here." She felt born again. She discovered her health, her body, the experience of moving about freely. She also discovered that the Thing was the terrible force pushing her way from the path she was supposed to follow to please her mother, making itself known every time she displeased her. The Thing protected the integrity and truth about her self. And now it would be the Thing, her insanity, that would lead her to her true self.

Yet beyond the Thing was her own nothingness. With the metabolization of her hallucination, she is thrown into an incomprehensible void. By removing the eye at the end of the tube, she had removed her own eye as well. She was now thrown fully into her own non-existence and emptiness. The center and structure of her life had always been her mother, that shaming eye that would impose its discipline. She didn't know anything other than to revolve around her mother and her fantasies, principles, passions and sorrows. Marie was now reduced to a disheveled nebula revolving around an indefinable center, firmly attached to a vortex "which was now the unseeing eye of (her) mother" (p. 167). She had no vision of her own eye, and treatment could only be complete when she was capable of taking responsibility for her own thoughts and actions, and to be less at the mercy of others. This took another four years to accomplish.

She now had to come face to face with herself. Her own existence depended on her realization of what the Thing fed on, in what corner of her cranium the madwoman hid. It was the only way to create a separate existence from her mother as an independent person with her own character. She had to come to own what she knew, she now needed to come face to face with herself, and achieve her own eye-sight and vision of things.

More memories. She had splattered vomit all over her mother's beautiful tablecloth as she threw up her soup. Mother's face tightened with an hysterical expression while she screamed tyrannically, "She is going to eat all her soup all the same!" Marie eats the vomit of her soup, sensing something sick, something stronger and more horrible in her mother. The child in her had an eye, "an eye which was above all sensitive to the Thing, an eye which the Thing had overthrown, an eye which had seen the Thing in her mother" (Cardinal, 1975/1996: 199), the Thing that tried to kill her off, the Thing that had taken over her own mother who had a taste for death and held the dead as objects of affection.

Wanting to be the dutiful daughter in order to be loved by her mother, she found that she was really a rebel, and had been one since birth. With this revelation, she exclaims "I existed" (p. 200). She could begin to accept her real shortcomings which also helped to enhance her virtues. In fact, her shortcomings became dynamic instead of annihilating. "Thanks to my anus I understood that everything was important, and that what had been called dirty, small, shameful and wretched was quite different in reality" (p. 261). She found that when she encountered the world she wanted to have a car so she could go faster, farther. She was in a hurry to make up for lost time, to see everything, to know everything. Most importantly, however, she encountered her own violence and murderousness, a suppressed but constant force rumbling inside of her, like a storm, and the greatest source of nourishment for the Thing. With the removal of her shame around her violence, she could feel vitality and generosity. She felt almost complete after separating out her healthy feelings from the murderousness surrounding her mother. Yet there was still something lurking. There was that nausea her mother provoked in her, it totally unnerved her. The Thing was now the only link she had with her mother, who had nevertheless been living with her for the past five years. Having passed the Thing on to her, her mother knew it well. When Marie was in the grips of it, her mother showed keen interest. When it was clear that the Thing was losing ground, her mother was lost in confusion:

> Her face had about it a look of sadness and fatigue. Indeed, there was an angry flame in the green of her eyes although nothing she ever said in words revealed the source of it. She walled herself off ... maintaining a growing inaccessibility in her expressionless face ... in the middle of her universe, ravaged and destroyed, there remained only me with new energy emerging. This she could watch happening with her own eyes as she tried clumsily to hang on to me.
>
> (Cardinal, 1975/1996: 244–5)

The castle of cards that she lived in with her mother was going to collapse.

> I had made my decision. It was without difficulty or shame that I went to find my mother in her room. She was on her bed, surrounded by the relics of her dead: photographs, portraits, objects. "I wanted to tell you that I've made a serious decision: we're going to separate ..." She didn't say a word ... I thought only of building my own life, I was absolutely determined ... She knew very well what my early years had been, my childhood, my adolescence, her indifference to me and her occasional peevishness. She had nothing to say.
>
> (Cardinal, 1975/1996: 275)

From this point her mother ages quickly, horrible to behold. "There was no one behind the eyes in that ravaged face. It was as if the eyes had turned inwards away from anyone or anything which might come her way now" (p. 277). Her mother was without shame, without the instinct to hide herself. One night Marie witnesses her mother possessed by the Thing:

Sitting on her bed as usual, her nightgown pulled up over her stomach so that I could see her hairless vagina. She had done it where she sat, and her shit was oozing out down to the floor. On the table beside her there were two square bottles of rum . . . She was vile . . . She looked at me, she looked at her dirt, then she went to search in the depths of herself, I don't know where, for an expression. I experienced everything she was going through . . . I saw surprise on her face but that wasn't what she wanted . . . Then I saw her face transformed, the folds of her skin changed direction, stretched out . . . She was smiling . . . Her eyes went back and forth from her excrement to me with a mischievous look, and then she put her smile back on her ravaged face.

(Cardinal, 1975/1996: 281).

The following day her mother dies. Rigor mortis had fixed the look of horror on her face. They would be unable to lay her out with her look of saintliness, or compose her face serenely. She would be exposed and carry her own shame. "As a farewell, I leave them my mother's grimace of horror before a life that was false from beginning to end, her features, tortured by all the amputations to which she had submitted, this mask worn in the great Punch and Judy show which was her life" (p. 289). The Thing was now safe where it belonged, and could no longer torment Marie who was free to go on with her life.

Psychotic anxieties

Margaret Little began analysis "paralyzed with fear" following a friend's three-year bout with severe depression and suicide. This analyst didn't even pretend to understand what she was facing, but therapy did enable her to break free from her dominating, clinging friend. The analyst also made an interesting remark: "You seem to be always thinking of other people and apologizing for your existence, as if you thought you had no right to it" (Little, 1990: 26). He saw her shame and she confirmed it, saying that she always felt sickly, bad, "in the way" and a "trouble." These feelings went all the way back to being a small child, when she and her mother and sister had the whooping cough. She was a vile, evil germ that could make her sister and mother cough if she coughed. And then there was her friend who chose her, but died shortly thereafter. She hadn't written to her, which made her selfish and uncaring. This analyst simply told her to "be herself," and she replied, "I don't know how, I don't know what myself is" (p. 27). She ended this first round of treatment in a place of not knowing – but that was not to be the end of her quest to have a self.

Later, Margaret resumed analysis with a woman analyst who stirred up the issues connected to her relationship to her mother. During her first visit, she had a very disturbing experience. She saw her in a kind of grey mist, like a spider in a web that was her hair. She knew it was delusional, and its implications terrified her. Despite her first analyst's determination that all she needed was "synthesis," she knew that her disturbance was far more profound. Psychoanalysis for her was coming to mean total annihilation, and her fears of it were unbearable. In her first session with this woman she lay petrified and "rigid on the couch, again unable to speak or move" (Little, 1990: 32). She felt her fear was even more than a fear of death, far more than any mortal fear. No, her fear "was of utter destruction, being bodily dismembered, driven irretrievably insane, wiped out, abandoned, and forgotten by the whole world as one who had never been – cast into outer darkness" (p. 33). Her analyst interpreted these fears as they may have related to infantile sexuality, whereas Margaret insisted that they related to matters of existence and identity, and felt strongly that sexuality was irrelevant so long as these basic needs of survival could not be taken for granted. She kept insisting that she wanted to be somebody, a real person, not the nobody or the evil, uncaring non-person that she felt herself to be.

Once again she was abandoned in her infantile chaos. Neither analyst could help her come into her own existence. Neither was willing or able to see or understand the depth of her disturbance, and this resulted in a repetition of the same lethal dynamic contained in the relationship with her mother: she would not be seen or reflected as a person in her own right. The best she could do was to maintain some stability and rebuild defenses.

Finally, 13 years after first initiating her search for psychiatric help, she went to see D. W. Winnicott. He could see the depth of her disturbance, and with him she would make a full regression in search of her true existence. He writes of his work with Margaret:

> I have had a patient . . . who had had an ordinary good analysis before coming to me but who obviously still needed help . . . although the diagnosis of psychosis would never have been

made by a psychiatrist, an analytical diagnosis needed to be made that took into account a very early development of a false self.

(Winnicott, 1992b: 279–80)

Her first session with him brought a repetition of the delusional terror she felt with the female analyst. She shut him out by lying curled up tightly in the fetal position, completely hidden under a blanket, unable to speak or move. This was her petrifaction in the eyes of mother. There was no safe place on earth, not even the womb, and all she wanted to do was hide. The world became very small, and she wanted to take up as little space in it, and be as unobtrusive, as possible. Shortly thereafter, she smashed a vase in his room in a desperate attempt to unleash and make visible her level of despair and chaos, and how she felt smashed to pieces inside.

Margaret's mother was "tragically damaged." Mainly, she was severely depressed, and could only live by turning everything into a game. Her parents would tease each other and their children sadistically. When it came to childbirth, "it was a sheer horror, warded off by padding her body so that her pregnancy could not be perceived, and avoiding labor (which would inevitably be fatal) by 'not thinking about it' until this became impossible." Her mother had no mind of pregnancy, which is unnatural. Being afraid was "cowardice, contemptible" (Little, 1990: 50). Margaret was delivered before the arrival of the doctor or midwife. This was probably due to her mother's belief that "if you don't think about it the pain will go away," and partly because of fear lest the "midwife should hold back the head." The absence of maternal reverie is unmistakable. These misunderstandings inevitably led to disasters, so that chaos always threatened at every turn. Margaret could not imagine that her mother was capable of any "primary maternal preoccupation," because she could never think of her baby except as part of herself. The very idea of separation aroused an anxiety of annihilation. Her mother's thoughtlessness and intrusiveness is depicted in Margaret description of her mother as in an infantile state herself, when she couldn't leave anything alone. Whenever her mother found an infant's mouth open, she would close it; whenever a baby sucked her thumb she would remove it. If the baby lay on its back or left side, she would turn it to the right side, "so as to prevent pressure on the heart."

Interestingly, by studying a portrait of her face, Winnicott got a very intimate idea of the rigidity of Margaret's mother's defenses (Winnicott, 1971: 115). From this he goes on to describe Margaret as a woman who shows little interest in seeing her own face in the mirror, unlike other women. She looks in the mirror only "to remind herself that she looks like an old hag" (again, a reference to the Baba Yaga) (p. 116). Margaret was also in search of Winnicott's face, asking him for a large picture of his face so that she could "see the lines and all the features of this 'ancient landscape' " (p. 116). He understood this as her need to see that his lined face had some features that forged a link with the rigidity of the faces of her mother and nurse (the depressed caregiver mother picked so as not to compete with her). He also felt that it was important that he understood her need for her mother's face to reflect her as a person. Margaret's lack of existence, and her need for a good holding mother to make this possible, is expressed in a poem she wrote entitled "Life in Death or Death in Life":

> I live among the shadows
> Unseeing, unhearing
> unknowing, unthinking
> Unfeeling, uncaring,
> All is unreal,
> Chaos, deceit
> I have no focus
> No mainspring, no God.
> Had I a framework,
> A structure, a holding,
> A scaffold, or cross,
> There might thorns pierce me,
> Thrust inward, infiltrate,
> There might the chaos
> Cling, focus, and form.
>   (Little, 1993: 217)

Her father also became a nonentity with her mother. He systematically destroyed all of his relationships and outgoing activities. He could seldom stand up to her and eventually became irritable and short-tempered. All of her siblings became disturbed to some degree, especially since mother would consistently express her fear that each one would "turn out badly." Given her level of intrusiveness, what choice did they have?

Margaret was sickly as an infant and child, and needed a lot of attention, probably owing to congenital hiatus hernia together with a coeliac condition. These, however, were not diagnosed until she was in her sixties, because her mother thought of them as "fuss," "imagination," and later "psychogenic," but always something that she "should control." Margaret was scolded for being "a baby" or "thin-skinned" if she made any fuss at all.

Overall, she felt under her mother's possession. Her delusion contained the idea that she was indistinguishable from her mother. Her only defense was to withdraw in shame. This was the reason she did not exist in her own right, and like her father was a nonentity. She needed to find a healthy way to separate from her mother, "and find health stronger than sickness that originally was hers, and with which (she) had been identified" (Little, 1990: 100).

Several years into the analysis which "seemed unending," she asserted herself by exploding at her mother for the first time in her life in retaliation for some piece of her trivial jibing and clever nonsense. Her mother completely ignored the explosion and attempted to make it useless by coming back with further demands, implying that whatever was Margaret's really belonged to her. Margaret maintained her stance by not seeing her mother again for two years, until she was dying, but at the same time felt helpless rage which she discharged against her own body. On a hike she started stomping around like a baby and ended up breaking her ankle. This resulted in a long period of immobility, her petrifaction now in full possession. Winnicott interpreted this as a serious suicidal attempt, an attack on self. On the other hand, it was also an attempt to break free of her mother's hold in order to destroy the pattern of repetition. Margaret desperately felt that something had to snap in order for her to be free. Memories surfaced in conjunction with this incident: her mother gripping her wrists while saying emphatically "you must control yourself," when really, her mother was controlling her. The other was a time when she had become quite ill with pneumonia and was moved to her mother's bedroom. Her mother told her that she clung to her day and night; Winnicott understood that her mother would not let her die. Margaret felt that "she would not let me choose whether to live or die. I had to live for her" (Little, 1990: 58). On some level she believed that freedom from mother meant to be ill and die (probably the reason she was a sickly child). Death felt like the only defense against being taken over by her. These feelings are expressed in Margaret's poem entitled "Words":

My words were stolen, years ago.
Now, behind bars, I cannot find
What is my own.

Henceforward I am dumb –
Dumbfounded,
Dumbly, doubly dumb.

Words that *should* rise
Swell in my throat and choke
In salt and bitter tears I cannot shed.

Between my words and me,
Between my thoughts and words
Cold bars, unshakeable, are fixed.

Beyond the bars an iron will,
A will that none can fight,
Strong as my life itself.
So am I dumb, undone.
I have no speech, no words,
No mother tongue.

(Little, 1993: 219)

When Winnicott next went on holiday, he arranged for Margaret to go to the hospital in order to prevent a suicide. She raged against this. But after a period of feeling forlorn and abandoned, followed by a period of rage, she felt "regressed to dependency" and in a safe place, a place where she would "go on being." She could rely upon Winnicott's care. Now she could decide for herself whether to live or die. She began to write poetry and paint. One day she painted a sea, and suddenly added a huge monster's head with flaming eyes and fierce jaws. She also wrote the following poem, entitled "Mental Hospital". This poem gives imagery to her psychosis and the faces that plagued her:

This place is
So full of faces;
They come too near
I long to flee.

They come and peer,
They come and leer,

They come and jeer,
Or – is it me?

There's Dr. Prozy
And Sister Cozy,
And Mrs. Dozy,
And then – there's me.

There's Mrs. Bit,
And Mr. Spit,
And old Miss Hit,
And – then there's me.

This place is
Full of faces
And I can't flee,
For they're all me!
(Little, 1993: 218)

Suicide eventually came to feel like a victory for the crazy world her
mother had created and in which she was forced to live. From that
point of realization she never considered it again. Her experience of
extinction was validated. Winnicott told her that "such fear of
annihilation as she felt belonged to 'annihilation' that had already
happened; I had been annihilated psychically, but had in fact survived bodily, and was now emotionally reliving the past experience"
(Little, 1990: 62). She says of this interpretation: "It was true that I
had been annihilated, before I even existed. I was not a person in my
own right, only an appendage of someone else" (p. 62). Being human
became the all important thing. Her abilities to value herself grew,
and she began to be herself for her own sake. She could gradually
relinquish her omnipotence and false caretaker self in order to have
her infantile needs met. As she approached a resolution of her
shame, Margaret was in the process of discovering her own body,
herself, and her world. She quotes a poem entitled "The Salutation"
to describe her process of discovering the good-enough mother. It
also provides a beautiful description of a being coming into a full
existence:

The little Limbs,
These Eyes and Hands which here I find
This panting Heart wherewith my Life begins;

Where have ye been? Behind
What Curtain were ye from me hid so long?
Where was, in what Abyss, my new-made Tongue?

When silent I
So Many thousand Years
Beneath the Dust did in a Chaos lie,
How could I Smiles, or Tears
Or Lips, or Hands, or Eyes, or Ears perceive?
Welcome ye Treasures which I now receive.

I that so long
Was Nothing from Eternity,
Did little think such Joys as Ear and Tongue
To celebrate or see:
Such sounds to hear, such Hands to feel, such Feet,
Such Eyes and Objects, on the Ground to meet.

From Dust I rise
And out of Nothing now awake;
These brighter Regions which salute mine Eyes
A Gift from God I take:
The Earth, the Seas, the Light, the lofty Skies,
The Sun and Stars are mine; if these I prize.

A Stranger here
Strange things doth meet, strange Glory see,
Strange Treasures lodg'd in this fair World appear,
Strange all and New to me:
But that they mine should be who Nothing was,
That Strangest is of all; yet brought to pass.
(Little, 1993: 123–4)

Conclusion

No two stories are alike. There are countless variations on the theme
of shame, but the images and feelings remain the same. Eyes, faces,
stones, and petrified affects that create a sense of non-existence predominate. Petrifaction, in fact, is the only way to go on being with
any feeling of solidity. The suffering and ways to free oneself from
core shame are also unique. Each of the stories just told were narrow
escapes from death that led to deep reconciliations, the setting free of
each from their shame to become separate human entities, and to

life. It is important to remember, however, that the work on shame can just as easily lead to suicide. In shame, one stays merged with the eyes of mother (hence her deepest psychic disturbance). The looking of mother is a looking at, not a looking after or into. It is distant and unempathic. Shame is this entrapment, and yet protects an inner conflict between the need to establish connections with others and the need to preserve the integrity of the self. Vision, however, can mean both petrifaction and movement, and in the next chapter we will look at the ways that shame is transformed into a symbol of creativity through the image of the eye, and how its emergence out of the richness of one's inner life takes place. Only in this way does shame take on its very important, consciousness-raising, life-affirming role. Shame has the singular capacity to disclose the self to the self, and its relational nature contains a revelatory capacity. Restoration of the reflective object restores the possibility of love, which is, ultimately, the only antidote for shame. Eyes can then become a symbol for the totality of the self.

Chapter 7

The eyes of love

Lovers look into each other's eyes, not at other parts of their bodies. For in the eyes Aidos [shame] dwells.

(Aristotle, 384–32 BC)

Eyes which see are the same thing as a heart which understands.

(Deuteronomy 29:4)

Shame is the sign of timidity, which is born of true love.

(Unknown)

The birth of love by the eyes alone finds a passage to the soul; for as, of all inlets to our senses, sight is the most lively, and most various in its motions, this animated quality most easily receives the influences which surround it, and attracts to itself the emanations of love.

(Heliodorus, *fl.* 3rd and 4th century AD)

Anyone who suffers the kind of absolute shame which has been the subject of this work does not feel loved, and is therefore incapable of loving oneself or others. One feels oneself to be nothing of any value, empty, and frozen like a stone. This work has been an attempt to show how the earliest experiences of unlovability have their roots in being rejected through eye-to-eye contact as a means of taking in the world. This rebuff is a tearing from mother that results in a deep fissure in the self. Reality loses all concreteness, and a part of the self becomes stone. This narrow crack in the rock face keeps one fragmented and apart from a sense of being loved. In shame, the ground beneath one's feet literally opens, and the earth swallows you up.

A main point expressed consistently throughout this entire work is that the unconscious fear that petrifies in shame is separation and annihilation – the threat of a loss of love. In order to hold onto any feeling of existence and a love that may never come, the infant ends up merging with mother's deepest disturbances. Shame in this sense is the pining away in vain for the loving object that will affirm empathically one's experiences. The cry of shame splits the crevice in the earth wider. Where an infant is used unconsciously or consciously as a dumping ground for the mother's psychic illness, loving is lost and shame takes over. The infant ceases to exist where withholding, envy, or rage take over a mother's mind. The mother is possessed by a narcissistic feeling that the fact that she has been wounded is more important than what she may have done wrong. Wurmser captures the reality of this human trauma when he writes:

> Shame at its deepest layer is the conviction of one's unlovability, an inherent sense that the self is dirty, untouchable, rotten . . . this abyss of unlovability contains such a depth of wordless and imageless despair that any more delimited shame comes as a welcome friend – its visibility and concreteness protect against the gray ghost of that absolute shame . . . The two risks are to offer oneself and be proved unlovable, and to merge or to conquer by sight and expression, and be proved helpless . . . To be unlovable means not to see a responsive eye and not to hear a responding voice . . . the helplessness of the searching eye and of the cry is the helplessness of feeling doomed to unlovability. Function and content are one in this primary trauma; they remain combined in the affect of shame.
>
> (Wurmser, 1997: 96–7)

Another consequence of being an infant suckled by a stone mother is the damage done to the development of symbolic activity. During the earliest phases of development, many aspects of psychic life are taking shape. Intelligence is dawning. The organization of personal psychic content is forming, and this will eventually provide the basis for dreaming and living relationships. If the lack of reverie in mother's mind does not provide a container with transformative potentials, psychosis is created. Real existence doesn't make sense; being petrified is the only way to go on existing. Shame is psychotic because the active use of eyes and looking – hence love and existence – got twisted. It is this distortion that blocks the development of the capacity to symbolize.

Symbols of transformation

As was shown clearly through the four case examples, it is no small undertaking to create movement out of what is petrified. The stone is wisely depicted by Yeats (quoted by de Vries, 1984) as "the unyielding face of the universe, which will not give up its mysteries, or the calcified parts of Self, which guard a similar secret life" (p. 444). Shame has also been protecting the true self, which reveals that contained secretly in it is a basic, archetypal instinct to exist. The drive to come into the world as a human being compels movement despite the "unyielding face of the universe." Shame points to something beyond will, something of power within the human. On the level of the collective unconscious, this is the life instinct and primary experience to restore creation. On an individual level, the movement is to find love in order to create a whole self. Lispector offers a description of the compelling force to move:

> If I talk to you will I frighten you and lose you? but if I don't I'll lose myself and in losing myself lose you anyhow . . . A step away from the climax, a step away from the revolution, a step away from what is called love. A step away from my life – which, because of a strong reverse magnet, I wasn't making into life . . . I didn't need the climax, the revolution, or even that prelove that is so much happier than love itself. Was the promise all I needed? Yes, just a promise.
>
> (Lispector, 1964/1994: 11–21)

She echoes the sentiments of Van Gogh expressed in a letter to his brother Theo almost a century earlier:

> What am I in the eyes of most people – a nonentity, an eccentric, or an unpleasant person – somebody who has no position in society and never will have, in short, the lowest of the low. All right, then – even if that were absolutely true, then I should one day like to show by my work what such an eccentric, such a nobody, has in his heart,
>
> (Van Gogh, quoted by Moffett, 1998: 29)

As well as containing the power to annihilate, shame is the power in one's being to destroy the Terrible Mother irrevocably. It is as though in shame there is an Athene, the motherless goddess who incited Medusa's beheading, and a Medusa, the horribly ugly face that could change a person into stone only thereafter to become a protective charm. These goddesses symbolize two aspects of a single self constantly interacting with each other, separating and reuniting in a process to transform powerful, unconscious energies. Therapy for shame is about transforming the stone into a symbol. A stone which is simply a stone has no feeling, no being, no life at all. A stone cannot experience loving or being loved. Facing the concrete, the petrified, the superficial of the earth, means coming eye to eye with psychosis. In summarizing her experience of coming face to face with the most despicable and insane part of her self imaged as a cockroach with beady eyes, Lispector says:

> But in the final analysis, the lowest of all acts was what I had always needed. I had always been incapable of the lowest of acts. And like that lowest of acts, I had deheroized myself . . . By not being I was. To the edge of what I wasn't, I was. What I am not, I am. Everything will be within me, if I am not; for "I" is merely one of the world's instantaneous spasms . . . But now I was much less than human . . . and would realize my specifically human destiny only if I gave myself over, just as I was doing, to what was not me, to what was still inhuman.
>
> (Lispector, 1964/1994: 172–3)

Shame is an original feature of human existence. One must meet the inanimate thing that lives inside, and out of this one will begin to exist. Just as one cannot face the Baba Yaga without protection, one cannot face unimaginable darkness until the good mother, a being capable of love, has been restored. Out of this confrontation, ego develops with the capacity to symbolize, and this provides the opportunity for a deeper, intact ground. This restorative process requires the integration of projected internal objects. Marie Louise von Franz explains:

> The possibility of integrating projected contents instead of apotropaically casting them out into extrapsychic space does not arise until symbols of the Self begin to appear. From this center impulses proceed to a contemplative, thoughtful recollection of the personality. The contents now seen to have been projected are at the same time recognized as belonging to one's own psychic wholeness. Consequently the psychic energy belonging to

these contents now flows toward one's own inner center, strengthening it and heightening its intensity.

(von Franz, 1987: 169)

In shame, the eye is a symbol of the self that begins to appear. With this strengthening that makes a connection to one's inner self, the concretized images of shame can undergo a symbolic transformation. The stone and eye become living symbols of the self. Introjection of its contents leads to the development of a symbolic capacity.

A stone as a symbol is the densest, oldest, and most enduring aspect of life on earth, an image of the Great Mother's eternal life. In fact, many deities are said to have been born from stone. It has the property of being able to bring creation into being, and the archetypal Terrible Mother is restored in her capacities as the source for all creativity. On an individual level, the stone becomes "an emblem of Being" (de Vries, 1984: 444). In alchemy this rock is called the Philosopher's Stone, the conjunction of opposites. As prima materia, shame contains the spirit of Mercurius, the "philosopher's child, the first purification, feeling, and imagination" (p. 444).

Symbolization of the stone makes it possible for the creative imagination to extend from a secure base. Internally, the mother that could petrify becomes the mother as stabilizer, and the inert infant becomes the infant as binder and settler (Wurmser, 1997). The fissure scarring the face of self becomes a process of separation and division. Separation is no longer the fear of a loss of love, but an opportunity for consciousness. In therapy, a shared reverie can occur that allows for the transcendent function to take its rightful place as the complex function that facilitates a transition from one attitude to another to bring different parts of the self into a whole. The eye is no longer petrifying, representing original shame with its terrifying effects, but takes on symbolic motifs with a nuance of one's previous feelings of being watched. At first the eyes of others see us, and then through those eyes we are able to see ourselves. The eye becomes one of insight, of the self looking at one's own self. "The eye with which I see God is the same eye with which God sees me." Shame becomes a source of unqualified self-knowledge. The eye is a soul "in the Eternal Abyss, a similitude of Eternity" and "a ball of fire or a fiery Eye" (Boehme, quoted in von Franz, 1987: 166). The many eyes of others become the one internal eye, an idea captured in the following passage:

Many authors of an earlier day have described how, after seeking this kind of self-knowledge . . . many lights or eyes gradually grow together into one great inner light or eye that is the image of God or of the light "which faith gives us."

(von Franz, 1987: 166)

Psychologically, the eye represents and expresses the light, or positive aspects, in the unconscious. In the language of shame, one would say the flickering whiteness in the blackness, the warmth of love and truth at the heart of the stone. Like the visible face, shame becomes a source of light, ego awareness and conscious energy. This light is the opposite of the petrifying qualities of shame, as it expresses every emotion in the human soul. With this eye, the world becomes a whole and balance of opposites.

The Self has for millennia been depicted as full of suns and eyes. Franz Boas (quoted in Pope, 1968) says that "the eye is drawn, when it is desired to represent the individual in his totality. The eye is the person himself, and possession of the eye gives control over the whole energy of the owner and power over his life" (p. 6). Van Gogh was quoted as saying:

I prefer painting people's eyes to cathedrals, for there is something in the eyes that is not in the cathedral, however solemn and imposing the latter may be – a human soul, be it that of a poor beggar or a streetwalker, is more interesting to me.

(Van Gogh, quoted by Moffet, 1998: 34)

When shame is transformed, the staring eyes of the world, depicted in Figure 1.1 as a "Universe of Eyes," are channeled into the birth of a human being (see Figure 7.1). This drawing depicts Hildegard of Bingen's vision of many eyes descending out of the stars through a cord to a baby in mother's womb. A soul comes out of God's shining body into the body of a growing child in his mother. This is the beginning of human life, the connection between the body and the soul. In German it is said *Leib und Seele auf dem Weg* – "Body and Soul on their way." Healed shame becomes the gift of self-reflection that makes subjective consciousness visible. The eye becomes a mirror for one's insight into the total reality of one's own being. Huxley (1990) says that those in whom inner life is just beginning describe being surrounded by eyes of light. Jung diagnosed this as polyopthalmia, a state in which complexes are made visible to the mind's

Figure 7.1 "The Soul and Her Tent" from Hildegard of Bingen's *Scivias*, 1141

eye by the light they give off. These sparkling eyes become phos-phenes of the imagination, "those organizations of the visual field that bring sensation to its focus in the world of meaning" (p. 80).

When the stone, or petrified self, is loved, shame is transcended. The eyes of shame become the eyes of love, and the face serves as mirror. Wurmser writes:

The answer to where both strands combine is clearly this: Love resides in the face – in its beauty, in the music of the voice and the warmth of the eye. Love is proved by the face, and so is unlovability – proved by seeing and hearing, by being seen and heard . . . I believe the two merge in the original experience – the nourishing breast (or at least milk) and the loving face and voice.

(Wurmser, 1997: 97)

The eyes of love

The process of transforming the eyes of shame into the eyes of love requires the kind of love depicted in the following biblical passage:

Love is patient and kind; love is not jealous or boastful; it is not arrogant or rude. Love does not insist on its own way; it is not irritable or resentful; it does not rejoice at wrong, but rejoices in the right. Love bears all things, believes all things, hopes all things, endures all things. Love never ends. But as for prophecies, they will come to an end; as for tongues, they will cease; as for knowledge, it will come to an end. For we know only in part, and we prophesy only in part; but when the complete comes, the partial will come to an end. When I was a child, I spoke like a child, I thought like a child, I reasoned like a child; when I became an adult I put an end to childish ways. For now we see in a mirror, dimly, but then we will see face to face. Now I know only in part; then I will know fully, even as I have been fully known. And now faith, hope and love abide, these three; and the greatest of these is love.

(I Corinthians 13:4–13)

This kind of love is the only antidote to the narcissism, rage, envy, and other causes for mother's absent mind. It is a love that makes it safe enough to come face to face with one's emptiness, hence the possibility of wholeness. This kind of love is rare and priceless. Rilke (1984) had this to say of loving in this way: "For one human being to love another human being; that is perhaps the most difficult task that has been entrusted to us, the ultimate task, the final test and proof, for which all other work is merely preparation" (p. 68).

The pain of shame evokes the endless moments of agonizing fear and disconnection in infancy. Maternal love is vital to a sense of wholeness and acceptability, and so, while its absence creates core shame, its presence has the potential to heal the disconnection that produces it. Even when healed, however, one must never forget the other side of mother's nature, her archetypal being as absence and deprivation. Shame will remain a gnawing sense of lack, although integrated as the way of nature.

Archetypal images that serve as containers for shame's transformation

Jung (1959) said that is was essential to continually keep before the eyes the original images of childhood in order to maintain a conscious link with them. In the same way, throughout this work shame has continually been kept before the reader's mind as an eye to establish a conscious link with the earliest days of infancy. This image has been amplified through infant research, literature, the visual arts, clinical and analytic theory, personal dreams and archetypal images to show how shame is generated through eye contact with mother, perpetuated through repeated mergers, and amplified by the archetypal images of the collective unconscious. The eye in particular has the quality of revealing the emotional, and therefore largely unconscious, elements of the mind.

What has not been said so far is that the basic instinct in shame that moves to find loving eyes brings about the transformation of it through either death or a living existence. When shame becomes death, it is much as it was for Cain, who lived in fear of the eye of God. In the following passage, Victor Hugo impressively depicts how shame can drive someone right into the grave:

> After killing his brother Abel, Cain flees from God; with his family he stops to rest on a mountain but is unable to sleep; he sees "an eye, wide open, in the darkness," fixed upon him. "I have not gone far enough," he calls out, trembling, and continues his flight. For thirty days and nights he hurries on until he comes to the seacoast, but as he settles down there he sees the eye again, in the heavens. He cries out to his family to hide him from God! They build a tent for him but the eye is always there. Finally at his request his family digs him a deep grave in the earth. He sits down on a little seat, and his family pushes the heavy gravestone over him. As the grave closes he sits there in darkness.
>
> (Hugo, quoted in von Franz, 1987: 167)

The inescapable Eye of God pursues the evil deed, and the mark of Cain is the tattooing of the crime that creates a desire to commit suicide – in other words, his shame. It is the motion of running, hiding or staying petrified in shame that creates the turn towards death.

This fate befalls the wicked Queen in Snow White. Driven by her narcissism, a pursuit of love based on superficial and self-centered principles combined with insatiable envy, the Queen insists that she will be the most beautiful woman alive in the land. She is so obsessed with the mirror reflection of her face that she attempts to murder her rival for beauty whom the mirror proclaims is lovlier – Snow White. The mirror is actually working to make the Queen conscious of her real form, a murderous witch; the mirror reveals the face that she should never show the world, revealing her own psychic truth to her – a truth for which the queen is not aware that she should be ashamed.

Remember that Snow White was put into a glass coffin instead of the black earth (hidden in shame), so that even while she was in her death-like sleep, she was watched by others who loved her. By contrast, whenever the Queen is talking into her mirror she is alone. Snow White is to marry her beloved prince, the man who stumbles and brings her back to life. They invite the Queen to their wedding, who is so petrified by her shameless acts that she cannot budge, but is nevertheless made to dance in red-hot iron slippers until she falls down dead.

A similar fate awaits the tragic figures of Narcissus and Echo. Like the Queen, Narcissus is killed by his own reflection, caught by his power of attraction. Upon recognition of his own image he says:

> O, I am he! I have felt it, I know now my own image. I burn with love of my own self; I both kindle the flames and suffer them. What shall I do? Shall I be wooed or woo? Why woo at all? What I desire, I have; the very abundance of my riches beggars me. Oh, that I might be parted from my own body! and, strange prayer for a lover, I would that what I love were absent from me!
>
> (Ovid, trans. Miller, 1916/1977: 10)

Ultimately, it is Narcissus's refusal to separate from the power of the Terrible Mother, who reveals herself in his strange prayer that what he loves be absent from him. He is totally merged with his mother Liriope, shown by the fact that he is both the lover and the beloved.

Poor Narcissus is bound towards his destiny of being sacrificed for the sake of Liriope's equilibrium, who has been ambivalent towards Narcissus since his birth. He was fathered by the river god Cephisus, who raped and nearly drowned her. This ambivalence is manifest in her concern with whether Narcissus will live a long life or die young. Her trauma prevented her from being an adaptive mother who could empathically connect to her son.

Narcissus was also cursed by the envy of others, namely a scorned youth who prays and curses him: "So may he himself love, and not gain the thing he loves" (p. 10). While Narcissus seeks to slake his thirst, he catches his own reflection and is smitten by the sight he sees:

> He looks in speechless wonder at himself and hangs there motionless in the same expression, like a statue carved from Parian marble. Prone on the ground he gazes at his eyes, twin stars, and his locks, worthy of Bacchus, worthy of Apollo; on his smooth cheeks, his ivory neck, the glorious beauty of his face, the blush mingled with snowy white: all things, in short, he admires for which he is himself admired. Unwittingly he desires himself; he praises, and is himself what he praises; and while he seeks, is sought; equally he kindles love and burns with love . . . What he sees he knows not; but that which he sees he burns for, and the same delusion mocks and allures his eyes . . . why vainly seek to clasp a fleeing image? What you seek is nowhere; but turn yourself away, and the object of your love will be no more . . So great a delusion charms his love.
>
> (Ovid, trans. Miller, 1917/1977: 11)

Separation would have been possible only if he had developed insight at the moment he sees his own reflection. Instead, he simply sees the beauty of his face, and became completely self-absorbed. Narcissus is doomed to repeat his infantile experience of the extreme despair he felt in the presence of the loved object who couldn't nurture and love him. In defense of the anxieties caused by this dim awareness, and to prevent the dissolution of his personality, he rallies all of his psychic resources towards eliciting other's love with disastrous consequences. The death of his soul eliminates any desire to live. "Hanging there motionless" where "no thought of food or rest can draw him from the spot . . . he gazes on that false image with eyes that cannot look their fill and through his own eyes perishes." He dies a shamed but a shameless self never having felt love; "death is nothing to me, for in death I shall leave my troubles; I would that he is loved would live longer; but as it is, we two shall die together in one breath." He dies replicating the relationship he had with Liriope by wasting away, a symbol of the mother's inability to soothe his help-lessness and fears of annihilation. Ultimately, it is his inability to separate from his own internal, absent mother that eventually kills him. Yet even death doesn't free him from his shame: when he is received into the infernal abodes he is fixed at the reflection pool, gazing upon his own face.

Both stories of the wicked Queen and Narcissus demonstrate that the kind of love that heals shame must be derived from insight developed in connection with the loving eyes of others, and returned to others in kind. Beginning in a self-absorbed love that excludes an awareness of shame only invites disaster, much as Agamemnon's hubris at stepping onto the red carpet punctuated his death sentence. One is eventually killed through the malignant abuse of power to prevent the dissolution of oneself.

The lovesick Echo is trapped in the same developmental place as Narcissus, completely regressed and dependent for her life upon this uncaring person who is not attracted to her. She assumes Narcissus's self-hatred much as an infant merges with mother's psychic disturb-ance to maintain her equilibrium. His contempt almost adds to his attractiveness – both are stripped of any respect and bound towards death. As Narcissus dies shamelessly merged with the Terrible Mother, the non-existent Echo can't hold her feelings:

> Scarce does his form remain which once Echo loved so well. But when she saw it, though still angry and unforgetful, she felt pity; and as often as the poor boy says "Alas!" again with answering utterance she cries "Alas!" . . . His last words as he gazed into the familiar spring were these: "Alas, dear boy, vainly beloved!" and the place gave back his words. And when he said "Farewell!" "Farewell!" said Echo too. He dropped his weary head on the green grass and death sealed the eyes that marveled at their master's beauty.
>
> (Ovid, trans. Miller, 1917/1977:11)

Despite her memory of his ruthless rejection, she is victim to Hera's rageful curse (image of the negative mother), and echoes Narcissus until his end. Her inability to separate from the unreflecting object brings about her dematerialization, an irretrievable loss of self in the face of absolute shame. As the reader will recall from Chapter 3, Echo's death comes to epitomize the petrifying qualities of shame: she hides her face, and in her isolation becomes increasingly gaunt, until all the moisture faded from her skin. Her bones turn to stone, and only her voice is left alive.

Echo meets the same fate as Narcissus and the wicked Queen. A transitional figure is She-who-must-be-obeyed, who in her death falls ambiguously in the space between the next life and death. Her shame, like that of the wicked Queen's, Narcissus's and Echo's, remained unconscious in life – but her story has a twist. In trying to possess an illegitimate love, She steps into the Pillar of Life again. Similar to the sacrament of baptism, one can't be impregnated with its power more than once, for otherwise the effects of the flame will be neutralized. As She greedily reaches for life, She is turned to death, and her petrified 2000-year-old face reveals her shame. In reaching to possess love in this way, She is turned into a pile of ashes.

The moment of death, however, becomes her moment of transformation. Unlike the other three characters who met tragic endings, She is able to begin a process of separation by letting go of Kallikrates, the man for whom She had clung to unending life. A head of mummified skin with frightful age graven on her gnarled countenance, her body disintegrated into a pile of ashes, her only dying words are "Kallikrates. Forget me not, Kallikrates. Have pity on my shame; I shall come again, and shall once more be beautiful, I swear it – it is true. Oh-h-h" (p. 336). She fell upon her face to stir no more, dying at the same spot that she had killed Kallikrates 20 centuries earlier. She lived a false life, and in her death the whole length of her 2000 years took effect upon her, showing that her aging had never stopped. She had only been existing, locked up in the living tomb of her deceptively beautiful body. She had been living her death, and so in her death would have hope for life:

> Having once looked Ayesha in the eyes, we could not forget her forever and ever while memory and identity remained. We both loved her now and for always, she was stamped and carven on our hearts, and no other woman or interest could ever raze that splendid die.
>
> (Haggard, 1957: 342)

For Ayesha, the hope for love in life lived on. She had a future to look forward to. She stood against an eternal law, and strong though she was, she was swept back to nothingness with shame and mockery. Coming face to face with her shame in her moment of death reconnects her to true love. She may be united with Kallikrates in a future life after all.

Shame can only be transformed into life by maintaining consciousness, coming face to face with the deepest stratas of the unconscious, despite severe pain. In this way the eyes of shame become the immediate experience of the voice of self within. Something numinous has survived despite the death, or absence, of one's mother, or a constellation of the Great Mother. When the Terrible Mother is integrated, she is revealed as not so evil after all.

The Baba Yaga eventually shows herself to be more human than evil in the story of Wassilissa. This is made possible through the protection of the good mother, and the respect Wassilissa demonstrates around the Baba Yaga's shame. With the good mother's help, Wassilissa is helped to sort and integrate both bad and good, depersonify the archetype of the Terrible Mother, and eventually comes to terms with the Baba Yaga as a natural phenomenon. If Wassilissa had dared to ask about what she saw inside the hut, the Baba Yaga would have taken on the full force of her devouring side and eaten her on the spot. Instead, as a reward for not probing, Wassilissa is given the skull with fiery eye that burns her stepmother and stepsisters to death. In other words, Wassilissa comes face to face with her shame, integrates its power, and presents the same to her stepmother and stepsisters who are petrified by their own shame. The secrets of the hidden side are often associated with death, but the story supports the spark of human awareness in shame when it teaches us that death becomes evil only when there is no respect for the duality of forces contained in shame.

The second that Wassilissa does not ask the question, and the Baba Yaga gives her the skull, is the moment of transformation for them both. The Baba Yaga shows herself to be more human by experiencing shame about the filth inside her hut, while Wassilissa has come face to face with the Terrible Mother and been empowered by her so that she is no longer victim to her stepmother and stepsisters. The effects of the Terrible Mother have been integrated and humanized.

A secret that tempts one to look into the dark side of shame is a common motif in myths and fairy tales. Psychodynamically, this is the infant seeing mother's disturbance, and relinquishing self in relation to it. There is a secret that should not be looked into in the story of Psyche. As you will recall from Lewis's (1956) retelling of the myth, Orual is the evil sister and mother figure to Psyche who pushes her to look into the mysterious secret of her husband's identity. Following this heinous act, Orual undergoes facing her own ugliness (envy) and transforming her shame. Her mother had died when she was quite young, and her father despised her as ugly. Her most beautiful sister Psyche was born when her father remarried because her own mother died in childbirth. Orual becomes Psyche's possessive mother. Fueled by her feelings of betrayal, she incites Psyche to expose her husband's face, which results in Psyche being cast out into a desperate world of abandonment to survive numerous tasks. Like Inanna, Orual finally comes to face her most despicable parts when she is exposed and naked, and judged before the gods. She then finds real love. The title of the book, *Till We Have Faces*, is based on the following biblical quote (I Corinthians 13:12): "Now we see in a mirror, dimly, but then we will see face to face. Now I know only in part; then I will know fully, even as I have been fully known." After seeing the mother's face, one's own true face is finally, after much brutal suffering, a relief. There is just no alternative for someone so afflicted (except perhaps actual death).

God also does not want to reveal his mysteries in the Garden of Eden, and when Adam and Eve eat the apple they are exposed in their sin of disobeying His edict. The moment of the exposure of their shame is the same moment they realize their humanity. A nice contrast to the story of the Garden of Eden is an Assyrian version of the Epic of Gilgamesh and early history of the hero Enkidu, who represents the transformation of savage man to civilized man. In the beginning, Enkidu was a wild man living as an animal among animals, but a woman named Ukhat was sent to seduce him. She waited for him at a watering hole and "exposed her breast, revealed her nakedness, and took off her clothing." She enticed him without shame. Enkidu responded at once to his desires (also without shame), the consummation took place on the spot, and the hero forsook the animals to remain with Ukhat and learn the arts of civilization.

This story is so different from the biblical account of Adam and Eve, for whom awareness and nakedness caused annihilating shame and eventual expulsion from the Garden of Eden. Their exposure became mankind's Original Sin, the reason for our fall from grace. They would live in their shame and create the history of the human race. On the other hand, learning to accept shame was the psychological task articulated by Milton (1667/1978) in *Paradise Lost*. He writes:

> Love was not in their looks, either to God
> Or to each other, but apparent guilt,
> And shame, and perturbation, and despaire . . .

After God discovers why Adam and Eve are wearing such faces, Adam tells Eve:

> What better can we do, then to the place
> Repairing where he judg'd us, proftrate fall
> Before him reverent, and there confefs
> Humbly our faults, and pardon beg, with tears
> Watering the ground, and with our fighs in the Air
> Frequenting, tent from hearts contrite, in fign
> Of Forrow unfeign'd, and humiliation meek.
>   (9th book)

And now we turn to the creation myths of Egypt. Pope (1968) interprets the Egyptian myth of Ra's wrath as expressing in archetypal terms the transformation of the destructive powers of the eye into eros. The reader will recall from Chapter 5 that Ra sent out his Eye (of Death) in the form of Hathor to kill mankind. When eros was absent, Ra ruled mankind exclusively by power, revealing the goddess Hathor in her terrible aspect. But her wrath was so dangerous that Ra was forced to reflect, and came to his senses. When Hathor sees her reflection in the mirror of Red Beer, a mirror that reveals her deepest shame – the unconscious murderer of life in her own soul – Hathor calms down and acts with love. Ra withdraws his projection of his own murderous intentions from Hathor, which facilitates her transformation from a wild animal into a beautiful goddess. Hathor as the terrible goddess is brutally destructive only when personified by projections into the external. When internalized, Hathor acts with kindness and becomes mankind's salvation.

The Great Mother in her most extreme negative form as the Eye of Death evolves into beneficent goddesses whose worship extends throughout the Western world. In Ancient Egypt, the most popular and important of all the maternal goddesses is Isis, the prototype of motherhood and the embodiment of wifely love and fidelity. She is the sister spouse of Osiris and the mother of his son, Horus, whose name means eye. The name of Isis translates to "seat" or "throne," which means that it is very probable that "the throne which made the king" is the Great Mother charged with the mysterious power of kingship (James, 1959). Isis personifies all that was most vital in the maternal principle, its attributes, functions, and duties. In order to restore life to the dismembered Osiris, she receives him into her left eye, creating the symbol of the eye as womb (Pope, 1968). She is otherwise known as the Goddess of Many Names, and eventually, despite her subservience to Osiris, was equated with the Great Mother of Western Asia, Greece, and Rome, as well as the entire Nile Valley.

The transformation of the Terrible Mother into her loving aspect that promotes Self is articulated well by Wolkstein and Kramer, who in their notes on the hymns of Inanna, poetically describe her resurrection:

> Once Inanna takes up the me, the holy form of things, she assumed her destined role, and her spiritual force moves from the wild and unpredictable "heart" to the all-knowing and all seeing "eye." So, too, the animals, people, and gods who are governed by their uncontrollable instincts go before their queen in order to discover their own form and destiny. What they discover is the experience of being linked to the "eye" or inner light of their goddess. The incredible energy of the storming goddess, now brought into the social order, emanates with such luminosity and intensity that the people are captured and lifted into a state of "greater light." This spiritual impulse is given grounding in the many forms of expression offered in the holy me.
>
> (Wolkstein and Kramer, 1983: 71)

The Evil Eye of Medusa that could cause death becomes an eye amulet that protects life. As a talisman her potency lies only in her head, which begins to take on beneficent powers once it is severed from her body (Harrison, 1922). Its power becomes a paradox of the evil eye, now becoming the eye that wards off evil or bad luck. As a form of protection, Medusa's visage was used to warn intruders that her rites were in progress, and to ward off demonic assaults. This explains why pottery workers affixed it to their ovens to stop their pots from breaking, and smiths put it on their furnaces; why it was placed in tombs and over hot springs, those conduits from the underworld and the unconscious; and on shields, to demoralize the enemy. It was, in fact, the emblem of the eye that reflected evil back upon its source, and was therefore an amulet against what it looked like. Even Athene, who was born without a mother, wore the face of Medusa on her breastplate, perhaps as an attempt to replace the absent mother with a good one.

And last, we turn from the archetypal level to a personal one to see the transformation of the eyes of shame into the eyes of love for the four individuals whose therapeutic processes were presented in Chapter 6. Throughout their struggles, one wonders what will come in the end. Each in her way transforms the eyes of shame into loving eyes by no longer being identical with her mother's disturbance. In this movement each advances significantly in her process of separation and individuation. From what I know, Barbara went on explore the rock further, remarried and became more of a mother to her son. Margaret's mother died a year after she confronts her with her own illness. She eventually finds peace with herself and enjoys her first real romantic relationship. Alexandra literally turned the death of her mother into life through the birth of her own son whom many people spontaneously named "bright eyes." Marie's mother died, at which time Marie finally found love with her mother and rekindled her dying marital relationship. Marie went to the graveyard to talk to her mother in much the same way her mother went and talked to her deceased daughter:

> I have never seen you more beautiful than on that night in your long white dress tied in back at the waist with a huge sash as green as your eyes . . . I love you. Yes, that's right, I love you. I came here to declare it to you, once and for all. I am not ashamed to speak of it. It does me good to say it to you and to repeat it! I love you. I love you . . . It felt better to say it: three little words strung together and repressed a thousand times over throughout my life . . . It had taken this catastrophic death . . . to finally love her in the light . . . Two blind people armed to the teeth, claws exposed. What a blow she had struck me, what venom I had distilled! What savagery, what butchery! If I had not become insane, I would never have emerged.
>
> (Cardinal, 1975/1996, p. 292)

The role of eye-to-eye contact in psychotherapy

Therapy is a setting for the generation as well as the resolution of the kind of shame that will work to keep content both hidden and out of therapy. A thought from Nietzsche fits in very well here: "The attractiveness of insight would be small if there were not so much shame that, on the way to it, has to be overcome" (quoted in Wurmser, 1997: 307). An obstacle to dealing with shame therapeutically may in some ways be due to the asymmetrical therapeutic relationship that requires self-revelation only on the part of the patient, making her more needy and less autonomous than she may like. Moreover, there is an injunction in psychotherapy to tell all, whereas therapists will inadvertently use this material to shame their patients through the interpretations. I have found that therapists often like to ignore the fact that they have a vantage point of understanding that causes inhibitions. What may go unrecognized in this neglect is the fact that psychotherapists become shameless intruders, and patients may explode with negative affects the same way the Baba Yaga would have eaten Wassilissa had she asked her last question. This denial around intrusiveness inflicts a deep humiliation which professionals as well as the clientele have come to believe is simply in the nature of the undertaking and something the patient must get used to. This thinking has become a part of the therapeutic culture, so much so that Anthony (1981) has commented on the therapist as an "archetypal measure of all things."

Absolute shame arises from the self, not the therapeutic setting. Shame always hides, but a psychosis of shame may not evidence itself or even be heard by the therapist for quite some time. This is because this individual is wishing for reflection, acceptance, and existence while dreading catastrophe and annihilation, or the therapist is avoidantly trying to rush through a transformation as fast as possible. Under these circumstances, both patient and therapist really lose something. Facilitating its revelation and healing requires that certain therapeutic features be present in the situation. Keeping in mind that each individual is unique, in conclusion I would like to offer some therapeutic rules of thumb, so to speak, to keep in mind in treating such a patient. I am not trying to promote any disciplined thinking, which would only produce mirror-like unresponsiveness. Rather, I offer food for thought that may entice the psychotherapist to amplify or go deeper into my thoughts until the simplest and most direct inroad into shame is achieved.

Great emotional requirements that far exceed the care of a neurotic patient are demanded of the therapist when dealing with the type of shame that has been the subject of this work. This is due to a variety of reasons, most of which come under the heading of the significant role that countertransference will play, and the fact that projective identification dominates the process and tempts the therapist to replicate the terrible aspects of mother. The nature of the very early material contained in shame creates a strange relationship between the unconscious of the patient and that of the therapist. This is connected to the lack of existence which defines the patient's experience in the world and gets projected into the collective eyes of others, as well as the fact that the original trauma occurred through impingement. The petrifying occurrence of shame also demands its reenactment over and over again in an attempt to discharge unbearable tensions. In other words, the psychosis of shame, fraught with powerful affective potentialities, will inevitably and unavoidably act itself out between the therapist and the patient. This is what therapists seek to avoid by keeping things as if, and yet when acting out occurs it offers rich material that cannot be gained by any other means. It must be mined, and the therapist must contribute her own work on herself. The reenactment in therapy is an unconscious attempt on the part of the patient to free herself from mother's impinging hold and finally put an end to the repetitious pattern dogging her life. It is the therapist's responsibility to hold the situation in mind and maintain contact on every level with what is going on in the relationship. Winnicott had this to say about psychosis:

> From this is derived the fact, if it be a fact, that it is from psychosis that a patient can make spontaneous recovery, whereas psychoneurosis makes no spontaneous recovery and the psychoanalyst is truly needed. In other words, psychosis is closely related to health, in which innumerable environmental failure situations are frozen but are reached and unfrozen by the various healing phenomena of ordinary life.
>
> (Winnicott, 1992b: 284)

Shame is a very provocative and contagious affect which may incite the therapist to overreact. Initially shame may present as anger, cockiness, or depression. It will likely surface, however, when there are lapses of attention, failures of acknowledgement, or unresponsiveness on the part of the therapist which mimic maternal failures. The patient will feel fragmented, disconnected, or dismissed. Deficits in the therapist will also become poignantly painful, so that she needs constantly to examine her emotional participation in the process. We all defend against the awful sting of shame, but if the therapist defends or has not been treated on her issues of shame, it will be hard to recognize, much less access. The therapist must resist her own feelings of shame lest she dismisses something important or worse, impinges. Maintaining objectivity is the only way to compensate for this. Winnicott's work provides a model for how this can be done:

> He did not defend against his own feelings but could allow their full range and, on occasion, expression. Without sentimentality he was able to feel about, with, and for his patient, entering into and sharing an experience in such a way that emotions that had had to be dammed up could be set free.
>
> (Little, 1990: 46)

Although the hidden content in shame stings deeply when revealed, the individual wants so much to exist and is compelled by a universal need for recognition. In shame resides the unconscious desire for the other despite its walls. Marie Cardinal had this to say about finally coming to face the eye at the core of her shame:

> I always ended up by lifting the mask to tell the exact truth. I understood very well, without needing him to tell me, that if I concealed certain images it was because of an unconscious fear they would hurt even more when brought into the light, whereas, on the contrary, it was by lancing the wounds and cleaning them all out that the pain would go away.
>
> (Cardinal, 1975/1996: 143)

In a similar vein, Joyce Maynard (1998) wrote: "I have to believe that my greatest protection comes in self-disclosure. It's shame, not exposure, that I can't endure" (p. 48). Little relates her moment of desperation:

> In one early session with D.W. I felt in utter despair of ever getting him to understand anything. I wandered round his room

trying to find a way. I contemplated throwing myself out the window . . . finally I attacked and smashed a large vase filled with white lilac, and trampled on it. In a flash he was gone from the room.

(Little, 1990: 43)

The absence of a containing environment was made real by the breaking of the vessel and Winnicott's departure. On the other hand, a petrified patient who does not feel safe may give no clues, making certain that the therapist can do nothing in order to make the therapist feel exactly as she feels. She will look like a stone, the tears will dry up, and there won't be a communicative sound.

Shame is very caught up with vision, and so it can be brought into therapy directly and simply through eye contact. While shame may remain hidden, the face and eyes, which are always visible, will eventually reveal what the person is prone to hide. Historically, eye contact has been avoided with our patients, especially by putting the patient on the couch. This avoidance leaves a whole line of clinical thinking around the use of eye contact untouched. Its absence thus far is hard to understand, however, given that sustained eye contact is the most intense and intimate form of interpersonal communication. In fact, the earliest deprivations may result in a heavy compensatory reliance on nonverbal communication such as eye-to-eye contact. If this interchange is blocked and warped, the core of the self-concept will become warped. The true self will never match one's own expectations or those of others.

The face is the most expressive part of the human body, and much of what a patient communicates in psychotherapy is through facial expression and eye-to-eye contact. When she is angry she will snarl. When pleased, she will make positive eye contact, looking directly at you with perhaps a laugh. If she thinks you have said something stupid, she will roll her eyes or stare blankly, as though to communicate her wondering what planet you come from. When shame is present, the gaze will be averted and cheeks will turn red.

Among many other things, eye contact is a means to forming a viable transference. The mother's face is the infant's first emotional mirror (Winnicott, 1971), and in this same way the therapist's face comes to serve as a kind of mirror image of the patient. To an infant, mother's face is the environment which tells her who and what she is. Therefore, the therapist's face needs to be open to scrutiny. Coping with face-to-face interaction requires a different set of skills, and a relaxed openness to what is going on within as well as a receptiveness to what is coming from without (Wright, 1991: 7). Any therapist under such scrutiny will feel on guard, but such reluctance will impede the work. Winnicott articulates well how the therapist's face can serve the actualization of a true self:

> Psychotherapy is not making clever and apt interpretations; by and large it is a long-term giving the patient back what the patient brings. It is a complex derivative of the face that reflects what is there to be seen . . . If I do this well enough the patient will find his or her own self, and will be able to exist and to feel existing; it is finding a way to exist as oneself, and to relate to objects as oneself, and to have a self in which to retreat.
>
> (Winnicott, 1971: 117)

The dialogue in psychotherapy can incorporate a watching of the facial expressions and eye contact in order to replicate the mother–infant relationship. The processes of Alexandra and Barbara show how the rhythms of looking between therapist and patient is useful in revealing how the comings and goings of mother were experienced, and the nature of a person's grip on existing. Mother's face represents security for an infant (seen most dramatically in the first days of life), and the same is true of the psychotherapist's. In other words, the creation of self depends upon mother's perceptions, which are reflected in her face. Therefore, in a process of psychotherapy, the patient must be able to read the therapist's face so that the patient is able to gain knowledge of her therapist in much the same way as an infant gains knowledge of her mother, hence the world. Her face becomes a mirror where the patient can see not an objective truth, but the therapist's subjective responses. This leads to integrative processes that promote a healthy, human sense of self.

Eye contact can also establish deeper contact through the countertransference relationship. Moody (quoted in Pope, 1968: 34) gives a beautiful example of the penetrating and fertilizing aspects of the eye that got things moving with a 7-year-old girl. Nothing was happening in the treatment, except that the girl would stare and embarrass Moody. He finally "gazed back into her eyes for a long time" as if "trying to penetrate her mind." Therapeutic movement began at that exact moment.

The practice of psychoanalysis is most responsible for setting a precedent on the dismissal of eye contact. Analysis has historically taken place in a vacuum, and the analyst is taught to be non-visible and to remove any emotional responses. This deprivation of the visual modality discourages shame ideation, and the absence of the human element perpetuates shame. It was the originator of psychoanalysis who, due to his own shame sensitivities, constructed an absence of vision in the psychoanalytic relationship. Given his self-deprecating comments, it appears that Freud didn't like his own appearance, and he also disliked being constantly looked at by his patients. For these reasons, among other factors, he created the practice of placing the patient on the couch with the analyst sitting behind him (Pines, 1987: 17). Not only does the couch remove vision, but reality as well. Little had this to say about her experiences on the couch in her prior analysis with Ella Freeman Sharpe:

> Always on the couch reality had to be set aside, including observations of her age and her health, and specifically her heart condition . . . I, much younger and in good health, was not allowed to help but had to stand by useless, while she, who was in danger of heart failure, dragged a heavy couch from one end to the other of a long room . . . (My mother used to say I was spineless, always taking the line of least resistance. "What use would you be on an Arctic expedition?" and quoted Milton "On his Blindness.")
>
> (Little, 1990: 35)

If the therapist is practicing psychoanalysis, the rigors of a traditional analytic stance need to be toned down. If someone goes on treating the patient afflicted with core shame according to the strictest of analytic principles, one is acting destructively, becoming the withholding mother without transformative potentials. To circumvent a more delimited kind of shame that can become an obstacle to uncovering absolute shame, the therapist and patient need to be on more of an equal footing. This requires a great versatility of therapeutic attitude (although there are elements in analytic technique, however strictly interpreted, that can provide for legitimate transference gratification). The absence of flexibility towards the patient's spontaneous movements will result in excessively severe frustration. Shame is the failure to form palpable human relationships, so that substituting direct interpersonal response for the analysis of emergent elements, for example, is crucial at times to the resolution of the transference psychosis. This type of response is necessary due to what Wurmser (1997) describes as the very powerful, relentless, self-attacking, and masochistic elements in shame which can make analysis of it very difficult. Furthermore, how can interpretations be given if the individual in her psychotic part does not have access to the symbolic function? Revelations that are derived from empathic human contact and communications that the patient is understood are more important than interpretations. Another reason for giving at times a reasonable human response is the patient's need to feel that the therapist accepts what she is saying despite her sickening illness, and to create a real functional, human relationship with another individual.

Great humanness can be revealed in empathically reacting with shame. During Margaret Little's analysis with Winnicott, he came in looking grey and very ill, but claimed he was suffering from laryngitis. She knew better and said, "You haven't got laryngitis, you've got a coronary. Go home" (1990: 48). He called later that night to tell her in fact she was right and it was a coronary. This moment became a landmark separation from her earliest maternal environment. At last, she says, she was allowed to know the truth. She could be right and trust her perceptions. Little describes Winnicott this way:

> I found D.W. essentially a truthful person, to whom "good manners" were important; he had respect for the individual . . . To demand "associations" or to push an "interpretation" would be "bad manners," as well as being useless. He was as honest as anyone could be, responding to observations and answering questions truthfully unless there was a need to protect another person, but it was essential to know when his answer was not wholly true, and why. He would answer questions directly, taking them at face value, and only then considering why it was asked? Why then? and what was the unconscious anxiety behind it?
>
> (Little, 1990: 47)

In order to bring movement to a catatonic part, the patient's feeling must be attuned to and reflected adequately. Another example of this is that offered by my patient Alexandra, who consistently confronted me when she experienced or dreamt that countertransference issues were impinging, and her uncanny intuitive perceptions needed to be consistently validated, rather than deftly avoided and turned back on her. I had only to make this mistake once. On one occasion she had brought a dream about reluctantly driving my mother around on the back of a motorcycle along with a bed of impatiens (a pun for both the words patient and impatient). My questions formed an attempt to open up some awareness about her own mother, and following the session she became quite frustrated and enraged. She called to address this by phone and, since I was unavailable, we scheduled a time to talk by phone first thing the next morning. Yet before we could talk she had another dream of a picture book entitled "No Tears," which contained childhood photographs of my mother. Impressed on its cover was a stamp of authenticity. This book was in fact a matter I kept close to my heart, an album of my mother's childhood photos that I had made during a private time of enormous grief around my mother. Obviously I had not cried or worked through enough. This incident taught me that I had to trust her impulses, and allow her to know what she knows. In the same way that, when things do not go well, the infant can become aware of maternal failures, my patient could intuit my impingements.

Shame is the deprivation of satisfactions which the patient should have been able to expect of her mother, so that refusing to gratify only petrifies and freezes the reaching when the patient may only be clamoring for something which has hitherto been impossible to achieve. To deny the patient's reality is to replicate the original absent, withholding mother and undermine the basic, affirmative elements (see the above quote again from Little regarding her mother's opinion of her). Bending the technical structure may produce increasingly transparent communications by the patient, which will in turn diminish projective identification, facilitating the resolution of the psychosis.

Unlocking the fears of annihilation through exposure brings out the need for, and the presence of, unconditional love. Furthermore, since love is the only true transcendence of shame, it is imperative that a maternal kind of love be present. This affect creates another kind of therapy. Above all shame needs protection, so that the therapeutic love that heals provides a safe container and the therapist's adaptation to the individual's pace. Anything else results in impingement. In Marie Cardinal's words:

> I would learn much later that the mind doesn't just present itself at the gate of the unknown. It isn't enough merely to want to penetrate the unconscious so that consciousness can enter. The mind procrastinates. It goes back and forth. It delays. It hesitates.

It keeps watch. And when the time has come, it stands motionless in front of the gate like a setter, paralyzed.

(Cardinal, 1975/1996: 96)

The active presence of love also requires the therapist to be fully present to her own humanity. The patient needs to understand the fallibilities of the person to whom she is entrusting her mental and emotional life. In a way, the patient needs to see the therapist as she actually is. This demands honesty, openness, and responsiveness without the revelation of personal content. Specifically in relation to shame, this means that the therapist's face must be able to read like an open book, much as an infant is able to scrutinize mother's face eight inches away during breastfeeding. The building up of object constancy in shame takes place through the eye, and so this object increasingly gains importance in the therapeutic setting. The unconscious and hence symbols are activated when the therapist is able to penetrate the psychosis of shame with genuine interest and love. Eventually shame comes under ego control. This contact will manifest as the image of the eye, which will appear in dreams with special clarity. Moreover, this manifestation often marks significant turning points of new emotions that foster different behaviors.

The Evil Eye of the life-threatening mother becomes the eye of sight and insight in the heart of the self. The moment at which the transforming insight is ripe depends on the archetype of the self. When the inner eye of self-recognition emerges, shame can serve as mediator between the inner self and the world. It is only once one has become aware of one's true and separate identity that one is no longer petrified by it, and an interplay occurs between inner and outer worlds. When shame becomes an eye at the center of consciousness, the psychosis is resolved. Subjective realities are connected to and reflected by objective realities. One feels at home inside oneself and in the world. Instead of the ground beneath one's feet opening to swallow one up, the earth becomes the ground of one's being. The absence of love becomes mature object love, the concrete becomes symbol, and one connects to one's human realities.

Conclusion

The eye as an interpersonal object of study is curiously missing throughout the history of psychoanalysis. This avoidance is not only a glaring oversight in the literature, but barriers have even been built into the physical structure of psychoanalysis itself. The "regressive" position on the couch with the analyst seated behind the patient, or angled chairs that "invite a third" reinforce the avoidance of eye contact. This chapter has explored the implications of this avoidance specifically in relation to the analysis of absolute shame. Always true to its nature, shame hides and is at first very difficult to reach in a process of psychotherapy. It will normally enter the room via the therapist's eyes and face, and replicates the infant self's facial inter-action with mother. The process of making this affect conscious entails a long process of self exposure and separation from the reject-ing mother of one's personal experience, and the Terrible Mother of the collective unconscious. It is through this process that the eyes of shame are transformed from an unmentalized, concrete experience to a symbol of wholeness and life. The patient's transformation makes considerable emotional demands upon the therapist.

The main premise of this chapter is that the primary curative element for shame is what was initially missing in the mother's face – Eyes of Love.

I close with a prayer that evokes images of the genesis and creative transformation of shame.

Hail Holy Queen, Mother of Mercy;
Hail, our life, our sweetness, and our hope.
To you do we cry, poor banished children of Eve.
To you do we send up our sighs, mourning and weeping in this
     valley of tears.
Turn then, most gracious Advocate, your eyes of mercy towards
     us.
And after this our exile show unto us the blessed fruit of your
     womb, Jesus.
Oh clement, oh loving, oh sweet Virgin Mary.

Epilogue
Clinical implications for the field of depth psychology

My review of the literature in Chapter 1 culminated in the primitive shame experience described by Broucek (1991) as caused by the still-faced mother that produces a shriveling infant, and Wurmser's (1997) depiction of a mother's contemptuous face that produces a wordless infant with searching eyes frozen in stone. To be sure, the infant does not see herself reflected: but I wondered also what she must see that creates such a profound feeling of damage. What is in a mother's face that has the power to come between an infant and her own subjectivity, arresting development and creating shame in the core of the self? This aspect of self then becomes a pariah that should drop off the face of the earth. This loss of self is supported by Anthony's (1981) observation that in the more disturbed cases of shame, one is often confronted by the individual's immaturity and proneness towards regressive processes, conducive, at times, to experiences not only of object loss but also to a sense of the "loss of self."

During the initial stages of my research, then, the eyes of the contemptuous, unreflecting or still mother's face caught my eye, becoming my point of contact with shame. The regressive and chronic nature of shame, the high recidivism rate among patients suffering from shame, as well as the extensive spectrum of shame-related phenomena, demanded a look into the eyes of that face. It has also been observed (Lansky and Morrison, 1997; Nathanson, 1987) that contributors on shame have approached shame separately, which results in a lack of integration in the literature. The resurgence of interest in this topic has created a vast body of explorations that include contributions from the fields of psychoanalysis, biology, social theory, and research psychology. Many controversial issues have arisen and continue to be debated. These include its time of onset, the factors necessary for its development, and whether it is intrapsychic and connected to drives or issues of identity, or intersubjective and related to processes of separation. Focussing on the eyes of shame thus also became an attempt to synthesize these varied contributions and issues, and to uncover shame at its deepest intrapsychic place as a way of understanding its multiple manifestations in a broad variety of clinical disorders. This effort drew me into many areas. Infant research supported my inquiry, providing the scientific data on the importance of mother's face in processes of attachment between mother and infant, and demonstrated the onset of shame states in early infancy. Metapsychological literature provided the theoretical framework. The empirical methods of depth psychology required that I approach the eye as an image, and so myths, fairy tales, literature, philosophy, archaeology and the arts provided the means for this exploration into the eye's complex psychic meaning on personal, historical, and cultural levels. This material then provided guidelines for my interpretations.

My venture into this vast and prolific world of shame has been precise, small, and detailed (imaged earlier as looking at a tree in the forest). This kind of looking has excavated another layer of the meaning of shame, a strata barely visible to the naked eye but which manifests through eye contact. What does this synthetic piece contribute to the wide scope of shame? How may this layer affect psychology's understanding of shame? How does my theory stand in relation to its predecessors, and what are its clinical implications? The following is an effort to answer these questions.

Many theorists have understood shame as an intersubjective phenomenon. The essence of this position is best captured by Morrison and Stolorow:

A basic idea of intersubjective theory is that recurring patterns of intersubjective transaction with the developmental system result in the establishment of invariant principles that unconsciously organize the child's subsequent experiences . . . it is these unconscious ordering principles, forged within the crucible of the child-caregiver system, that form the basic building blocks of personality development . . . From early, recurring experiences of malattunement, the child acquires the unconscious conviction that unmet developmental yearnings and reactive feeling states are manifestations of a loathsome defect or of an inherent inner badness.

(Morrison and Stolorow, 1997: 79)

Theoretical orientations vary in that the transactional factors at play are different, or more stress is put on either the subject or object in the intersubjective space, or the shared space in between becomes the focus. Wurmser (1997) sees that shame bridges two poles: the "object pole" or factor in front of which one is ashamed; and the "subject pole," or the aspect of which one is ashamed. Kaufman (1992) describes shame as caused by a breakdown in what he calls the "interpersonal bridge." Broucek (1982, 1991, 1997) conjectures that shame vulnerability is generated by the parent's failure to respond to an infant's gestures and pleasures. For him, the intersubjective origins of shame emphasize the caregiver's failure to respond to the child's experiences of efficacy and intentionality. The child ends up experiencing life as an object rather than as a subject. This environmental failure contributes to the infant's experience of incompetence, inefficacy, and the inability to influence, predict, or comprehend an event which the infant expected to be able to control or understand.

This thesis explicates the intersubjective dimension that generates shame at an earlier level than previously done. This is one that occurs before subject and object are distinct, when conditions provide for a confused perception between the two. The object (mother) is emphasized as overwhelming the subject (infant) to the point of her nonexistence. This intersubjective space is not one of mutual influence, but of the infant merged in mother's psychic space.

This idea about the intersubjective field is then extended by delineating its intrapsychic consequences. Intrapsychic shame is deeply pathological and can be re-experienced without interpersonal interaction. The eyes of shame reveal that the mother's misattunement creates the reality for the child that she has never been born. The child distinctively feels that her own affective states are unwelcome or damaging to mother, and must therefore be sacrificed in order to maintain the desperately needed tie. In this view, shame is the feeling of a human being who should become nothing – a deeply significant derailment of developmental processes.

Shame has also been identified by several authors as constituting the principal source of pain in narcissistic states. The term narcissism is defined as a grandiose need to be special, an excessively positive state of loving oneself. When this self is not responded to, it leads to exquisite narcissistic vulnerability and shame sensitivity. Shame in this context refers to some sort of failure, weakness, flaw, or injury of the self which delimits the range of social interaction. It is a traumatizing disappointment in love; a good and loving connection with the other is turned into self-absorption. This keeps relationships on a very primitive level.

Morrison (1987, 1989) in particular has understood shame in the framework of self psychology and the work of Kohut, which he believes provides the optimal means for understanding shame and its relationship to narcissism. In this endeavor he also emphasizes the intrapsychic dimensions of shame, which he calls the "eye of the self gazing inward." For Kohut, states Morrison, "shame is exclusively a reflection of the self overwhelmed by infantile and split-off grandiosity" (p. 274). However, he expands Kohut's work by adding that the notion of an ideal self is required in order to incorporate into self psychology a full understanding of shame. In order to do this, he focuses on the term selfobject, emphasizing its level of responsiveness to the infant. Shame, he states, is the selfobject's failure to respond to the self's idealizations. It is the infant's early quest that leads to the defensive grandiosity constituting the so-called narcissistic personality disorder.

Looking at shame as a core affect in psychotic anxieties brings several thoughts to mind about the work on shame and narcissism. First, narcissism is a self-based experience that occurs during the stage of omnipotence. It is the result of a failure to achieve grandiose tasks or to be reflected by an idealized object. However, this thesis has looked at core shame as developing during the holding phase of development, a stage earlier than the development of narcissism. The roots of shame can develop before an objective sense of self. The quest at this primary stage is to become a human being who exists. Shame here is not about a defective self that has failed in some attempt, but one that has never been born. Further, understanding shame at this depth grasps the level of fragmentation and emptiness that lies at the heart of absolute shame, a non-self lacking cohesion that the experience of petrifaction defends against. This sense of absence is compounded later by the developmental need to be special and absolutely unique in the eyes of the idealized other, but starting at this point does not account for the psychotic elements in shame. Later experiences of environmental failure that create a sense of flaw and deficit certainly complicate the picture, but the core of the unbearable pain in absolute shame is the sense of "being swallowed up by the earth."

Second, in narcissism the self has attempted to exclude a part of its experience, most frequently the infant turning away mother. Contained in narcissism, then, is the infant's rejection of mother due to her failures. It is considered a defense against shame. Narcissistic individuals focus on themselves and their desires shamelessly. Shame as a psychotic anxiety, on the other hand, contains the infant's petrifaction in the face of mother's rejection, as well as the infant's desperate and longed for connection to her. This difference is depicted well by the figures of Narcissus and Echo: Narcissus dies without shame by his own reflection, whereas Echo becomes petrified by her shame, pining away for a reunion with Narcissus and disappearing into the woods to remain unseen by the eyes of the world. Both endings are the result of a refusal to separate from the Terrible Mother, but are different due to the level of shame present.

Lastly, the focus on shame as a narcissistic injury leads to the extensive use of the word mortification as a synonym to describe what the shame-prone person suffers. For example, Wurmser states:

> The more ambitious and peremptory [narcissistic] the ego ideal is, the more painful is the wound about failing and the more pervasive is the narcissistic anxiety about yet more mortifications of such nature – in other words, the more shame-prone that person is.
>
> (Wurmser, 1997: 76)

Morrison (1987) believes that Kohut is speaking of shame throughout his writings (even though he only mentions the word shame once) when he writes of mortification, a term used to refer to the self's defeat in realizing its goals (p. 279).

Mortification is indeed a shame word. It means "a feeling of shame, humiliation, or wounded pride" (*The American Heritage Dictionary*, 1980). But more interesting for my purposes is its further meanings "to cause (a bodily part) to die, as by gangrene . . . to become gangrenous or necrosed, as a part of the body" (p. 855) (necrose meaning the pathologic death of living tissue). This part of its definition brings into vivid relief the murderous roots of shame to self (which as the case examples have shown can become quite literal). Shame in the deepest sense is a pathological symbiosis with mother, a parasitic relationship in which a part of the mother lives off her baby, devouring her sense of existence as the only way of seeing her. However, when shame is understood as an affect generated through early eye contact with mother, the killing process is not a mortifying one, but a petrifying one. The word petrify captures the process wherein a subject, a person, is turned into an object or thing – in the case of shame, a stone. An infant is turned to stone in the process of becoming a container for a mother's psychic illness. The human element ceases to exist, and shame becomes the nonexistent aspect of one's own being. Shame essentially thwarts the self from becoming a subject that is capable of forming her own relationship to the world. Freud may have inadvertently captured this idea when he referred to certain states produced in narcissism as "stone walls" (quoted by Nathanson, 1987: 214).

In the fairy tale of "The Beautiful Wassilissa," the stepsisters' and stepmother's deaths are not described as a process of mortification, where after they are exposed for their heinous deed they decay into putrid, rotting flesh. Rather, their deaths are described as a transformation of human flesh into an inhuman pile of ashes. The skull's "flowing eyes stared unceasingly . . . right down to their very souls . . . they tried to hide but the eyes followed them everywhere, and by morning they were burnt to ashes." The fiery eyes that follow one anywhere and everywhere so that nothing can stay hidden contain the power to petrify. This shaming without cessation incinerates.

Looking at shame intrapsychically (rather than intersubjectively) as an affect in psychotic anxieties (not only as a core affect in narcissistic states, although shame may comprise the psychotic core of a narcissistic condition) makes a very important clinical distinction. The mere change in a theory on shame, though helpful, is simply inadequate to provide the depth of healing that is required for such an affliction. A change in theory, therefore, necessitates a change in therapeutic approach. The patient who suffers core shame needs more than empathy, adequate mirroring, or sophisticated, analytic interpretations in order to be healed. In fact, these therapeutic tools may only stir more shame and cause premature terminations. When dealing with shame at the level of catastrophic anxieties, it becomes a matter of transforming a psychosis, unlocking the real but unimaginable early experience of becoming a container for mother's mental illness, originally experienced as the infant's inherent badness or weakness. This process is the only one that can transform the concreteness of psychosis into a symbol of the self. The single most important clinical difference is that this kind of patient needs what she feels, thinks, perceives or intuits to become real in order to exist in the face of another. This basic necessity of treatment requires a genuine and honest relationship with another vulnerable human being.

Apart from clinical theory, this analysis has shown the petrifying function of shame active in the infant's first days of life as well as the dawn of humankind's beginnings with the emergence of the Terrible Mother and her Eyes of Death. This feature may offer some insight as to why psychologists, as well as biologists, sociologists, philosophers, novelists and other students of the humanities have in recent times turned to focus on shame. Clearly psychologists are compelled by something much deeper than shame's intractability, prevalence in clinical disorders, or the high recidivism rates among our patients. What stalemate on a global scale are we are hoping to understand? I believe that we seek a solution to the widespread experiences of maternal deprivation, rejection, hatred and destruction in the world today – universal issues in countless human circumstances that attack life itself. Historically, the emergence of the Terrible Mother coincided with the dominance of masculine values over feminine ones. Perhaps deep within the collective unconscious humankind has remained petrified in this shameful moment. We now wish to acknowledge our shame and yearn for the light of consciousness that only it can engender. On a collective level, this means the restoration of the Great Mother's fertile and creative qualities that can inspire us towards humanness, in addition to progress.

Similar to the historical neglect of shame, another major lacuna in psychological theory is an investigation of eye contact and, more importantly, its role in the therapeutic encounter. Many theorists have speculated that the long neglect of shame in the history of psychology is its stinging, contagious quality that stimulates the therapist's own shame reactions. Clinicians have eclipsed shame in order to avoid dealing with this most painful affect. Perhaps in a similar way, the eclipse of eye contact is linked to an avoidance of shame, or the inability of professionals in psychology to tolerate the mutual intimacy and exposure which it entails.

Without language, the face becomes the major means of information transfer between mother and infant. The eye, however, has been overlooked as a point of contact in favor of the breast in psychological discourse. This is hard to fathom, despite the attempts of several early thinkers to link the breast with the eye. For example, as far back as 1955, Spitz seemed to understand the importance of the infant's perceptions of mother's face and came to the conclusion that the first visual precept is the human face. He advanced his hypothesis thus:

> When the infant nurses and has sensations in the oral cavity while staring at the mother's face, he unites the tactile and the visual perception, the perceptions of the total situation, into one undifferentiated unity, a situation Gestalt, in which any one part of the experience comes to stand for the total experience.
>
> (Spitz, 1955: 222)

Spitz went on to surmise that "under conditions of deep regression the percept of the face may re-emerge from its condensation with the breast image, which may be said to act as a screen for the face" (Almansi, 1960: 65). However, this opening into the role the face plays in early development was investigated by only a few psychologists, including Kenneth Robson (1967), who published a short article entitled "The Role of Eye-to-Eye Contact in Mother-Infant Attachment," and Kenneth Wright's (1991) book, *Vision and Separation between Mother and Baby*, which is, in part, about the role that mother's eyes play in the formation of self.

This work entailed amplifying shame's quintessential phenomenological image, the human eye. This necessitated an exploration of the part that eye contact plays in the earliest stage of psychological development, the creation of the intersubjective space, and in particular the part that it plays in the formation of attachment between mother and infant. For it is only in seeing and being seen, in hearing and being heard, that the matching can occur between our own self-concept and the concept that others have of us. Tomkins states:

> The significance of the face in inter-personal relations cannot be exaggerated. It is not only a communication center for the sending and receiving of information of all kinds, but because it is the organ of affect expression and communication, it is necessarily brought under strict social control . . . the shared eye to eye interaction is the most intimate relationship possible between human beings.
>
> (Tomkins, 1982: 376)

Due to the intimacy of eye contact between mother and infant, it becomes the means by which the infant becomes prematurely aware of separateness and a container for mother's mind – in other words, can develop absolute shame.

In this respect, eye contact, the ways it can facilitate the development of and understanding of the transference and countertransference, and what eyes can tell us about regressive states and the infant self's experience of mother become particularly important. Therapeutically, eye contact can become a way of touching the infant body without enacting the actual, physical mother–infant holding. In the same way that eye contact with mother damaged the infant self, so it is also true that holding the patient before the therapist eye's, noticing her, and hence holding the patient in mind, can provide the necessary healing.

A hope is that my preliminary venture into the therapeutic uses of eye contact has opened up a new territory for the exploration into and healing of primitive, infantile states of mind. I also hope that this look into the eyes of shame has contributed to the creation of an atmosphere where we as professionals no longer need to be ashamed of our shame, and that absolute shame (which is particularly contagious and stinging), as well as eye-to-eye contact, can come into a fuller existence in psychological discourse and practice.

And for the individual who suffers core shame? I hope that I have imparted enough therapeutic insight to assist the psychologist in facilitating her catastrophic regression back to the earliest days of life in order to consciously endure the horrendous experience of the Terrible Mother with the annihilating eyes. This will help her find, in the background of her soul, an Isis or Virgin Mary who will, with love and wisdom, recapture the humanness locked in stone, restoring her shame to its rightful place as the spark of self-awareness.

Bibliography

Ainsworth, M. D. (1969) 'Object relations, dependency, and attachment', *Child Development*, 40: 969–1025.

Aleksandrowicz, M. and Aleksandrowicz, D. (1976) 'Precursors of the ego in neonates', *Journal of the American Academy of Child Psychiatry*, 15: 257–68.

Almansi, R. J. (1960) 'The face–breast equation', *Journal of the American Psychoanalytic Association*, 8: 43–70.

Ambrose, J. A. (1961) 'The concept of a critical period for the development of social responsiveness', in B. M. Foss (ed.) *Determinants of Infant Behavior*, New York: Wiley.

American Heritage Dictionary of the English Language (New College Edition) (1980) Boston: Houghton Mifflin.

Anthony, E. J. (1981) 'Shame, guilt, and the feminine self in psychoanalysis', in S. Tuttman, C. Kaye and S. M. Zimmerman (eds) *Object and Self*, New York: International Universities Press.

Ashbery, J. (1975) *Self-Portrait in a Convex Mirror*, New York: Viking Press.

Baring, A. and Cashford, J. (1991) *The Myth of the Goddess: Evolution of an Image*, London: Arkana.

Barnes, H. (1974) *The Meddling Gods: Four Essays on Classical Themes*, Lincoln, NE: University of Nebraska Press.

Beebe, B. and Stern, D. (1977) 'Engagement–disengagement and early object experiences', in M. Freedman and S. Grand (eds) *Communicative Structures and Psychic Structures*, New York: Plenum Press.

Benedict, R. (1977) *The Chrysanthemum and the Sword*, London: Routledge and Kegan Paul.

Bennett, S. (1971) 'Infant–caretaker interactions', *Journal of the American Academy of Child Psychiatry* 10: 321–35.

Berressem, H. (1995) 'The "evil eye" of painting: Jacques Lacan and Witold Gombrowicz on the gaze', in R. Feldstein, B. Fink and M. Jaanus (eds) *Lacan's Four Fundamental Concepts of Psychoanalysis*, New York: Albany State University.

Bible (Revised Standard Version) (1971) New York: American Bible Society.

Bion, W. R. (1962) *Learning from Experience*, London: Heinemann.

Bower, T. G. R. (1965) 'Stimulus variable deforming space perception in infants', *Science* 149: 88–9.

Brazelton, T. B. and Als, H. (1979) 'Four early stages in the development of mother–infant interaction', *The Psychoanalytic Study of the Child* 34: 349–71.

Brazelton, T. B., Koslowski, B. and Main, M. (1974) 'The origins of reciprocity: the early mother–infant interaction', in M. Lewis and L. Rosenblum (eds) *The Effect of the Infant on Its Caregiver*, New York: Wiley.

Bridger, W. (1961) 'Sensory habituation and discrimination in the human infant', *Journal of the American Psychiatric Association* 118: 991–6.

Broucek, F. (1982) 'Shame and its relationship to early narcissistic development', *International Journal of Psycho-Analysis* 63: 369–77.

—— (1991) *Shame and the Self*, New York: Guilford Press.

—— (1997) 'Shame: early developmental issues', in M. Lansky and A. Morrison (eds) *The Widening Scope of Shame*, Hillsdale, NJ: Analytic Press.

Cardinal, M. (1975/1996) *The Words to Say It*, trans. P. Goodheart, Cambridge, MA: Van Vactor and Goodheart. (Original work published in 1975.)

Clark, R. T. R. (1959) *Myth and symbol in Ancient Egypt*. London: Thames and Hudson.

Dalley, S. (1989) *Myths from Mesopotamia*, New York: Oxford University Press.

Darwin, C. (1965) *The Expression of the Emotions in Man and Animals*, New York: Philosophical Library.

DeCasper, A. J. and Fifer, W. P. (1980) 'Of human bonding: newborns prefer their mothers' voices', *Science* 208: 1174–6.

de Vries, Ad. (1984) *Dictionary of Symbols and Imagery*, Amsterdam: Elsevier.

Di Stasi, L. (1981) *Mal Occhio: The Underside of Vision*, San Francisco: North Point Press.

Donne, L. H. (1973) 'Infants' development scanning patterns of face and non-face stimuli under various auditory conditions', paper presented at the Meeting of the Society for Research in Child Development, Philadelphia, Pennsylvania.

Duchamp, M. (1958) *Marchand du Sel: Ecrits de Marcel Duchamp*, ed. M. Sanouillet, Paris: Le Terrain Vague.

Duplessis, R. (1980) *Wells*, New York: Montemora Foundation.

Dupree, J. (1978) 'Have mercy on me', Archive of Folk Music. Los Angeles: Everest Records Production.

Eckman, P. (2003) *Emotions Revealed*, New York: Times Books.

Elworthy, F. (1958) *The Evil Eye: The Origins and Practices of Superstition*, New York: Macmillan.

Emad, P. (1972) 'Max Scheler's phenomenology of shame', *Philosophy and Phenomenological Research* 32: 361–70.

Emde, R. N. (1981) 'Changing models of infancy and the nature of early development: remodeling the foundation', *Journal of the American Psychoanalytic Association* 29: 179–219.

Emde, R. N. and Harmon, R. J. (1972) 'Endogenous and exogenous smiling systems in early infancy', *This Journal* 11: 177–200.

Emde, R. N., Gaensbauer, T. and Harmon, R. (1976) *Emotional Expression in Infancy: A Biobehavioral Study*, New York: International Universities Press.

Erikson, E. H. (1950/1985) *Childhood and Society*, New York: Norton.

Estes, C. (1992) *Women who Run with the Wolves: Myths and Stories of the Wild Woman Archetype*, New York: Ballantine.

Eurich-Rascoe, B. and Kemp, H. V. (1997) *Feminity and Shame: Women, Men and giving Voice to the Feminine*, Lanham, MD: University Press of America.

Fantz, R. (1961) 'The origin of form perception', *Scientific American* 204: 66–84.

Feldman, S. S. (1962) 'Blushing, fear of blushing and shame', *Journal of the American Psychoanalytic Association* 10: 368–85.

Fenichel, O. (1945) *Psychoanalytic Theory of Neurosis*, New York: Norton.

Field, T. M. (1977) 'Effects of early separation, interactive deficits and experimental manipulations on mother–infant face-to-face interactions', *Child Development* 48: 763–71.

Fordham, M. (1965) 'The importance of analysing childhood for assimilation of the shadow', *Journal of Analytical Psychology* 10: 95–109.

—— (1985a) 'Abandonment in infancy', in N. Schwartz-Salant and M. Stein (eds) *Chiron: A Review of Jungian Analysis*, Wilmette, IL: Chiron.

—— (1985b) *Explorations in the Self*, London: Academic Press.

Frantz, G. (1986) 'Discussion: response to Peer Hultberg', in M. A. Mattoon (ed.) *The Archetype of Shadow in a Split World*, Einsiedeln, Switzerland: Daimon.

Freud, S. (1905) 'Three theories on the theory of sexuality', in J. Strachey (ed. and trans.) *The Standard Edition of the Complete Psychological Works of Sigmund Freud*, vol. 7, London: Hogarth Press. (Original work published 1923.)

Gadon, E. (1989) *The Once and Future Goddess: A Symbol for Our Time*, New York: Harper and Row.

Gifford, E. (1958) *The Evil Eye: Studies in the Folklore of Vision*, New York: Macmillan.

Gimbutas, M. (1993) *The Language of the Goddess*, San Francisco: Harper.

Goldstein, A. G. and Mackenberg, E. J. (1966) 'Recognition of human faces from isolated facial features: a developmental study', *Psychoneurological Science* 6: 149–50.

Gonzalez-Wippler, M. (1994) *Santeria: The Religion*, trans. C. Wetii, Maryland: Llewellyn Publications. (Original work published in 1989.)

Gravel, P. (1995) *The Malevolent Eye*, New York: Peter Lang.

Graves, R. (1962) *The Greek Myths*, New York: Penguin.

Greenacre, P. (1926) 'The eye motif in delusion and fantasy', *American Journal of Psychiatry* 5: 550–6.

Greenman, G. W. (1963) 'Visual behaviour of newborn infants', in A. Solnit and S. Provence (eds) *Modern Perspectives in Child Development*, New York: International Universities Press.

Grilikhes, A. (1981) *On Women Artists: Poems 1975–1980*, Minneapolis, MO: Cleis Press.

Grimm, Bros (1963) *Household Stories from the Collection of Bros. Grimm*, trans. Lucy Crane, New York: Dover. (Original work published 1886.)

Grinker, R. (1955) 'Growth inertia and shame: their therapeutic implications and dangers', *International Journal of Psychoanalysis* 36: 242–53.

Haggard, H. R. (1957) *She*, New York: Random House.

Haith, M. M., Bergman, T. and Moore, M. (1977) 'Eye contact and face scanning in early infancy', *Science* 198: 853–5.

Hake, T. G. (1894) *The Poems of Thomas Gordon Hake*, London: Elkin Mathews and John Love.

Harrison, J. (1922) *Prolegomena to the Study of Greek Religion*, New York: World Publishing.

Hart, H. (1949) 'The eye in symbol and symptom', *Psychoanalytic Review* 36: 1–21.

Heller, A. (1985) *The Power of Shame: A Rational Perspective*, London: Routledge and Kegan Paul.

Hendrickson, V. (1999) personal communication, August.

Herman, N. (1988) *My Kleinian Home*. London: Free Association Books.

—— (1989) *Too Long a Child: The Mother–Daughter Dyad*. London: Free Association Books.

Hultberg, P. (1986) 'Shame: an overshadowed emotion', in M. A. Mattoon (ed.) *The Archetype of Shadow in a Split World*, Einsiedeln, Switzerland: Daimon.

Huxley, F. (1990) *The Eye: The Seer and the Seen*, London: Thames and Hudson.

Jacobson, E. (1965) *The Self and the Object World*, New York: International Universities Press.

Jacoby, M. (1990) 'Shame: its archetypal meaning and its neurotic distortions', paper presented at the C. G. Jung Center, New York, April.

Jaffe, J., Stern, D. M. and Perry, J. C. (1973) ' "Conversational" coupling of gaze behavior in prelinguistic human development', *Journal of Psychology Resident* 2: 321–30.

James, E. O. (1959) *The Cult of the Mother Goddess*, New York: Barnes and Noble.

Johnson, B. (1988) *The Lady of the Beasts: Ancient Images of the Goddess and her Sacred Animals*, San Francisco: Harper and Row.

Jung, C. G. (1959) 'The psychology of the child archetype', in R.F.C. Hull (trans.) *The Collected Works of C. G. Jung*, vol. 9,1, Princeton, NJ: Princeton University Press. (Original work published 1951.).

Kagan, J., Henker, B., Hen-Tov, A., Levine, J. and Lewis, M. (1966) 'Infants' differential reactions to familiar and distorted faces', *Child Development* 37: 519–32.

Kaufman, G. (1992) *Shame: The Power of Caring*, Rochester, VT: Shenkman Books.

Keller, H. and Gauda, G. (1987) 'Eye contact in the first months of life and its developmental consequences', in H. Rauh and H.C. Steinhausen (eds) *Psychobiology and Early Development*, Amsterdam: Elsevier.

Kellogg, R. (1969) *Analyzing Children's Art*, Palo Alto, CA: National Press Books.

Kessen, W., Haith, M. and Salapatek, P. (1970) 'Human infancy', in P. H. Mussen (ed.) *Carmichael's Manual of Child Psychology* (3rd edn), New York: Wiley.

Klein, M. (1975) *Love, Guilt and Reparation and Other Works 1921–1945*, New York: Delacorte Press.

—— (1975) *Envy and Gratitude and Other Works 1946–1963*, London: Hogarth Press and The Institute of Psycho-Analysis.

Kramer, S.N. (1944) 'Sumerian mythology', *American Philosophical Society Memoirs* 21: 86–93.

Lacan, J. (1977) 'The mirror stage as formative of the I as revealed in psychoanalytic experience', in J. Lacan *Ecrits*, London: Tavistock.

Lagerlöf, S. (1978) *Gösta Berling's Saga*, Stockholm: Delfinserien, Bonniers. (Original work published 1891.)

Lansky, M. (1995) 'Shame and the scope of analytic understanding', *American Behavioral Scientist* 38, 8: 1076–90.

Lansky, M. and Morrison, A. (1997) *The Widening Scope of Shame*, London: Analytic Press.

Levin, S. (1967) 'Some metapsychological considerations on the difference between shame and guilt', *International Journal of Psycho-Analysis* 48: 267–76.

Lewis, C. S. (1956) *Till We Have Faces*, New York: Harcourt Brace Jovanovich.

Lewis, H. B. (1971) *Shame and Guilt in Neurosis*, New York: International Universities Press.

Lewis, M. (1995) *Shame: The Exposed Self*, New York: Free Press.

Lichtenberg, J. (1991) *Psychoanalysis and Infant Research*, Hillsdale, NJ: Analytic Press.

Lispector, C. (1994) *The Passion According to G.H*, trans. R.W. Sousa, Minneapolis: University of Minnesota Press. (Original work published 1964.)

Little, M. (1990) *Psychotic Anxieties and their Containment*, Northvale, NJ: Jason Aronson.

—— (1993) *Transference Neurosis and Transference Psychosis*, Northvale, NJ: Jason Aronson.

Lorde, A. (1973) *Collected Poems*, New York: Norton.

Lowell, A. (1925) *Complete Poetical Works by Amy Lowell*. Boston: Houghton Mifflin.

Lowenfeld, H. (1976) 'Notes on shamelessness', *Psychoanalytic Quarterly* 45: 62–72.

Lynd, H. (1958) *On Shame and the Search for Identity*, New York: Harcourt Brace Jovanovich.

Mackenzie, D. (1978) *Egyptian Myth and Legend*, New York: Bell.

Maynard, J. (1998) *At Home in the World: A Memoir*, New York: Picador.

Miller, S. (1985) *The Shame Experience*, Hillsdale, NJ: Lawrence Erlbaum Associates Inc.

—— (1996) *Shame in Context*, Hillsdale, NJ: Analytic Press.

Milton, J. (1667/1978) *Paradise Lost*, London: Paternoster.

Mitrani, J. (1996) *A Framework for the Imaginary*, Northvale, NJ: Jason Aronson.

Moffett, C. S. (1998) 'The artist as a whole man', *Washington Post Magazine*, 20 September: 11–18, 21–9.

Morrison, A. (1987) 'The eye turned inwards: shame and the self', in D. Nathanson (ed.) *The Many Faces of Shame*, New York: Guilford Press.

—— (1989) *Shame: The Underside of Narcissism*, London: Analytic Press.

—— (1996) *The Culture of Shame*, New York: Ballantine Books.

Morrison, A. and Stolorow, R. (1997) 'Shame, narcissism, and intersubjectivity', in M. Lansky and A. Morrison (eds) *The Widening Scope of Shame*, London: Analytic Press.

Moss, H. and Robson, K. (1968) 'The role of protest behavior in the development of mother–infant attachment', paper presented at Meeting of the American Psychological Association.

Nathanson, D. (1992) *Shame and Pride: Sex, Affect and the Birth of Self*, New York: Norton.

—— (1996) 'A Conversation with Donald Nathanson', Behavior Online.

—— (1987) 'A timetable for shame', in D. Nathanson (ed.) *The Many Faces of Shame*, New York: Guilford Press.

Neumann, E. (1974) *The Great Mother: An Analysis of an Archetype*, trans.

R. Manheim, Princeton, NJ: Princeton University Press. (Original work published 1955.)

Nichols, S. et al. (eds) (1962) *The Songs of Bernard de Ventadour*, Chapel Hill.

Nilsson, L. and Hamberger, L. (1990) *A Child is Born*, trans. C. James, New York: Bantam Doubleday. (Original work published 1990.)

Ovid (1955) *Metamorphoses*, trans. R. Humphries, Bloomington, IN: Indiana University Press.

—— (1916/1977) *Metamorphoses*, trans. F.J. Miller, Cambridge, MA: Harvard University Press.

Perera, S. (1981) *Descent of the Goddess: A Way of Initiation for Women*, Toronto: Inner City Books.

Perry, J. (1976) *The Far Side of Madness*, Englewood Cliffs: Prentice-Hall.

Piers, G. and Singer, M. (1953) *Shame and Guilt: A Psychoanalytic and Cultural Study*, New York: Norton.

Pines, M. (1987) 'Shame – what psychoanalysis does and does not say', *Group Analysis* 20: 16–31.

—— (1995) 'The universality of shame: a psychoanalytic approach', *British Journal of Psychotherapy* 11, 3: 346–57.

Plath, S. (1965) *Poems by Sylvia Plath*, London: Faber and Faber.

Pope, A. (1968) *The Eros Aspect of the Eye*, Zurich: C.G. Jung Institute.

Rheingold, H. L. (1961) 'The effect of environmental stimulation upon social-exploratory behavior in the human infant', in B. M. Foss (ed.) *Determinant of Infant Behavior*, London: Methuen.

Rilke, R. M. (1984) *Letters to a Young Poet*, trans. S. Mitchell, New York: Random House.

Robson, K. (1967) 'The role of eye-to-eye contact in maternal–infant attachment', *Journal of Child Psychiatry* 8: 13–25.

Salapatek, P. (1975) 'Pattern perception in early infancy', in I. Cohen and P. Salapatek (eds) *Infant Perception: From Sensation to Cognition*, vol. 1, New York: Academic Press.

Sartre, J. P. (1956) *Being and Nothingness*, trans. H. Barnes, New York: Simon and Schuster. (Original work published 1953.)

Schneider, C. (1977) *Shame, Exposure and Privacy*, Boston: Beacon Press.

Sherrod, L. R. (1981) 'Issues in cognitive-perceptual development: the special case of social stimuli', in M. E. Lamb and L. R. Sherrod (eds) *Infant Social Cognition: Empirical and Theoretical Considerations*, Hillsdale, NJ: Lawrence Erlbaum Associates, Inc.

Sidoli, M. (1988) 'Shame and the shadow', *Journal of Analytical Psychology* 33: 127–42.

—— (1989) *The Unfolding Self: Separation and Individuation*, Boston: Sigo Press.

Siebers, T. (1983) *The Mirror of Medusa*, Berkeley: University of California Press.

Spero, M. H. (1984) 'Shame: an object-relational formulation', *Psychoanalytic Study of the Child*, 39: 259–82.

Spitz, R. (1955) 'The primal cavity: a contribution to the genesis of perception and its role for psychoanalytic theory', *Psychoanalytic Study of the Child* 10: 215–40.

Spitz, R. and Wolf, K. (1946) 'The smiling response: a contribution to the ontogenesis of social relations', *Genetic Psychology Monogram* 34: 57–125.

Stern, D. N. (1971) 'A micro-analysis of mother–infant intereaction: behavior regulation social contact between a mother and her 3½ month old', *Journal of the American Academy of Psychiatry* 5: 517–25.

—— (1974) 'The goal and structure of mother–infant play', *Journal of the American Academy of Psychiatry* 13: 402–21.

—— (1977) *The First Relationship*, Cambridge, MA: Harvard University Press.

—— (1990) *Diary of a Baby: What Your Child Sees, Feels, and Experiences*, New York: Basic Books.

Stone, I. F. (1988) *The Trial of Socrates*, Boston: Little, Brown.

Super, C. and Harkness, S. (1982) 'The development of affect in infancy and early childhood', in D. Wagner and H. Stevenson (eds) *Cultural Perspectives on Child Development*, San Francisco: W.H. Freeman.

Surrey, J. (1991) 'The self in relation', in J.V. Jordan et al., *Women's Growth in Connection: Writings of the Stone Center*, New York: Guilford Press.

Thrane, G. (1979) 'Shame and the construction of self', *Annual of Psychoanalysis* 7: 321–41.

Tomkins, S. (1962) *Affect, Imagery, Consciousness, vol. 2: The Positive Affects*, New York: Springer.

—— (1963) *Affect, Imagery, Consciousness, Vol. 3: The Negative Affects*, New York: Springer.

—— (1982) 'Affect theory', in P. Ekman (ed.) *Emotion in the Human Face*, 2nd edn, New York: Cambridge University Press.

—— (1987) 'Shame', in D. Nathanson (ed.) *The Many Faces of Shame*, New York: Guilford Press.

Tomkins, S. and Izard, C. (1965) *Affect, Cognition, and Personality: Empirical Studies*, New York: Springer.

Tourney, G. and Plazak, D. (1954) 'Evil eye in myth and schizophrenia', *Psychiatric Quarterly* 28, 478–95.

Trevarthen, C. (1974) 'Conversations with a two-month-old', *New Scientist*, May: 230–35.

Tronick, E., Adamson, L., Wise, S., Als, H. and Brazelton, T. (1975) 'The infant's response to entrapment between contradictory messages in face to face interaction', paper presented at the Society for Research in Child Development, Denver.

Turner, F. (1995) 'Shame, beauty and the tragic view of history', *American Behavioral Scientist* 38: 1060–72.

von Franz, M. L. (1986) *The Feminine in Fairy Tales*, Dallas, TX: Spring Publications.
—— (1987) *Projection and Recollection in Jungian Psychology*, trans. W. Kennedy, London: Open Court. (Original work published 1978.)
Walker, B. (1985) *The Crone: Woman of Age, Wisdom, and Power*, San Francisco: Harper and Row.
Wallace, L. (1963) 'The mechanism of shame', *Archives of General Psychiatry* 8: 80–85.
Ward, H. (1972) 'Aspects of shame in analysis', *American Journal of Psychoanalysis* 32: 62–73.
Weaving, W. (1916) *Star Fields and Other Poems*, Oxford: Blackwell.
White, B., Castle, P. and Held, R. (1964) 'Observations on the development of visually-directed reaching', *Child Development* 35: 349–64.
Winnicott, D. W. (1960) 'The theory of the parent–infant relationship', *International Journal of Psycho-Analysis* 41: 585–95.
—— (1965a) 'Ego integration in child development', in D. W. Winnicott *The Maturational Processes and the Facilitating Environment*, New York: International Universities Press.
—— (1965b) 'Psychiatric disorder in terms of infantile maturational processes', in D. W. Winnicott *The Maturational Processes and the Facilitating Environment*, New York: International Universities Press.
—— (1971) 'Mirror-role of mother and family in child development', in D. W. Winnicott *Playing and Reality*, London: Tavistock.
—— (1992a) 'Hate in the countertransference', in D. W. Winnicott *Through Pediatrics to Psycho-Analysis: Collected Papers*, New York: Brunner/Mazel.
—— (1992b) 'Metapsychological and clinical aspects of regression within the psycho-analytical set-up', in D. W. Winnicott *Through Pediatrics to Psycho-Analysis: Collected Papers*, New York: Brunner/Mazel
—— (1992c) 'Primitive emotional development', in D. W. Winnicott *Through Pediatrics to Psycho-Analysis: Collected Papers*, New York: Brunner/Mazel.
—— (1987) 'Environmental health in infancy', in C. Winnicott, R. Shepherds, M. Davis (eds) *Babies and their Mothers*, Reading, MA: Addison-Wesley.
Wolff, P. H. (1963) 'Observations on the early development of smiling', in B.M. Foss (ed.) *Determinants of Infant Behavior*, New York: Wiley.
Wolkstein, D. and Kramer, S. (1983) *Inanna Queen of Heaven and Earth*, New York: Harper and Row.
Wright, K. (1991) *Vision and Separation between Mother and Baby*, Northvale, NJ: Jason Aronson.
Wurmser, L. (1987) 'Shame: the veiled companion of narcissism', in D. Nathanson (ed.) *The Many Faces of Shame*, New York: Guilford Press.

—— (1997) *The Mask of Shame*, Baltimore, MD: Johns Hopkins University Press.

Yorke, C., Balogh, T., Cohen, P., Davids, J., Gavshon, A., McCutcheon, M., McLean, D., Miller, J. and Szydio, J. (1990) 'The development and functioning of the sense of shame', *Psychoanalytic Study of the Child* 45: 377–409.

Index

Lewis, C.S.: *Till We Have Faces*
162–3, 202
Lewis, H.B. 9, 20, 29
Lewis, M. 1
Lewis, Helen Block 24
Lichtenberg, J. 51, 53, 55, 57
Lispector, Clarice 83, 84, 190, 191
Little, Margaret 74, 147, 148,
179–86, 208, 209, 211, 212, 213;
"Life in Death or Death in Life"
182; "Mental Hospital" 184–5;
"Salutation, The" 185–6;
"Words" 183–4
Lorde, A. 168
Lowell, Amy 7, 146
Lowenfeld, H. 11
Lucy of Syracuse 108
Lynd, H. 15, 20, 25

Maat 117
Mackenberg, E.J. 55
Mackenzie, D. 110
Magritee, René: *Difficult Crossing,
The* 46; *False Mirror, The* 84–5;
monde poétique, La 47; *Painted
Object: Eye* 43, 44
Main, M. 57
masculininity 76, 77
masochism 9
maternal failure 86
maternal failure of adaptation 73–4
maternal reverie 64–5
Matthew, St 100, 108
Maynard, Joyce 208
Medusa myth 33, 132–6, 144, 191,
204–5
Mencius 75
mental illness: evil eye in 107–8;
maternal 95
Miller, S. 26, 80
Milton, John: "On Blindness" 211;
Paradise Lost 203
mirror, eye as 63–72; false, eye as
72–97
misogyny 77
Mitrani, J. 12–13, 78
Moffett, C.S. 190, 193
Moody, R. 210
moon, evil eye and 109

Morrison, A. 9, 11, 25, 29, 30, 32,
59, 216, 217–18, 219, 220
mortification 220
Moss, H. 59
mother as world 78–9

narcissism 8, 25, 32, 29, 30, 77,
219–20
Narcissus, myth of 77, 89–93, 102,
197–200
Nathanson, D. 1, 2, 8, 9, 13, 15, 25,
26, 216, 221
neonatal reflexes 53
Neumann, Erich 112
Nichols, S. 61
Nietsche, F. 15, 206
Nilsson, L. 37
Ninhursag, Sumerian goddess 117
nipple as eye 54–5

object/self distinction 63–4
objective self-awareness 31
Oedipus complex 9
original sin 23
Osiris, Eye of 129, 130–1
overt, consciously experience shame
9
Ovid 91, 135, 197, 198, 199

paranoia 101–2
peacock feathers 103–5
Perera, S. 123
Perry, John 54, 157
Persephone, myth of 21
petrifaction 72, 78, 83 100, 101–2,
145, 150, 157–169, 186–7, 221
phenomenology of shame 12–24, 32
Philosopher's Stone 192
phobia of stranger's face 42
physiology of shame 15
Piaget 53
Piers, G. 8, 20, 24, 27
Pines, M. 19, 78, 211
Pirandello 99
Plath, Sylvia: "Mirror" 35–6;
"Moon and the Yew Tree, The" 76
Plazak, D. 107
Pliny 108
Plutarch 131